LEE BAILEY'S
California Wine Country Cooking

LEE BAILEY'S
California Wine Country Cooking

by Lee Bailey

Photographs by Tom Eckerle

Design by Impress

Recipe Development and Research with Lee Klein

CLARKSON POTTER/PUBLISHERS

NEW YORK

**To my dear friend and former editor,
Carolyn Hart Bryant,
for years of encouragement, plain hard work, and help
—but mostly for all the fun we had
working together.**

Published by Clarkson N. Potter, Inc., 201 East 50th Street,
New York, New York 10022, and distributed by Crown Publishers, Inc.
Member of the Crown Publishing Group.

CLARKSON N. POTTER, POTTER and colophon are trademarks of
Clarkson N. Potter, Inc.

Manufactured in Japan

Library of Congress Cataloging-in-Publication Data
Bailey, Lee.
[California wine country cooking]
Lee Bailey's California wine country cooking/by Lee Bailey;
photographs by Tom Eckerle; recipe development and research with Lee Klein.
p. cm.
Includes index.
1. Cookery, American. 2. Cookery—California, Northern. 3. Wineries—California, Northern. 4. Menus.
I. Klein, Lee. II. Title. III Title: California wine country cooking.
TX715.B1562 1991   90-7771
641.5973—dc20   CIP

ISBN 0-517-57450-0

10 9 8 7 6 5 4 3 2 1

First Edition

Acknowledgments

❦

MY SINCEREST THANKS to all the dedicated winery owners who so generously contributed toward getting this book together. In alphabetical order: at Alexander Valley, all the Wetzel clan, especially Maggie, Katie, and the two Hanks; at Beaulieu, Heublein Inc., the Sullivans and Eschers; at Beringer, Wine World Inc.; at Buena Vista, Marcus and Anna Moller-Racke; at Cain, Jerry and Joyce Cain; at Cakebread, Jack and Dolores Cakebread, sons Bruce and Dennis; at Ferrari-Carano, Don and Rhonda Carano; at Fetzer, Kathleen Fetzer and the Fetzer siblings; at Heitz, Joe and Alice Heitz, sons David and Rollie, daughter Kathleen, and Rollie's wife, Sally; at Hess, Donald Hess; at Inglenook, Hueblein Inc.; at Iron Horse, Barry and Audrey Sterling; at Jordan, Tom and Sally Jordan, daughter Judy; at Martini, Louis and Liz Martini, son Michael, daughters Carolyn and Patricia; at Matanzas, Sandra and Bill MacIver; at Mondavi, Robert Mondavi and wife, Margrit Biever, sons Michael and Tim, daughter Marcia; at Monticello, Jay and Marilyn Corley; at Newton, Peter and Su Hua Newton; at Quivira, Henry and Holly Wendt; at Schramsberg, Jack and Jamie Davies; at Sonoma-Cutrer, Brice Jones; at Stag's Leap, Warren and Barbara Winiarski; and at Trefethen, John and Janet Trefethen.

Also at Alexander Valley, Randi Middleton; at Beaulieu, Charlotte Combe and Craig Root; at Beringer, Toni Allegra, Tor and Susan Kenward, Maxine Seidenfaden, and Joseph Costanzo; at Buena Vista, Sharon Lydic, Stuart Tracy, Don Surplus, and his crew from Napa Valley Balloons, Inc.; at Cain, Michael Osborn; at Cakebread, Brian Streeter; at Ferrari-Carano, Marie Gewirtz, Donna Freitas, Shannon Beglin, and Elaine Reese; at Fetzer, Rusty Eddy; at Hess, Elizabeth Pressler, Jean Mazza and Denis Corey; at Inglenook, Jamie Morningstar; at Jordan, Jean Reynolds, Barbara Bowman, and Maria Mondrigan; at Martini, Mr. and Mrs. Olivia Piero and Susan Smith; at Matanzas, Marc Roumiguiere and Judy Ortiz; at Mondavi, Ada Moss, Linda Borelli, Estefana, and Fume the poodle; at Monticello, Kathleen Clark and Roger Thoreson; at Newton, Claudia Schmidt and John Kongsgaard; at Quivira, Jan Mettler; at Schramsberg, Robert Kaspar and Rita Escalante; at Sonoma-Cutrer, Leslie Litwak, Nancy Freeman, and Robert Reboschatis; at Stag's Leap, Mary Jane Bowker; at Trefethen, John Bonick.

And thanks and appreciation for invaluable advice from Bob and Harolyn Thompson, Belle and Barney Rhodes, and Penni Wisner.

For being so willing to share their beautiful wares: John Nyquist, Charles Gautreaux, and Kathy Vanderbilt of Vanderbilt Inc., St. Helena.

Also my appreciation to—in no particular order—Claudia Appleby, Michael Florian, John Duff, Bill and Lila Jaeger, Scott Chappell, Howard Lane, Susan Contesini, Elaine Bell, Joan Comendant, Anne Grace, Cynthia Lindway, Gil Rogers, Arthur Foster, and Bill Blum.

For my old friend and fellow food enthusiast Lee Klein, who made me aware of what was going on in the wine country over the years and guided us during our stay in California. I can't imagine how we could have done it without you. Thanks, pal, for making it all run so smoothly!

As usual my deep appreciation to Tom Eckerle for his truly spectacular photographs, with an able assist from Bill Keene and Jimmy Eckerle.

Also to Hans Teensma for once again giving us such a beautifully designed book.

Thanks to all my diligent friends at Clarkson Potter, especially my new editor, Roy Finamore, who made the transition so seamless and pleasant.

And to my friend and agent, Pam Bernstein.

A reluctant farewell to Alan Mirken, who was always so unfailingly supportive of not only me but each of his writers. Your warm, sympathetic presence will be remembered by all of us.

Contents

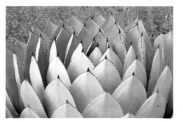

Introduction

THE FIRST TIME I visited the northern California wine country in the mid-1970s, it was to take a look and lend a bit of moral support to Lee Klein, an old friend, journalist, and publisher who had courageously decided to kick it all over and open a small restaurant in Sonoma County, something he had always wanted to try.

Sterling Vineyards had only recently completed its gleaming white Greek village–like buildings, which included a funicular to transport visitors up the hillside. As we ascended, looking back across an ever-widening view of the lovely cultivated parquet valley floor below, I remember thinking what a perfect, quiet paradise it all seemed. The weather had been glorious during my stay, with soft warm air and the good smells of spring—all made doubly welcome for my having so recently left New York City where April had played one of its usual dirty tricks by concluding several achingly promising spring days with freakish snow showers and high winds.

We visited several other wineries during the next days, had some nice but unmemorable meals, and debated going aloft in a balloon.

And I really had no inkling of what had already begun to happen there.

Over the intervening years the number of wineries had proliferated like grasshoppers, bringing with them a new breed of local denizen: people with a fresh and keen awareness of the great food potential the area offers.

In Europe it's a given that if you want really good food, you go where wine is made. Without much fanfare beyond that generated by local boosterism and word sent out by devoted foodies, the same was quickly becoming true in California. Only the region's tranquil valleys offered an advantage even their aging and aloof European counterparts couldn't match: the opportunity for an almost endless variety of produce created by the vastly differing microclimates nestling between its gentle hills.

Very soon the demands of this new awareness produced a great local outpouring of familiar vegetables and fruit. Then, as winemakers gained expertise and confidence, food tastes refined and expanded along with them, adding greater culinary innovation to the mix. What had once been new and exotic became commonplace—a startling spectrum of tomatoes, from palest yellow through orange to deepest red, found their way into local kitchens; peppers appeared in colors and flavors unimaginable a few years before; there were all sorts of garden greens, from buttery tender to peppery sharp. Eggplants that previously had only been seen in their bulbous dark, shiny shapes, took on other forms and creamy white skins. No longer did cooks have to be satisfied with one kind of thyme or mint or garlic. All sorts of other many-faceted flavors began cropping up in these and other old standbys.

And there was the fruit—everything from the ubiquitous kiwi to persimmons with a texture as crisp as an apple's, which could be eaten raw, skin and all.

There's more of course, but you see what was going on.

While this was happening, people took to cheese making or baking wonderful breads in newly resurrected brick ovens. Free-range chickens and other animals were raised in natural environments without the use of chemicals. Curiosity and freedom were suddenly the order of the day. One local fellow, not content with the imported product, even started making his own prosciutto.

The result of this amalgam of experimentation and imagination is a way of cooking, a taste for food, and a style of entertaining that I think is perfectly in tune with today's evolving palates and busy schedules. Based on freshness, diversity, and abundance, it also prides itself on spontaneity, unpretentiousness, and simplicity. And much of it is fast, flexible, and easy to prepare. I've been told by

more than one cook in California that if they are out of something, they merely substitute whatever is at hand and go on from there.

So forget overwrought food. Forget artifice. It's back to basics, but basics as you never quite knew them before. They can be as simple as Tomatillo Soup with Cilantro and Orange or as intricate as a poached cold king salmon dressed for a party.

In short, welcome to California Wine Country Cooking.

Now, about the wines. As you go over these menus, you'll notice that in lots of cases, separate courses are each accompanied by a different wine (with the cook's own comments about his or her choices). And often this doesn't include the wines served before dinner. Obviously, the average host or hostess seldom, if ever, serves this many wines at a single meal. As a matter of fact, I've never done it and probably never will. Two wines are enough in usual situations for me, and even more often one is plenty. But wine is these people's business, and although I found their deep concern for quality and variety bracing and reassuring whether I intend to follow their example or not, it's certainly not just business to them. They love what they are doing with a devotion and concentration that can, and does, elevate plain hard work and dedication to an art.

Be that as it may, what this comes down to as far as you and I are concerned is that there's much to learn from the reasoning behind pairing food flavors with particular types of wines, which will be handy when selecting wines for oneself. I don't think you, any more than I, must do exactly as the people here do, and many I spoke with in Napa and Sonoma got around to agreeing that, in the final analysis, personal taste should be your guide; but, as with anything else, an open mind on the subject is a great plus. For instance, I almost never drink white wine if I have a choice, but during my stay in northern California I tasted everything that came my way, and though not exactly converted, I discovered whites that I particularily liked and that I'll look for again—or for ones with characteristics similar to them. I also rediscovered just how good sweet wines can be with dessert. I don't know why this should have taken me by surprise, since for years I've been encouraging cooks to spike dessert whipped cream with generous amounts of bourbon or eau-de-vie. Not the same thing obviously, but you get the connection.

Also, my wine-sampling adventure made me appreciate more fully that although there may certainly be plenty of jargon and ritual to it all, much of what is too often seen as pretense to the uninitiated actually rests on a solid foundation. So understanding the "why" of swirling wine in the glass—it's to release the wine's bouquet so you can inhale it—and other gestures that can be off-putting or intimidating to the novice can lead to your following these rituals and can actually enhance your pleasure. The more you become acquainted with the subtleties of a wine's taste, the greater will be your enjoyment of it. It's as simple as that but it's up to you.

Perhaps the best thing about the wine country is that everyone connected with the business seems honestly pleased and delighted, not just to exclaim but to explain—to help visitors understand what they are tasting so as to make wine drinking more pleasing. Everyone, especially those who have had only big city wine merchants to deal with or some fancy sommelier, will be thrilled with the openness and the desire to educate that the wine community exhibits. It was an experience I encourage people who have curiosity about wines to make time for on their next visit to this splendid part of the world.

I should add that although the very articulate cooks and chefs I talked with were definite about what characteristics make for a good marriage between wines and their food, I hope their brief (usually) comments will guide you toward the larger purpose of understanding what general qualities to look for in wines. That's step one. Specifics and subtleties can come later.

Although I am certainly no expert on the subject of wine—and after all, this book is meant to be essentially about food—I hope the remarks about wine by these professionals and my own reactions will make you feel freer to experiment, especially after you have gone through and used this book. There's fun out there to be had and I wouldn't want you to miss out on it.

Incidentally, this would probably be a good place to say that some of the vintage wines photographed and mentioned here may not be available by the time you see this book. No matter. Forge ahead, for while obviously some years are better than others, this is often a question of degree. A good wine from a reputable vineyard is likely to be consistent enough for you to feel secure about it—regardless of the year.

One last thing about the recipes. They were contributed about equally by the owners of the wineries and by professional chefs. In each case the menus and recipes reflect the entertaining styles and preferences of the individual winery owners. And although we worked hard to make sure all the recipes were within the capability of the average cook, some menus devised by chefs still include dishes that need a bit of extra time or might require two ovens. Don't let this put you off! Even in such cases, there are plenty of individual *easy* dishes and techniques to be gleaned from such menus. For instance, the method of roasting lamb in the Jordan Winery menu couldn't be simpler and produces delicious results. You needn't even make the particular sauce from the recipe to enjoy it; also, you could substitute freshly whipped potatoes and another vegetable you like for the ones suggested and still come up with an elegant little dinner.

You'll find loads of good and interesting food in these pages even if you're not in the mood to re-create entire menus faithfully. You're in for a delicious adventure.

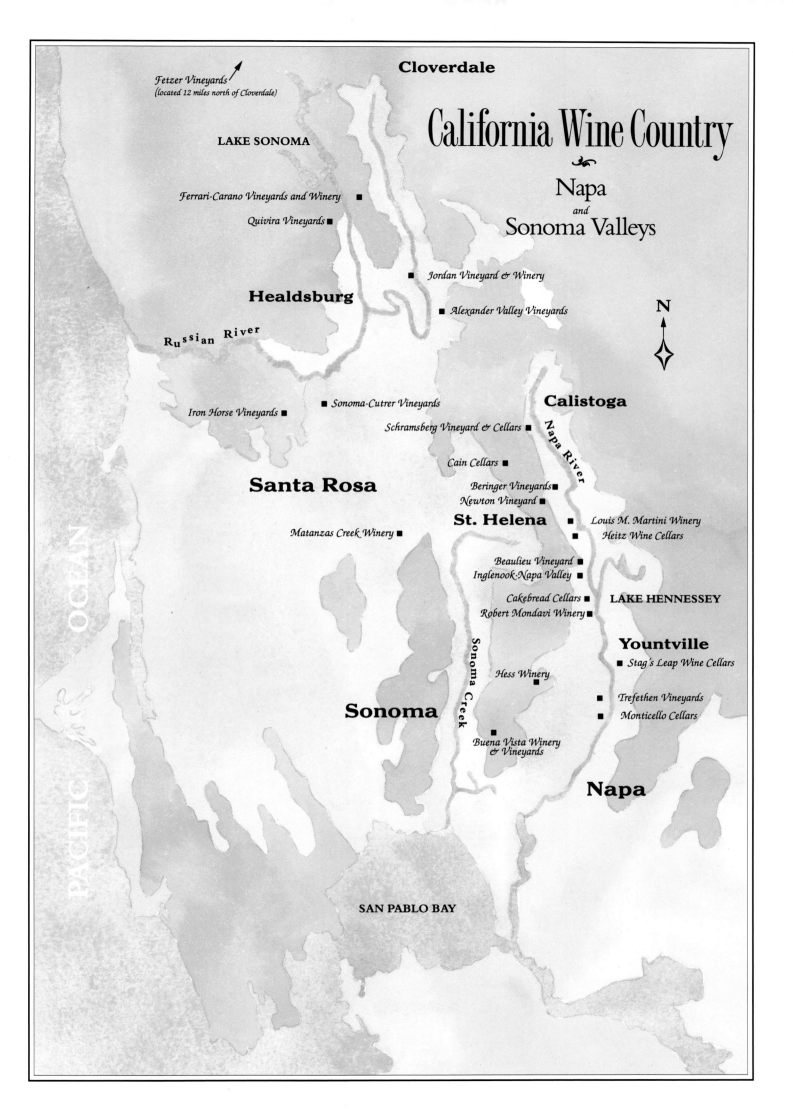

Fetzer Vineyards
(located 12 miles north of Cloverdale)

Cloverdale

California Wine Country

Napa
and
Sonoma Valleys

LAKE SONOMA

Ferrari-Carano Vineyards and Winery ■

Quivira Vineyards ■

Jordan Vineyard & Winery ■

Healdsburg

Alexander Valley Vineyards ■

Ru s s i a n River

N

Calistoga

Sonoma-Cutrer Vineyards ■

Iron Horse Vineyards ■

Schramsberg Vineyard & Cellars ■

Napa River

Cain Cellars ■

Santa Rosa

Beringer Vineyards ■
Newton Vineyard ■

St. Helena ■ Louis M. Martini Winery

Matanzas Creek Winery ■ ■ Heitz Wine Cellars

Beaulieu Vineyard ■
Inglenook-Napa Valley ■

Cakebread Cellars ■ **LAKE HENNESSEY**
Robert Mondavi Winery ■

Yountville
■ Stag's Leap Wine Cellars

Hess Winery ■

Sonoma Creek

■ Trefethen Vineyards
■ Monticello Cellars

Sonoma

Buena Vista Winery
& Vineyards ■

Napa

SAN PABLO BAY

PACIFIC OCEAN

Lunch in the Atrium

CAIN CELLARS

AIN CELLARS is one of the comparatively new kids in the valley (or more aptly, above it), having been founded in 1980. That's the year Jerry and Joyce Cain purchased the old cattle ranch that was to become their winery. Those who like to think we are occasionally guided by an unseen hand as well as those who simply like a good healthy coincidence will be intrigued by the curious way the Cains found the ranch. It seems that while having breakfast in Sonoma during one of their efforts to find suitable vineyard land, they overheard people at the next table talking about a large tract for sale on Spring Mountain. So, after their *petit déjeuner,* they immediately set out

for the unknown place, got lost, got found by helpful locals, and wound up two days later submitting a bid for the property.

After a year of preparation the Cains were finally able to plant their first Cabernet Sauvignon grapes. These were followed by Cabernet Franc, Merlot, Malbec, and Petit Verdot. People who know about such things have told me that Malbec and Petit Verdot are not often planted here, although they are regularly found in Bordeaux, where they are used for blending. You see, the Cains were particularly interested in the red wines of Bordeaux and wanted to create their own blended style.

I suppose that concern with style shouldn't be all that surprising when one knows that Joyce Cain is an interior designer among other things and her husband an entrepreneur involved in construction and real estate. They had often pooled their talents on projects in the past that required a keen sense of style, though admittedly of another sort. So this element was a natural goal for them—and is,

not incidentally, good news for the consumer.

Their commitment was such that in the very short time since the winery's founding, they and their staff have managed to create really distinctive and medal-winning wines.

Fortunately, the Cains' special interest in red wines has not caused them to neglect whites, particularily Chardonnays. They purchase the grapes from other vineyards in Napa and Carneros, and these wines have won high praise from all sides.

But because they have concentrated especially on blended wines, which utilize grape varieties they grow in their own vineyards, their experiments have been rewarded with a real winner in Cain Five. As the name implies, "Five" is made by skillfully blending five grape varieties, and it was a Double Gold Award winner at the Summer 1989 San Francisco National Wine Competition. If these early years are any indication, wine drinkers have lots of pleasure to look forward to from Cain Cellars.

Built along with the spectacular winery buildings was a residence, standing, as the winery buildings do, practically on the uppermost crest of the Mayacamus Ridge, which divides the Napa Valley from the Valley of the Moon. As you can imagine there is almost no place in the house that doesn't invite you to stop and be dazzled by the view, which looks down into the Napa Valley and across to St. Helena in the distance.

At the house's center is an atrium-kitchen, a lovely glassed-in spot for an intimate little lunch, which treats you to those views each time you glance up from your delicious meal. The peace and quite are almost palpable and the food superb.

OPPOSITE: **Looking up at the winery.**
ABOVE: **Jerry and Joyce Cain.**

Place the bok choy in a steamer with a small amount of water. Cook about a minute to wilt it.

To serve, spoon some of the butter onto individual heated plates, fan out the leaves of bok choy, and place the scallops at the stem ends. Garnish with chopped peppers and chives. Serve immediately.

Serves 6

❧

Roast Capon with Mushroom Sauce and Baby Vegetables

It's nice to see capon on a menu again. It seems to have gotten lost in the shuffle as chefs strive for innovation. I still love it.

1	capon, about 5 to 6 pounds
	Salt and freshly ground black pepper to taste
1/2	medium onion, coarsely chopped
1	medium carrot, broken into several pieces
3	celery ribs, broken into several pieces
	Unsalted butter, softened
1	to 1 1/2 cups chicken stock
1/2	pound white mushrooms, coarsely sliced
1	cup heavy cream
1	tablespoon cornstarch (optional)
	A small selection of fresh baby vegetables, steamed

Preheat the oven to 400 degrees.

Remove the giblets, neck, excess fat, and liver (reserve liver for another purpose) from inside the capon. Place everything except liver and fat in the bottom of a heavy roasting pan. Sprinkle inside of the bird with salt and pepper, and stuff cavity with the onion, carrot, and celery. Close opening and truss. Place bird in the roasting pan and brush the outside with the softened butter. Sprinkle with more salt and pepper. Roast for 20 minutes, then reduce heat to 325 degrees.

Pour 1 cup of the chicken broth over the capon and baste every 15 or 20 minutes. Add more of broth as necessary to maintain about a cup in the pan. After chicken has roasted for 30 minutes, add mushrooms to the pan to cook while the capon finishes

---

M E N U

**Scallops with Ginger–Soy Butter
on Bok Choy**
**Roast Capon with Mushroom Sauce and
Baby Vegetables**
**Mixed Baby Lettuces and Greens with
Honey-Lemon Dressing**
**Triple Chocolate Terrine with
Creme Anglaise and Raspberry Sauce**

*1987 Chardonnay
Cain Five*

Scallops with Ginger–Soy Butter on Bok Choy

I particularly like the way chef Stephen Benson explains the preparation of this dish's various simple elements, giving several alternative methods of cooking them so you may choose the one you are most comfortable with. For instance, notice the different ways he says you can cook the scallops.

1/2	bottle dry white wine
2	tablespoons rice vinegar
2	tablespoons finely grated fresh ginger
3	medium shallots, minced
1	cup (2 sticks) chilled unsalted butter, cut into small chunks
1	tablespoon soy sauce
18	to 24 ounces medium scallops (3 to 4 per person)
3	small heads baby bok choy, cut in half lengthwise

Diced red and yellow bell peppers and chives, for garnish
Olive oil (to just coat pan)

Place wine, vinegar, ginger, and shallots into a small saucepan and reduce over high heat until only about 1 tablespoon of liquid remains, about 5 minutes. Reduce heat and whip in the butter a piece or two at a time until all is emulsified, about 2 minutes. Remove from heat and stir in soy sauce. Sauce may be strained or not. Keep sauce warm over hot water while preparing the scallops and bok choy.

The scallops may be cooked under a broiler or in a very hot pan with a small amount of olive oil. If you broil the scallops, coat them with olive oil first. However they are done, cook them quickly over high heat, which will color them but allow the scallops to retain their natural juices.

roasting. Capon is done when the thigh juices run clear, about 1 hour.

When the capon is done, drain out any liquid from the cavity into the roasting pan. Set the bird aside on a warm platter and cover lightly with a sheet of foil. Tilt the pan and skim off surface fat with a small ladle.

Place roasting pan over medium high heat. Stir in the heavy cream and bring to a boil. Reduce sauce until only about 1½ cups remain, about 5 minutes. You may thicken it by dissolving the cornstarch in a small amount of water and drizzling it slowly into the sauce, stirring. Strain sauce into a saucepan. Discard mushrooms.

Remove breast meat of the capon by running a knife down each side of the breast bone, following the bone until you have 2 half-breasts. Remove leg and cut at leg thigh joint. Slice thigh meat and breast meat, and return to the heated platter.

Serve capon with sauce, accompanied by a garnish of the steamed vegetables.

Serves 6

❧

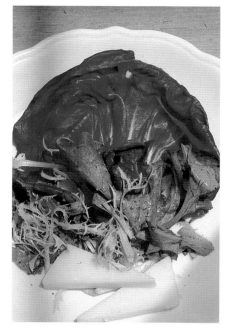

Mixed Baby Lettuces and Greens with Honey-Lemon Dressing

Many wine connoisseurs will tell you that wine cannot be served with the salad course because it reacts with the vinegar in the dressing. However, Stephen has devised a delicious and simple dressing that makes it possible to have wine with this course if you like.

- 2 medium shallots, minced, or 2 tablespoons minced onion
- 3 tablespoons honey
- 3 tablespoons fresh lemon juice
- 1 tablespoon olive oil
  Freshly ground pepper and salt to taste
- 6 generous cups mixed baby lettuces and greens or mesclun

Place all the above ingredients except greens in a small bowl and whisk.

Wash and dry greens thoroughly, then toss with dressing.

Serves 6

❧

OPPOSITE: **Scallops with Ginger-Soy Butter on Bok Choy with toasted bread.**
LEFT: **Roast Capon with Mushroom Sauce and Baby Vegetables.**
ABOVE: **Mixed Baby Lettuces and Greens with Honey-Lemon Dressing.**

Triple Chocolate Terrine with Crème Anglaise and Raspberry Sauce

Chocolate lovers, here it is!

- 10 ounces bittersweet chocolate
- 4 ounces milk chocolate
- 3 ounces white chocolate
- ¾ teaspoon unflavored gelatin
- ¼ cup water
- ½ cup plus 2 tablespoons warm Crème Anglaise (recipe follows)
- 2 egg whites
- 3 tablespoons sugar
- ½ cup plus 2 tablespoons heavy cream
- ½ cup finely ground walnuts
  Crème Anglaise
  Raspberry Sauce

Place the chocolates in a bowl over hot water and melt, stirring occasionally. Dissolve the gelatin in the water and add to the Crème Anglaise. Stir this mixture into the chocolates and set aside. Whip the egg whites and sugar until they become stiff. Set aside. In a large bowl, whip the cream until stiff. Fold in the chocolate mixture until incorporated completely. Fold in the egg whites, then fold in the walnuts. Pour into a 9¼ by 5¼-inch loaf pan 2¾ inches deep. Cover with plastic wrap and refrigerate overnight.

When ready to serve the terrine, dip the pan in hot water for about 15 seconds and turn out onto a serving dish. The terrine may not come out the first try; tap the pan over the platter until it does, or if it is really reluctant, dip it in hot water again. Once unmolded, smooth top of terrine with a spatula and refrigerate to set again, about 30 minutes. Slice with a knife dipped into hot water and serve with Crème Anglaise and Raspberry Sauce.
Serves 8 or more

CREME ANGLAISE

- 5 egg yolks
- ½ cup sugar
- 2 cups half-and-half
- 1 teaspoon vanilla extract

Place yolks and sugar in a bowl and whip until the mixture becomes thick and light colored. Bring the half-and-half to a boil over medium heat and slowly add it to the yolk mixture, stirring all the while. Pour the sauce into a double boiler and cook over gently

boiling water, stirring constantly, making sure you get into the edges of the pan. Cook until slightly thickened, about 5 minutes or more. Remove from heat, stir in the vanilla, and place pan into cold water, stirring occasionally until mixture is lukewarm.

Makes about 2¹/₂ cups

RASPBERRY SAUCE

2 cups fresh or frozen raspberries
Sugar (optional)

Place the berries in a blender or food processor and blend well. Strain through a fine sieve to remove seeds and add sugar to taste if desired.

Makes about 1³/₄ cups

ABOUT THE WINES

I must say I find executive chef Stephen Benson's obvious open-minded attitude to teaming food and wine very much in tune with my own feelings.

Here, in part, is what he had to say about the wines served at lunch. As you will notice, when describing Cain's wines, he is fully acquainted with their subtleties. For me, this makes his urging that one be unbiased about the whole thing carry even more weight:

"The 1987 Chardonnay should be poured with the scallops on through the salad course. The Cain Five should be opened for the entrée. I feel poultry can be served with red or white wine. The Chardonnay has the flavors of a multitude of fruits—apple, pineapple, mango, and papaya. The aromas match the intensity of the flavors; the fruit is enhanced by toasty and smoky oak aromas and flavors.

"Cain Five is an unusually complex red wine. Vanilla, anise, mint, cherry, blackberry, black currant, wood smoke, and tobacco elements can all be found in both the aroma and flavor. The wine has the silky, elegant-in-your-mouth feel, which is its hallmark. As enjoyable as this wine is now, it will improve with bottle age over the next ten to twenty years.

"Cain Cellars and I feel people should experiment and not have any set rules about pairing wine with food; for instance, try the red wine with the chocolate dessert."

LEFT: **Triple Chocolate Terrine with Crème Anglaise and Raspberry Sauce.**
ABOVE: **Winery chef Stephen Benson.**

A Fall Dinner

IRON HORSE VINEYARDS

❧

IF THINGS had gone according to their original plan, Barry and Audrey Sterling would now be contentedly living in France, making wine and enjoying great food. But since plans have a way of working out differently from how we imagine they will, instead of France it's California.

Barry and Audrey met as students at Stanford, where Barry was taking a degree in law. After his graduation, they married and moved to Washington, D.C., where they lived for several years.

Returning to Los Angeles in 1960 to open his own law office, Barry practiced corporate law and became active in Democratic party politics. The family also expanded to four with the birth of Joy and Lawrence.

Life was full and busy; both attractive young Sterlings loved entertaining and were also involved in the civic affairs of Los Angeles. Maybe they would be there yet, except for a trip to Europe—a 30th birthday gift to Barry from Audrey. It was love at first sight for him, and there followed years of travel abroad for both business and pleasure.

So it was a dream come true in the mid-1960s, when an opportunity presented itself to practice law in Paris. Without hesitation the family moved to a Belle Epoque apartment there, which was to be one of many residences they would live in over the next decade, including a house in the south of France and later a 300-year-old Queen Anne house when Barry opened an office in London.

During this period Barry and Audrey developed a keen interest in the wine and food of France. And on their trips to and from the south of France, they would zigzag across the country, trying new restaurants and wines as they went.

It must have been about this time, too, that the idea started to take hold of finding the "perfect" place to live in France where they could serve fine food and produce estate wines.

The search began in earnest in 1967 and was to continue until 1974 when, after several unsuccessful attempts to realize their goal, they abandoned it and decided to return to California.

Disappointed but determined to salvage at least part of what they had set their sights on, they began their search in the northern California wine country, which by then had started to show its wine-making muscle. Ultimately, they bought the old Iron Horse Ranch. Already at the ranch was Forrest Tancer, a man determined to see this property realize its full potential. So dedicated and knowledgeable was Tancer, in fact, that ultimately he became a partner with the Sterlings.

Over the years the vineyards and winery were renovated, and a frost-protection system, trellising, and fencing were undertaken. Meanwhile, Audrey had her hands full rebuilding the property's 1876 redwood gothic house and bringing the flower gardens, her special enthusiasm, into bloom.

At last in 1979 the first wines were made, which, when released, rewarded them for all their efforts. Today, with the operation working smoothly, it is hard to believe that it was only a little over a decade ago when the wines first started to flow from all their work.

So the dream did come true after all—as I think you will agree is abundantly borne out by this example of the subtle food and distinctive wines now enjoyed at Iron Horse.

I'm happy for the Sterlings that their dream panned out. I'm happier still that it happened here.

The table set with a fall bouquet.

Grilled Tuna, Salmon, and Sturgeon

Actually, any combination of fish would be fine here, but this is an especially pleasing threesome.

1 ¼   **pounds fresh tuna filet**
1 ¼   **pounds fresh salmon filet, cut into serving-size pieces**
1 ¼   **pounds fresh sturgeon filet, cut into serving-size pieces**
      Olive oil
      Salt and white pepper to taste
      Fresh Tomato Sauce (recipe follows)

Start the coals in an outdoor grill and place the grill rack 4 to 6 inches above the ash-covered coals (allow the rack to heat thoroughly before putting the fish on). Brush fish generously on all sides with olive oil and season with salt and pepper. Place salmon on first and cook until just flaky, about 2 minutes for each side. Remove to a warm platter. Place the tuna and sturgeon on next and cook the tuna about 2 ¼ minutes per side so it will be rare in the center; cook the sturgeon about 3 minutes per side, until flaky but still firm. Remove to a warm platter. You can also cook the fish in a preheated oven broiler with the rack set 4 to 6 inches from the heat.

Arrange the sturgeon and salmon around the tuna filet. Serve with sauce.

Serves 6 to 8

TOP (CLOCKWISE FROM BOTTOM):
Grilled Tuna, Salmon, and Sturgeon;
Green Beans with Yellow and Red Cherry Tomatoes; Yellow and Red Baby Beets; Beet Greens; and center, Fresh Tomato Sauce.
ABOVE: **Winery chef Martha Buser.**

FRESH TOMATO SAUCE

This sauce is cooked very briefly so it retains its fresh flavor. It is also delicious on pasta.

- ¼ cup olive oil
- 2 tablespoons minced garlic
- 8 medium to large tomatoes (about 4 pounds), peeled, seeded, and coarsely chopped
  Pinch of sugar
  Salt and freshly ground pepper to taste
- 3 tablespoons sliced fresh basil, in thin julienne

Place oil in a large skillet and heat over high heat. Add the garlic and cook about 1 minute, stirring. Add the tomatoes and continue cooking over high heat, stirring, until heated through and some liquid has evaporated, about 5 minutes. Add sugar and season to taste. Stir in the basil off the heat, then serve.

Serves 6 to 8

❧

Baby Beets and Greens

Many people think beet greens are too bitter, but if they are served with a bit of fresh lemon juice or a sprinkling of vinegar they can be very tasty. Besides, you will have bought them anyway, so you might as well give them a try.

- 2 dozen baby red beets with tops (about 2 pounds)
- 2 dozen baby yellow beets with tops (about 2 pounds)
- 2 medium shallots, minced
- 1 large garlic clove, minced
- 1½ teaspoons balsamic vinegar
- ¾ cup olive oil

- 1 tablespoon Dijon-style mustard
  Salt and pepper to taste
  Beet Greens (recipe follows)

Wash the beets well and cut off tops, leaving about 1 inch of stem. Reserve tops. Trim roots. In separate saucepans cover red and yellow beets with water and boil over medium heat until tender, 20 to 25 minutes. Drain and when cool enough to handle, slip off skins. Cut each beet in halves or quarters, depending on size, and place in a large bowl.

While beets are cooking, whisk together remaining ingredients and pour over cooked beets. Cover and marinate overnight in the refrigerator.

Drain beets and serve with greens.

Serves 6 to 8

BEET GREENS

- 24 beet tops
- 2 tablespoons olive oil
- 1 small garlic clove, minced
  Salt and pepper to taste
- 1 tablespoon balsamic vinegar, or to taste

Wash and stem the beet greens. Dry carefully. Heat the oil over medium heat in a large pot and sauté the garlic until wilted, 2 to 3 minutes. Add the greens and continue to cook tossing until wilted and tender, 6 to 8 minutes. Season with salt and pepper. Sprinkle with balsamic vinegar just before serving.

Serves 6 to 8

Green Beans with Yellow and Red Cherry Tomatoes

The colors of this dish are scrumptious.

- 2 pounds string beans, stemmed and tipped
- 1 dozen red cherry tomatoes (about ¼ pound), cut in halves
- 1 dozen yellow cherry tomatoes (about ¼ pound), cut in halves
  Salt and pepper to taste
- 2 tablespoons olive oil

Plunge the beans into a pot of rapidly boiling water and boil until tender but still crunchy, about 2 minutes. Drain and put into a bowl of ice water. Drain when cool.

Toss the beans and tomatoes together with the salt and pepper. Sprinkle with the olive oil and toss again.

Serves 6 to 8

❧

TOP: **Barry Sterling.**
BELOW: **Barn-red winery buildings.**

Mâche and Radicchio Salad with Sparkling Wine Vinaigrette

There is a lot of food here, so you may not want a salad, but here it is in case. You might want to serve double-cream Monterey Jack cheese with this salad, which is available most places these days.

Approximately 6 lightly packed cups mixed mâche and torn radicchio, carefully washed and dried

6 medium shallots, minced

1 tablespoon Dijon-style mustard

½ cup sparkling white wine

½ cup champagne vinegar

½ cup virgin olive oil

Salt and pepper to taste

Double-cream Monterey Jack cheese (optional)

Place the greens in a bowl and refrigerate, covered. Meanwhile, place shallots, mustard, wine, and vinegar in a bowl and whisk together. Whisk in oil, then salt and pepper. Check for seasoning and add more oil if desired. Do not refrigerate. (This makes about 1¾ cups of vinaigrette.)

Place greens in a bowl and toss with a few tablespoons of vinaigrette, adding more to taste as well as more salt and pepper if desired. Serve with a wedge of the cheese.

Serves 6 to 8

✣

Cabernet and Honey Poached Figs

This looks as good as it tastes. It's easy, too.

24 medium figs, stems removed Cabernet to cover, about 1½ bottles

¼ cup honey, or more to taste Mint sprigs, for garnish (optional)

Place the figs in a stainless steel saucepan. Cover with wine and add honey. Bring quickly to a boil and immediately turn back to simmer. Cook figs until tender but not falling apart, 4 to 5 minutes. Cool in the liquid.

When cool, remove figs and reduce liquid until very slightly thickened, about 5 minutes over high heat. Allow to cool and refrigerate.

To serve, place figs in individual glass bowls and pour sauce over. Garnish with mint. Leftover sauce may be used again to poach more fruit.

Serves 6 to 8

ABOVE: **Audrey Sterling.** BELOW: **Mâche and Radicchio Salad with Sparkling Wine Vinaigrette.** OPPOSITE: **Cabernet and Honey Poached Figs with Cayenne Pound Cake.**

Cayenne Pound Cake

Here is an interesting twist on an old Joy of Cooking *recipe.*

- 1 cup (2 sticks) unsalted butter, softened
- 1 cup sugar
- 5 eggs, at room temperature
- 1 teaspoon vanilla extract
- 2 cups all-purpose flour
  Scant pinch of cayenne pepper
- ½ teaspoon cream of tartar
- ½ teaspoon salt

Preheat the oven to 325 degrees and grease a 9 by 5-inch loaf pan. Set aside.

Cream the butter and sugar until light and fluffy. Add the eggs one at a time, mixing well after each. Stir in vanilla. Sift the flour and measure, then sift again with the other dry ingredients. Gradually add to the butter-sugar mixture, stirring. When well mixed, pour into the pan and bake for 1 hour, or until a cake tester comes out clean.

Serves 8 to 12

Pepper Sugar Cookies

This cookie is similar to one of my favorites, so I was bound to like it.

- 1 cup (2 sticks) unsalted butter, softened
- 1 ¼ cups sugar
- 2 eggs
- 1 teaspoon vanilla extract
- ½ teaspoon salt
- 1 teaspoon cream of tartar
- 2 ¼ cups all-purpose flour
- 1 tablespoon ground allspice
- ½ teaspoon black pepper

Cream the butter and 1 cup of sugar until light and fluffy. Add the eggs one at a time, beating well. Add the vanilla and mix. Sift together the salt, cream of tartar, and flour, then add to the batter, beating until you have a semistiff dough. Refrigerate for 20 minutes. Meanwhile, preheat the oven to 350 degrees.

Mix the remaining ¼ cup of sugar, allspice, and black pepper in a bowl and spread on a sheet of wax paper. Roll dough into balls by the spoonful, then roll in the spiced sugar to coat. Place on a cookie sheet, allowing space for them to expand.

Bake until lightly golden, about 10 to 12 minutes.

Makes 4 to 5 dozen

ABOUT THE WINES

I especially like the way Iron Horse's executive chef, Martha Buser, explains why she and Mrs. Sterling selected the wines for this meal. Martha not only lists the qualities that led to their final selection but also tells why the Pinot Noir, which was considered, was not served.

"We chose Chardonnay to serve with the fish because it stands up to the flavors of all three fish better than a fumé, not being as fruity in character. We had considered a Pinot Noir but decided on the Chardonnay because of the light flavor of the sturgeon. Pinot would have been fine with the tuna and salmon, if they were the only two fish being served.

"Cabernet with both the salad and dessert seemed right because of the cheese and hearty bread served with the salad—and the figs were poached in Cabernet. I especially like Cabernet's peppery and berry flavor with the figs."

An Hors d'Oeuvre and Dessert Party

BERINGER VINEYARDS

❧

BERINGER VINEYARDS came into being in 1876, six years after Jacob Beringer had emigrated to America determined to find the proper climatic and physical conditions to establish a winery. His search brought him to California on the same tide as the Gold Rush. But gold prospecting was of no interest to Jacob, and he ultimately found what he was looking for in Napa Valley, the location of Beringer today.

Fortunately, Jacob's older brother, Frederick, had settled in New York in 1865. And Jacob, who had worked as a winemaker and cellarmaster in their native Germany, was able to convince Frederick to join his wine-making venture as partner and business manager. Jacob was to be the winemaker, which he continued being for the rest of his life.

Immediately upon Frederick's arrival in California, the brothers set about laying out the facilities. From his experience in the vineyards of Germany and France, Jacob knew that the best way to store and age wine was in rock caves or tunnels, and the hills rising at the back of the winery property were perfect for such a scheme. This task of excavating took several years to complete, most of the work being done by Chinese laborers who, after completing work on the Transcontinental railroad expansion, had returned to nearby San Francisco.

While the tunnels were being tediously bored and chiseled out of the rocky hillside, the balance of the facility was developed. Vines were planted and buildings completed.

With major winery construction finished, Frederick, who wanted to re-create the family home overlooking the Rhine River in Germany, cleared a large plot on the winery property and began building "Rhine House" in 1883. Jacob was already occuping Hudson House, built in 1854, into which he and his wife moved during construction of the tunnels. Both structures are still standing.

Jacob's instinct for locating the winery in this tranquil valley and his notion to create tunnels for aging and storage, which maintain a temperature of 58 degrees year round, are part of his living heritage. These tunnels are still in use today.

Jacob's descendents lived in Hudson House up until 1971, when Beringer Brothers was acquired by Wine World Inc.; over the years the new owners have continually updated the complex with such ambitious projects as augmenting the production facilities, reinforcing the original cellar and tunnels, remodeling and refurbishing Rhine House (which was listed on the National Register of Historic Places

Historic Rhine House, which was begun in 1885.

in 1972), and purchasing new lands and buildings.

Finally, in 1989, the Beringer Culinary Center was opened in the remodeled Hudson House as the permanent home for their culinary program.

Today this school for chefs is headed by the renowned teaching chef Madeleine Kamman and ensures that Beringer will go into the new century not only as a leader in the wine industry but in the community of professional cooking schools as well.

M E N U

PHYLLO CUPS WITH GOAT CHEESE, PINE NUTS, AND SUN-DRIED TOMATOES
MANDARIN GRILLED QUAIL
OYSTERS IN ARUGULA CREAM
PICKLED SHRIMP
NAPA VALLEY APPLE TART
STRAWBERRY AMARETTO CUSTARD TART
BLACK WALNUT SORBET
LEMON WALNUT BARS

1987 Sauvignon Blanc
1987 Knights Valley Gamay Beaujolais

Phyllo Cups with Goat Cheese, Pine Nuts, and Sun-dried Tomatoes

As you can note from the photograph, these make a spectacular presentation and are remarkably easy to prepare.

- 12 sheets phyllo dough
- ¼ cup hazelnut oil (walnut or vegetable oil may be substituted)
- 8 ounces mild goat cheese
- 4 ounces cream cheese
- 3 eggs
- ⅓ cup toasted pine nuts
- ¼ cup sun-dried tomatoes, tightly packed, finely chopped
- 6 scallions, both white and green parts, finely chopped
- 2 tablespoons finely chopped fresh dill
  Freshly ground black pepper to taste
  Salt to taste (optional)

Preheat the oven to 350 degrees.

It is best to use 2-ounce (¼-cup) mini-muffin tins for this recipe. Cut the phyllo into 8-inch squares and brush with hazelnut oil. Stack in 4-sheet batches and push one batch into each muffin cup, folding the edges to form "petals." Cover with plastic and chill for 1 hour. Blend the goat and cream cheeses in a bowl. Add the eggs one at a time, and mix. Add remaining ingredients, mixing until well blended. (Mixture may be made in advance and refrigerated up to this point. Bring filling back to room temperature before proceeding.)

Fill phyllo cups three-fourths full. Bake until phyllo is golden and filling puffs, about 12 to 15 minutes.

Makes 3 dozen

Mandarin Grilled Quail

When you buy quail, ask your butcher to remove the backbone and rib cage; it will make this recipe much simpler. Or you can halve them through the breast and backbone, then cut out the rest of the backbone with poultry shears.

- 1½ cups low-sodium soy sauce (tamari)
- ½ cup water
- ½ cup hoisin sauce

- 6 tablespoons dark brown sugar
- 3 tablespoons rice vinegar
- 4 medium garlic cloves, finely minced
  2-inch piece fresh ginger, peeled, thinly sliced, and minced
- 2 medium shallots, finely minced
- 6 scallions, white and green parts, finely chopped
- 1 tablespoon hot sesame oil
- 24 small quail, butterflied

Mix the first 10 ingredients, stirring until the brown sugar dissolves. Place the quail in a shallow nonmetallic dish and cover with the marinade. Refrigerate, covered, turning occasionally, for at least 3 hours. (They are best if allowed to marinate overnight.)

Remove quail from marinade and pat dry. Grill over hot coals approximately 3 to 4 minutes per side. Or cook the quail under a preheated broiler for the same amount of time.

Serves 12 or more

Note: Tamari, hoisin sauce, and hot sesame oil are available in the Chinese or Japanese section of your market.

Oysters in Arugula Cream

If you buy shucked oysters—and unless you know how to open them, you should—be sure to get the liquor and the 36 bottom shells.

- 36 oysters, shucked, with liquor saved and bottom shells scrubbed clean
- ½ pound arugula, stems removed (spinach may be substituted)
- 1 cup heavy cream
- 3 tablespoons unsalted butter
- 3 medium shallots, finely minced
- 2 medium garlic cloves, minced
- ⅔ cup oyster liquor, fish stock, or bottled clam juice

TOP: **Phyllo Cups with Goat Cheese, Pine Nuts, and Sun-dried Tomatoes.**
LEFT: **Mandarin Grilled Quail.**

1 tablespoon Pernod or
  Ricard, or 1 pinch anise seed
Salt to taste (optional)
Freshly ground black pepper
  to taste
Rock salt
Grated Parmesan cheese to
  taste
Arugula, for garnish

Rinse each oyster in reserved juices to remove any shell fragments. Strain liquor and refrigerate oysters.

Boil the bottom shells in water for 10 minutes to sterilize. Drain.

Blanch the arugula in boiling water for ½ minute. Drain, squeeze dry, and chop fine. In a small saucepan over medium heat, reduce cream to ½ cup, about 15 minutes.

Place butter in a small skillet and when bubbly, add the shallots. Sauté over medium heat until transparent, about 3 minutes. Reduce heat to low and add the garlic. Continue sautéing for a few more minutes. Add the reserved oyster liquor or stock, increase heat to medium and reduce until only a few tablespoons of liquid remain, about 5 to 7 minutes. Add the arugula and reduced cream. Stir and then flame with Pernod. Check seasoning and add salt and pepper as needed.

To assemble, spread the rock salt on a rimmed cookie sheet large enough to hold the shells. Place an oyster in each shell and top with a tablespoon of the arugula cream. Sprinkle with cheese and place under the broiler until the cream bubbles. Served garnished with extra arugula.

Serves 12 or more

Note: To flame Pernod place it in a large metal measuring cup or ladle, heat to almost simmer and flame with a match. Pour into cream mixture while stirring.

TOP: **Oysters in Arugula Cream.**
RIGHT: **Pickled Shrimp.**

Pickled Shrimp

Not only do jumbo shrimp look better for this dish, they also are a lot easier to peel and devein. Prepare this 2 to 3 days in advance for best flavor.

    1   cup cider vinegar
    2   teaspoons dry mustard
    ½   cup tomato or spaghetti
         sauce
  1 ½   cups corn oil
    2   tablespoons Tabasco sauce
    2   tablespoons Worcestershire
         sauce
    1   teaspoon salt
    ½   teaspoon black pepper
    3   tablespoons drained capers
    1   cup sliced bell peppers, cut
         into rings (red, yellow, and
         green mixed, if available)
    2   cups thinly sliced red onions
         (use small onions)
2 ½ to 3 pounds jumbo shrimp,
         cooked, peeled, and de-
         veined, leaving the tip of
         the tail shell on

In a large nonmetallic container, combine vinegar, mustard, tomato sauce, corn oil, Tabasco, Worcestershire, salt, and pepper. Layer capers, pepper rings, onion rings, and shrimp in a storage container. Pour marinade over all. Seal tightly and refrigerate until ready to serve.

Serve with slices of French bread or crackers.

Serves 12 or more

Napa Valley Apple Tart

Neatness counts here.

PASTRY

- 2 cups unbleached all-purpose flour
- ½ teaspoon salt
- 2 teaspoons sugar
- ¾ cup (1½ sticks) unsalted butter, chilled
- ⅓ cup cold water

ASSEMBLY

- 6 to 8 Golden Delicious apples, peeled, halved, cored, and sliced ¼-inch thick
- ½ cup sugar
- 4 tablespoons (½ stick) unsalted butter
- ½ cup sieved apricot preserves
- 1 to 2 tablespoons Calvados (apple brandy)

Make the pastry. On a table or work surface, place flour, salt, and sugar. Mix well. Blend in the butter, using your fingers to make coarse crumbs. Make a well in the center of the mixture and add cold water. Bring flour in from sides and mix gently. (This step may also be done in a food processor.)

With the heel of your hand, press out small bits of the dough, then gather it into a mound. Wrap in wax paper and chill approximately 2 hours.

Preheat the oven to 400 degrees.

Assemble. Roll out the pastry into a large round or rectangle approximately ⅛-inch thick. Roll dough onto rolling pin and transfer to a large 12 by 16-inch cookie sheet. Place apple slices on top, slightly overlapping, leaving a 2-inch border all around. Fold border back onto the apples. Sprinkle with sugar and dot with pieces of butter. Bake for 1 hour, until golden.

When cool, mix apricot preserves and brandy in a small bowl and brush carefully over the apples.

Serves 12 or more

TOP: **Napa Valley Apple Tart.**
LEFT: **The outdoor living room set for a party.**

29

Black Walnut Sorbet

As most of you know, black walnuts have a distinctive taste. If you like them, you'll love this. There is really no substitute for the black walnut extract or the liqueur, so if you can't find it, don't make this.

- 3 cups water
- 1 cup sugar
- 1 cup shelled black walnuts, toasted and finely chopped
- 1 tablespoon black walnut extract, or ½ cup black walnut liqueur (see Note)
- 2 tablespoons fresh lemon juice

Bring water and sugar to a boil. Remove from heat and add black walnuts, and allow to macerate overnight.

Add extract or liqueur and lemon juice. Strain and freeze mixture in an ice cream freezer according to manufacturer's directions. Or you may freeze this without straining.

Makes about 1 quart or 20 scoops

Strawberry Amaretto Custard Tart

Raspberries or blueberries may be substituted for the strawberries—or combine all three.

PASTRY

- 1 cup all-purpose flour
- 2 tablespoons sugar
- ¼ teaspoon salt
- 6 tablespoons (¾ stick) chilled unsalted butter
- 3 tablespoons iced water

AMARETTO CUSTARD

- 2 cups milk
- ¾ cup sugar
- ½ cup all-purpose flour
- ⅛ teaspoon salt
- 2 egg yolks, beaten
- 5 tablespoons unsalted butter, cut in small pieces
- 1 teaspoon vanilla extract
- ¼ cup Amaretto liqueur
  Heavy cream (optional)

ASSEMBLY

- 1 10-ounce jar apricot preserves
  Kirsch or other liqueur (optional)
- 2 pints strawberries

Make the pastry. Place the flour, sugar, and salt on a table or work surface and mix well. Cut in the butter using your fingertips, making coarse crumbs. Make a well in the center of the mixture and add the ice water. Bring flour in from the sides and very gently mix. With the heel of your hand, press out small bits of dough, then gather them into a mound. Wrap in wax paper and chill about 2 hours. (You may also mix the dough in a food processor.)

Roll out dough to fit a 10-inch tart pan with a removable bottom, pressing it firmly against bottom and sides. (May also be made into individual tarts.) Prick with a fork and chill for 1 hour.

Preheat the oven to 425 degrees.

Fit the pastry with foil and cover bottom of shell with dried beans or rice. Bake for 12 to 15 minutes. Remove foil and beans and continue to bake 10 to 12 more minutes, until crust is light golden brown, being careful not to let it burn.

Make the custard. Scald the milk. Mix the sugar, flour, and salt in a bowl. Add to the hot milk and cook over very low heat until it thickens, stirring all the while, 4 to 5 minutes. Add the egg yolks, stirring constantly, and continue cooking for another 3 minutes, until quite thick. Stir in the butter, vanilla, and Amaretto. If filling is too thick, thin with a bit of cream. Stir occasionally as filling cools. (May be refrigerated until tart is assembled.)

Assemble. Melt preserves in a saucepan and put through a fine sieve. You may want to thin this slightly with water, kirsch, or any other liqueur. Strain and spread the custard evenly over the baked crust. Top with a layer of berries, whole or sliced. Brush with the melted preserves.

Refrigerate until ready to serve.

Serves 12 or more

Note: Grutzmacher's black walnut liqueur is available at some liquor stores and Wagner's black walnut extract is available at good specialty food stores.

꒜

Lemon Walnut Bars

Lemon bars are just about everyone's favorite.

BASE

1	cup all-purpose flour
1/3	cup confectioners' sugar, sifted
1/2	cup finely ground walnuts
1/2	teaspoon grated lemon zest
2/3	cup unsalted butter, cut in small chunks

FILLING

2	eggs
1	cup granulated sugar
7	tablespoons fresh lemon juice
2	tablespoons flour
1/2	teaspoon baking powder
	Confectioners' sugar to taste

Preheat the oven to 375 degrees.

Make the base. Combine the flour, confectioners' sugar, walnuts, and zest in a bowl and blend well. Add the butter chunks. Using your fingers, combine until mixture resembles coarse meal. Press mixture into an ungreased 8-inch square pan. Bake until set, about 20 minutes.

Make the filling. Beat the eggs and granulated sugar in a bowl until light in color. Add the lemon juice and continue beating another 5 minutes. In a separate bowl, combine the flour and baking powder. Add the flour mixture to the egg mixture slowly, stirring all the while until smooth.

Pour the filling over the partially baked base and return to the oven and continue baking until set, about 25 minutes. Remove from the oven and cool. Sift confectioners' sugar over the top and cut into squares or bars.

Makes 12 to 16 bars

꒜

Beringer's resident chef, Pat Windisch, planned the assortment of tempting hors d'oeuvres and desserts for our party. The following are her views on putting together wines and food. Incidentally, Pat was a student of Madeleine Kamman, who now heads Beringer's chefs' cooking school:

"The basics of food and wine pairing come down to a balancing of sugars and acids. The acid in the pickled shrimp and in the goat cheese and sun-dried tomatoes helps to pair each to a very nice acid level in our 1987 Sauvignon Blanc. Its herbaceousness ties well to the dill and other herbs in the recipes. Because of the cream in the Oysters in Arugula Cream, you may want to try a Chardonnay or add the juice of a lemon to it to bring it closer to a Sauvignon Blanc.

"Mandarin Grilled Quail is paired to our 1987 Knights Valley Gamay Beaujolais because of its light fruitiness. The low fat and light texture of the quail is complemented by the lighter bodied red wine."

OPPOSITE TOP: **Strawberry Amaretto Custard Tart.** LEFT: **Black Walnut Sorbet, and Lemon Walnut Bars.** ABOVE: **Winery chef Pat Windisch.**

A Healthful Celebration Dinner

CAKEBREAD CELLARS

AKEBREAD CELLARS started with a good honest deal. Jack and Dolores Cakebread had decided they wanted to be in the winemaking business when they happened upon a piece of land at Napa Valley's Rutherford Bench. It was owned by an elderly couple named Sturdivent, family friends. The Sturdivents were ready to retire and the Cakebreads were ready to buy. A deal was struck whereby the Cakebreads would buy the ranch and the Sturdivents would live there for their remaining days—which they did. That was in 1972. Everybody was happy. But the work had just begun.

Land had to be cleared and vines planted since the place had been operated as a ranch for over half a century. Jack's mechanical ingenuity came in handy in creating the super-modern facilities. You see, he had owned and operated a sprawling auto garage, which he had bought from his father years before. But advanced technology was not all that he wanted. Aside from his mechanical skills, Jack was an accomplished photographer who had studied with Ansel Adams, and he wanted the whole thing to be aesthetically pleasing as well. So, with the help of San Francisco architect William Turnbull, buildings were designed and built to blend in with the land-

scape. The main building conceals what amounts to one big piece of high-tech equipment, which features such innovations as a drainage system that allows a single person to hose down quickly the whole thing— machines, vats, walls and floor, facilities for washing barrels—and a delicately structured air flow to keep electrical expenses down. Somehow in the midst of all this Jack managed to enroll in the viticulture and oenology program at U.C. Davis.

But this is a family affair. Also part of the squad are two of the three Cakebread sons. Bruce is the winemaker, and Dennis the "money man." Dolores has been on hand all the while serving as "camp cook," as she explains it, over time exhibiting exceptional talent at creating interesting and nutritious dishes. She's not just interested in taste, however; she wants her food to be low in calories and cholesterol. She has succeeded in this remarkably well.

For instance, the venison with red wine sauce in this menu has fewer calories and cholesterol than chicken. There is even a *seemingly* sinful chocolate dessert to finish the whole thing off. And all within her self-imposed rigid specifications. With great skill, she and Jack pair these dishes with the vineyard's wonderful wines.

Plans are afoot for slowly expanding the vineyards at the recently acquired Cakebread Hill Ranch, whose first harvest is expected in 1990. So it looks like this congenial and close-knit team will be hard at it well into the next century. Which suits them all just fine!

M E N U

**TORTELLINI AND WILD MUSHROOMS WITH
BUTTERMILK DRESSING**
**PEPPERED LOIN OF VENISON WITH
RED WINE SAUCE**
**PUREED CARROTS AND TURNIPS ON
ARTICHOKE BOTTOMS**
CHERRY AND CHOCOLATE TRIFLE

Sauvignon Blanc
Chardonnay Reserve
Rutherford Reserve Cabernet

OPPOSITE: **Tortellini and Wild Mushrooms
with Buttermilk Dressing.** ABOVE: **Bruce and
Dennis Cakebread.** ABOVE RIGHT: **Jack and
Dolores Cakebread.**

Tortellini and Wild Mushrooms with Buttermilk Dressing

White mushrooms, or a combination of mushrooms, may be substituted.

- 2 tablespoons light vegetable oil
- 2 medium garlic cloves, minced
- 2 shallots, minced
- ½ pound fresh shiitake or chanterelle mushrooms, sliced
- 1 cup dry white wine
- ¼ cup chopped fresh parsley
- 1 tablespoon fresh lemon juice
- 1 pound cheese-filled tortellini, cooked according to package instructions
  Buttermilk Dressing (recipe follows)
  Chopped nasturtiums, for garnish (optional)

Heat the oil in a large skillet. Add half the garlic and shallots and sauté over medium heat until wilted, about 5 minutes. Add the mushrooms and sauté 8 to 10 minutes over low heat, until mushrooms give up liquid and begin to get tender. Add the wine and remaining garlic and shallots along with half the parsley. Toss and sauté an additional 2 to 3 minutes, until mushrooms are tender.

Toss the cooked tortellini with the dressing, below. Sprinkle with remaining parsley and surround with mushrooms. Garnish with nasturtiums.

Serves 6 to 8

BUTTERMILK DRESSING

- 2 cups buttermilk
- 8 ounces low-fat cream cheese
- 2 medium garlic cloves, minced
- ½ teaspoon Tabasco sauce
  Freshly ground black pepper to taste

Place all ingredients except pepper in a food processor. Process until smooth. Add pepper and refrigerate until ready to use. May be made a day in advance.

Makes about 3 cups

Peppered Loin of Venison with Red Wine Sauce

This is absolutely delicious and very easy to prepare.

- 6 cups unseasoned beef stock
- 2 pounds trimmed axis venison loin (see Note)
  Salt
  Whole black peppercorns to taste
  Olive oil
- 16 to 24 cipollini onions, pearl onions, or shallots
- 1¼ cups Cabernet
- 1 tablespoon cornstarch
- 3 tablespoons cold water
- 2 tablespoons unsalted butter, cut into bits (optional)

Bring stock to a slow boil and reduce to 3 cups. This can take up to 45 minutes, so allow time for it. Season venison lightly with salt. Set aside. Coarsely crush the peppercorns with a rolling pin, then pat the crushed pepper on all sides of the venison.

Heat a large, heavy skillet or casserole until very hot. Add enough olive oil just to coat the bottom of the pan. Sear all sides and ends of the venison quickly, until well browned. Place a rack on a baking sheet and put venison on the rack. Set aside.

Reheat skillet and add onions; toss to sear until browned in spots. Reduce heat, then add wine and stock. Cover pan tightly and simmer gently until onions are tender, 15 to 20 minutes. Remove the onions with a slotted spoon and set aside, lightly covered. Reduce the sauce until you have 1½ cups, about 10 minutes. Stir cornstarch and cold water together in a small bowl, whisk into sauce, and cook over medium heat until sauce thickens. Whisk in butter if desired. Return onions to pan.

Meanwhile, preheat the oven to 450 degrees. Roast the venison 7 to 10 minutes, to desired degree of doneness. Let rest 5 minutes before slicing. Place each serving of venison on about 3 tablespoons of the sauce with several onions.

Serves 8

Note: If venison is not available in your specialty market, it may be ordered from Texas Wild Game Cooperative (see page 173).

There is another cut of venison that is often more available in local markets than the tenderloin. This is known as the Denver cut and may be substituted for the tenderloin.

LEFT: **The winery gardens.**
ABOVE: **Peppered Loin of Venison with Red Wine Sauce, and Pureed Carrots and Turnips on Artichoke Bottoms.**
OPPOSITE: **Cherry and Chocolate Trifles.**

Pureed Carrots and Turnips on Artichoke Bottoms

You can substitute any puree you like for the one suggested here. This one is mighty tasty, though.

- 8 medium to large artichokes
- 1 large lemon
- 8 medium carrots, scraped and cut into large rings
- 4 small turnips, peeled and quartered
  Salt, pepper, sugar, and nutmeg to taste

Remove all leaves and chokes from artichokes and peel all green from the bottoms. Bring a medium pan of water to a boil. Cut lemon into quarters and drop in water. When boiling, add artichoke bottoms and simmer until tender, about 15 minutes. Refresh with cold water and set aside, covered with a tea towel.

Boil the carrots and turnips separately until tender, 8 to 10 minutes. Puree the carrots until smooth and then, separately, the turnips. Add turnips to carrots in small amounts until pleasing to your taste. Add salt and pepper and mix. Add a pinch of sugar and a bit of nutmeg to taste.

Place puree on artichoke bottoms and serve at room temperature.

Serves 8

Cherry and Chocolate Trifle

Dried cherries seem to be popping up in lots of specialty shops, but they may also be ordered directly from American Spoon Foods (see page 173).

- 1 tablespoon sugar
- 1 tablespoon cornstarch
- ¼ cup liquid egg substitute or 1 egg, lightly beaten
- 1 cup skim milk
- 1 teaspoon vanilla extract
- 3 tablespoons dry sherry
- ¼ pound Angel Food cake, cut into 1-inch cubes
- ¾ cup dried cherries, reconstituted with Cabernet and heated until soft and plump; drained and chopped
- 4 ounces bittersweet chocolate
- ½ bottle dry red wine

Mix sugar and cornstarch in a small saucepan. Add egg substitute or egg and milk. Mix well. Heat to a simmer, stirring constantly, and continue to cook until thickened, several minutes. Remove from heat and add vanilla. Press a round of wax paper onto surface and allow to cool.

To assemble, sprinkle sherry over cake cubes and divide one-third of them among individual dessert bowls or wine glasses. Spoon one-third of the custard onto each serving, followed by one-third of the cherries. Repeat the layers—cake, custard, and cherries—twice more. Cover and refrigerate.

To serve, heat chocolate and wine together, stirring until chocolate melts. Drizzle this over the trifles.

Serves 4

About the Wines

Dolores Cakebread is as serious about their wines as she is about healthful food, expressing here an appealing balance between, and appreciation for, both:

"I work very hard to make our food tasty and healthy so you have enough room to enjoy a glass of fine wine! We like using our food to complement our wines, and vice versa. When we add our good friends to the table we are guaranteed a most pleasurable experience.

"The creamy richness of the buttermilk dressing and the earthy flavor of the mushrooms combine to enhance and complement the smooth, earthy richness of our Chardonnay Reserve. The subtle garlic in the sauce creates a little spice of life.

"Texas axis venison is a mild, tender, yet rich meat which can stand up to the tannins in our Rutherford Reserve Cabernet.

"Using Cabernet as a dessert wine works because the dried cherries are softened in the Cabernet and this works to emphasize the cherry-berry flavor of the wine."

A Champagne Dinner

SCHRAMSBERG VINEYARDS & CELLARS

❧

TO HEAR Jack Davies tell it, the only expertise he had in producing wine when he and his wife, Jamie, invested everything in an overgrown and dilapidated winery high on a hillside in Napa Valley was that he was a "wine fanatic." The fact that the property they bought was the oldest hill vineyard in the valley was interesting, but that didn't materially enhance their prospects— or did it? Was there past glory dozing there just waiting to be awakened?

Whatever, from the looks of their accomplishments since 1965, when they purchased the old Schram Estate, that fanaticism has served them both very well indeed.

actually stopped producing wines in 1911. In the intervening years a series of attempts by various families to revive the winery had all ended in failure. Not a very encouraging track record. However, the Davieses were not to be daunted.

First they decided that they would specialize—only in champagne. This was a daring decision, one that gave them a unique position among the wineries. Not incidentally, they still solely occupy this position, although the number of wineries in Napa has grown to more than 150. Next, they decided that their champagne would be made exclusively by the costly technique called *méthode champenoise*. This involves bottle fermenting and hand riddling, wherein fermented bottles are gently shaken individually so as to move spent yeast particles into the bottle's mouth. The final step is disgorging, in which the accumulated yeast is flash-frozen in place and removed. The champagne is then topped off, recorked, and aged three to six months longer. That sounds pretty complicated, but apparently it is not to the intrepid Davieses.

When they started, the entire U.S. production of *méthode champenoise* was hardly 50,000 cases. This year, with all the wineries that have followed their example, shipments will likely exceed 2.5 million cases.

Finally, aside from learning the wine business, Jack and Jamie had the Victorian house and gardens, which formed the centerpiece of the estate, to restore. And it is a California Historical Landmark. This is the very house in which Robert Louis Stevenson, on a visit in 1880, wrote a large part of his *Silverado Squatters*.

But that's all in the past. Along the way, Jack and Jamie have raised three sons, collected numerous awards, and become enthusiastic boosters of the Napa Valley. And Jamie has turned into one terrific cook, as the following meal will attest.

After talking to the Davieses, I'm willing to believe some people really *have* managed to live the great life.

Of course, it didn't hurt that Harvard-educated Jack had built a solid career in business management and that Jamie had been a founding partner in a very prestigious and successful San Francisco art gallery before they decided to take a chance on something they both really wanted. As they put it now, "We left the good life behind and found the *great* life."

However, in 1965 things were not really what you could call great—promising, maybe. The Schram Estate from which Schramsberg wine first came, aside from being in a terrible state of disrepair, had

Radish Canapés

I had forgotten just how tasty this simple canapé could be and was glad to rediscover it.

1 loaf homemade-style white bread, sliced medium thin
2 to 3 bunches red radishes
½ cup (1 stick) unsalted butter, softened
Finely chopped fresh chives

Cut the bread into 2½-inch rounds with a cookie cutter, making 24 in all. Spread each round generously with softened butter. Slice the radishes thin and arrange on bread in concentric circles. Sprinkle with chopped chives. Lightly cover with a damp cloth and keep chilled until serving time.

Any scraps and leftover pieces of bread can be made into bread crumbs.

Makes 24

❧

Ham and Rye Fritters

Here is another simple and delicious canapé devised by chef Robert Kaspar.

1 cup milk
½ cup (1 stick) unsalted butter
½ cup rye flour
½ cup all-purpose flour
3 eggs
1 ounce Monterey Jack cheese, cut into small cubes
2 ounces smoked ham, diced small
1 teaspoon caraway seeds

Preheat the oven to 425 degrees.

Heat the milk and butter in a saucepan until butter is melted and mixture boils. Sift in flours over medium heat, stirring all the while. Continue to cook and stir batter until it leaves the sides of the pan and forms a ball (1 to 2 minutes). Off the heat, beat in eggs one at the time. Beat in cheese, ham, and caraway seeds.

Form dough into 24 balls, about 1 inch in diameter and place 2 inches apart on a greased cookie sheet. (If dough is not firm enough to form into

balls, chill for about 30 minutes.) Bake for 15 minutes. Reduce oven heat to 325 degrees and bake for another 10 to 15 minutes, until golden.

Makes 24

ᕌ

Brioche with Mushrooms

Although served as a first course here, this would make a fine main course for a simple lunch, followed by the watercress salad and rice pudding.

- 2 tablespoons unsalted butter, plus additional
- 1 ½ pounds white mushrooms, brushed, trimmed, and sliced
- 1 tablespoon minced onion
- ½ teaspoon dried tarragon
- ½ cup champagne or dry white wine
- 1 ½ teaspoons fresh lemon juice
- 1 cup heavy cream
  Salt and pepper
- 1 tablespoon cornstarch blended with 1 tablespoon cold water
- 6 brioche, 4 inches in diameter, buttered

In a large, nonreactive skillet, melt the butter over medium heat and add the mushrooms, onion, and tarragon. Sauté for 3 to 4 minutes, until wilted. Add the wine, lemon juice, and ½ cup of the cream. Cook over medium-high heat until slightly reduced, about 5 minutes. Pour in the balance of the cream and add salt and pepper to taste. Stir in cornstarch mixture and simmer over low heat until thickened, 2 to 3 minutes.

To serve, remove tops from brioche and pull out soft centers. Butter inside with softened butter. Replace tops and warm in a 350 degree oven for 8 minutes.

Place brioche on individual plates and spoon mushroom sauce into each, surrounding with additional sauce.

Serves 6

ᕌ

OPPOSITE: **Ham and Rye Fritters with Radish Canapés.** ABOVE: **Dinner overlooking the pond.** LEFT: **Brioche with Mushrooms.**

pounds), peeled, cored, and coarsely chopped
- 2 large red bell peppers (about ¾ pound), cleaned and coarsely chopped
- 1 cup dried currants
- 1 cup coarsely chopped onion
- ½ cup peeled and finely chopped fresh ginger
- 2 large lemons, seeded and finely chopped (including rind)
- 2 teaspoons whole mustard seeds
- 1 tablespoon coarsely chopped fresh mint leaves
- 1 tablespoon salt

In a large, nonreactive pot, bring vinegar and brown sugar to a boil over high heat. Add all other ingredients and turn heat to a simmer. Cook, stirring occasionally, until thickened, about 45 minutes. Pour into sterilized jars and seal.

Makes 7 to 8 pints

- ½ pound bean sprouts
- 2 bunches watercress, washed and dried, tough stems removed
- 4 bunches scallions, sliced, with some green
- ⅓ cup olive oil
- 1 teaspoon sesame oil
- 2 tablespoons seasoned rice vinegar

String the peas and blanch. Cut into diagonal pieces. Blanch the sprouts. Place in a large salad bowl with the watercress and scallions. Toss.

Whisk together the oils and vinegar. Pour over vegetables and toss.

Serves 8 or more

ᕌ

- 1 large garlic clove, minced
- 3 tablespoons peeled and finely chopped fresh ginger
- ½ teaspoon hot red pepper flakes
- 1 ½ tablespoons sesame oil
- 1 large head green cabbage, shredded (about 10 to 12 cups)
- 2 large carrots, peeled and shredded

Heat the oil in a large skillet or wok over medium heat and add scallions, garlic, ginger, and red pepper flakes. Sauté for 3 minutes, until scallions have started to wilt. Add sesame oil, cabbage, and carrots. Stir-fry for 5 minutes, tossing. Cover and cook over low heat until tender, about 3 to 4 minutes.

Serves 6

Champagne Rabbit with Apple and Green Pear Chutney

I know not everyone is ambitious enough to make his or her own chutney, but just in case you want to give it a try, I am giving you the Schramsberg recipe and with it this delightful method of preparing rabbit. Incidentally, if you don't want rabbit, you can substitute chicken here. Not as interesting to my way of thinking, but good.

Incidentally, this recipe allows for very small portions because there is so much other food for this meal. If you would like to serve the rabbit accompanied simply by a first course, you should increase the recipe by another half.

- 1 **rabbit (2 to 3 pounds), cut into 6 or more serving pieces**
   Flour, for dredging
- 2 **tablespoons vegetable oil**
- 3 **tablespoons unsalted butter**
- 2 **tablespoons finely chopped**

- 6 **slices French bread, ¾-inch thick, cut on a diagonal so as to make them long enough to accommodate individual servings of rabbit (see photograph)**
   Melted butter or olive oil
- ¼ **cup pine nuts, lightly browned in 1 tablespoon butter**
   Chopped fresh parsley, for garnish (optional)
   Apple and Green Pear Chutney (recipe follows)

Snip off any protruding bones and trim pieces of rabbit. Dredge with flour, shaking off excess, and set aside.

Heat the oil and 2 tablespoons of the butter in a large, heavy skillet over medium heat. Lightly brown the rabbit pieces, 8 to 10 minutes. Add shallots, sauté another minute, and add champagne, brown sugar, lemon rind and juice. Cover and simmer over low heat until rabbit is tender, about 45 minutes.

Champagne Rabbit with Apple and Green Pear Chutney, and Sautéed Cabbage and Carrots with Ginger.

the simmering sauce. Continue to simmer, stirring, until it reaches the consistency of heavy cream, 2 to 3 minutes.

Brush the slices of French bread with melted butter or olive oil and fry until golden.

To serve, place a piece of rabbit on a slice of the fried bread (a crouton) and top with the sauce and a sprinkling of the pine nuts. Garnish with parsley if you like and a spoon of chutney (recipe follows).

Serves 6

OPPOSITE: **Rice Pudding with Blueberries.** RIGHT: **Jack and Jamie Davies, and their son Hugh.** BELOW: **A tumble of flowers in the rock garden.**

Rice Pudding with Blueberries

An old favorite—with or without blueberries.

¾ **cup short-grain rice (pearl)**
4 **cups milk**
½ **cup sugar**
   Grating of nutmeg
1 **cup fresh blueberries**
½ **cup heavy cream**
1 **teaspoon vanilla extract**

Combine the rice and milk in a saucepan or in the top of a double boiler and cook until very soft, about 45 minutes. Stir in sugar and nutmeg. Cool slightly. Fold in blueberries. Whip the cream and vanilla together. Pour the pudding into a broilerproof dish and top with whipped cream. Place under the broiler and brown top slightly. Sprinkle a few additional berries on top if you like. Serve at once.

Serves 6 to 8

ABOUT THE WINES

Jamie Davies's food and wine talents have developed in tandem during the years it took to bring the winery to its current position of leadership in its specialized field, and she has many useful thoughts about both to pass on. Regarding food and wine, Jamie feels very strongly that you should always offer a food item whenever you serve a wine. Food and wine are absolutely meant to go together:

"Our Blanc de Blanc is a fine apéritif champagne style that has crisp and delicate apple- and pear-like fruit flavors coming from Chardonnay, the main grape used in the blend. It finishes dry and is reminiscent of lemon zest. Neither the wine nor the appetizers overpowers the other; they are in harmony. The slightly salty ham plays off the fruit in the wine nicely. The effervescence provides a counterpoint to liven the palate. The bold Jack cheese also contributes smooth round flavors, and the caraway seed adds crunch. The bread of the canapés is relatively neutral, the butter relates to the Chardonnay with its delicate butterscotch flavor, and the mild radish contributes freshness, crunch, and color. The mouth remains fresh and clean in anticipation of the first course following these two appealing appetizers.

"The mushrooms have a woodsy, earthy flavor combined with cream and champagne for richness and complexity. The lemon juice brings up the acid and works with the crisp background in the wine. Our Blanc de Noirs is a lively, yet mellow, rich sparkling wine to stand up to this dish served in a butter brioche shell.

"With our Cuvée de Pinot Brut Rosé, the emphasis is on fresh, elegant fruit of Pinot Noir with a small amount of Pinot Meunier and Napa Gamay in the blend. The appealing, spicy fruit is highly complementary to the rabbit simply prepared and simmered in the same wine. Both are clean, tasty, and fresh. The pine nuts provide additional texture and a slight toastiness that brings out the toasted yeast flavors in the wine.

"The rice pudding has vanilla and spice, which relates to the same aspects in the champagne. The creamy, slightly sweet flavor matches the creamy texture and delicately sweet flavor in the wine with good acid structure. The blueberries add a luscious fruit flavor that brings out the fruit in the wine and pulls it all together. The gentle effervescence is appealing to the nose and palate at the end of a meal."

Lunch Under Grandmother's Arbor

BEAULIEU VINEYARD

❧

T HE GRANDMOTHER referred to here was Fernande de Latour, wife of the famed winemaker Georges de Latour. She had her gardeners lay out a great arbor forming an *allée* almost 200 feet long that opened into a space almost as long as, and double the width of, the *allée*. It required roughly thirty plane trees planted at twenty-foot intervals. Over the years these were pruned and trained until their branches created a canopy covering the entire area. Family lore has it that the year in which the tree limbs finally met over the top of the arbor, Fernande de Latour died. Fittingly, she had lived to see one of her favorite landscaping projects completed and for almost half a century now gatherings both large and small have been held under these sheltering branches.

But before there was the great arbor, there was Beaulieu.

Beaulieu Vineyard was ushered in with the new century in 1900. Georges de Latour, whose family name had long been associated with fine wine making in France, came to California looking for the right climate and rich soil to establish a vineyard in America and found what he was searching in the heart of the Napa Valley at Rutherford. Georges and Fernande de Latour also decided to build their large rambling house in Rutherford as well. They named it Beaulieu, meaning "beautiful place"— which indeed it certainly is.

Cuttings of the finest European grape varieties were imported and nurtured in vineyards that would bear, long beyond the couple's life span, remarkable wines ranking among the world's finest. Over the years the establishment grew to more than 800 acres,

ABOVE: **Paula Escher, the great-granddaughter of founder Georges de Latour.** RIGHT: **The buffet under the arbor.**

reaching as far as Carneros in the south valley.

However, there were two particular vineyards in Rutherford that de Latour was certain could produce the world-class Cabernet he was after. He persevered, and finally in 1939, his 1936 BV Private Reserve won the gold medal at the San Francisco Golden Gate International Exposition. And the rest, as they say, is history.

The vineyard also has the distinction of having ninety years of uninterrupted production; it managed even during Prohibition when they turned to making sacramental wines to weather the lean years.

Another distinction Beaulieu can claim is that all its wines are made exclusively from Napa Valley grapes, and all BV varietal wines but one blended Cabernet, Beau Tour, are made entirely from the specific varietal grape name on the bottle.

Georges de Latour insisted on perfection and was sternly commited to the consistency of quality. This heritage has been guarded and preserved by his successors, of which there have been only four in its long history.

Today, the grand old vineyard is getting ready to begin its second century as a leader in its class.

MENU

CHICKEN WITH TUNA SAUCE
ARTICHOKE SALAD
FRESH BEET SALAD
BABY GREEN BEAN SALAD
ORZO WITH MUSTARD BALSAMIC VINAIGRETTE
**LAYERED FRESH FRUIT WITH
RASPBERRY SAUCE**

1987 Reserve Chardonnay
1987 Carneros Reserve Pinot Noir
1982 Brut Champagne

ing ingredients except vinegar and artichokes, and bring to a slow boil. Add artichokes and cover. Cook over medium heat until tender, about 10 minutes. Remove artichokes with a slotted spoon. If any water is remaining in the pan, increase heat and boil until evaporated. Deglaze the pan with the vinegar, scraping any brown bits and herbs from the bottom of the pan. Pour over artichokes and toss.

Serves 6 to 8

Chicken with Tuna Sauce

This dish is as easy as it is delicious.

- 3 whole chicken breasts or 1 whole "oven roaster" breast, about 3½ pounds
- 1 celery rib
- 1 medium onion, thinly sliced
- 1 medium bay leaf
- 1 teaspoon dried thyme
- 1 tablespoon salt
  Dash of black pepper
- 1 6-ounce can *good* Italian tuna in oil, drained
- 3 flat anchovy filets, drained
- 1 heaping tablespoon drained capers
- 2 egg yolks
- 2 tablespoons fresh lemon juice
- ½ cup olive oil
- ¾ cup vegetable oil
  Lemon wedges and capers, for garnish (optional)

Place chicken breasts in a small saucepan and cover with cold water. Add celery, onion, bay leaf, thyme, salt and pepper. Bring to a boil over high heat and immediately reduce the heat. Simmer 10 minutes for chicken breast, 17 minutes for roaster breast. Allow to cool in the liquid. When cool, skin and bone the chicken, then slice.

Place tuna, anchovies, capers, egg yolks, and lemon juice in a blender and process a few seconds before adding the oils in a steady stream, blending until smooth.

To serve, smear the bottom of the serving dish with some of the sauce

and arrange a layer of the sliced chicken on top. Continue layering sauce and chicken, finishing with sauce.

Garnish with lemon and capers.

Serves 6

Artichoke Salad

All the salads in the menu are best served at room temperature, so if they must be refrigerated, be sure to allow time for them to warm up.

- 6 or 8 large artichokes
  Lemon juice
- ⅓ cup olive oil
- 2 large garlic cloves, finely chopped
- ¼ cup finely chopped shallots
- 1 tablespoon minced fresh Italian parsley
- 2 tablespoons chopped fresh mint
- ½ cup water
- 1 teaspoon salt
  Freshly ground black pepper
- 2 tablespoons red wine vinegar

Trim the artichokes by snapping off and discarding the coarse outer leaves. Using a small sharp knife, trim off the green fibrous parts, rubbing all cut surfaces with lemon as you work. Cut each artichoke heart in half and scoop out fibrous choke with a spoon.

In a shallow pan heat the olive oil over medium heat. Add garlic and shallots; turn heat to low and cook just long enough to soften the garlic and shallots, 2 or 3 minutes. Add remain-

Fresh Beet Salad

- 6 medium beets
- 1 tablespoon minced shallots
- 2 tablespoons olive oil
- 2 tablespoons balsamic vinegar

Preheat the oven to 400 degrees.

Wash the beets and cut off stems about 2 inches from the bulb. Leave root on. Place beets in a small foil-lined pan. Bake until tender to the touch, about 1 hour. When cool, peel and stem, cutting off and discarding the tops. Cut beets into ½-inch dice. Toss with shallots.

Whisk together the oil and vinegar. Pour over beets and toss.

Serves 6

Baby Green Bean Salad

- 1 pound baby string beans, with stems snapped off
- 2 tablespoons salt
- 1 tablespoon red wine vinegar
- 6 tablespoons olive oil
- 2 medium garlic cloves, minced

Bring a small saucepan of water to a boil. Add the beans and salt. Cook until the beans are just beginning to get tender, about several minutes. Drain and rinse in cold water to preserve color and stop their cooking.

Whisk together the vinegar, oil, and garlic. Pour over beans and toss.

Serves 6

Orzo with Mustard Balsamic Vinaigrette

This can be made in advance, but I like it better if it hasn't been refrigerated.

- ½ **pound orzo**
- 2 ½ **tablespoons balsamic vinegar**
- 1 **teaspoon salt**
  Freshly ground black pepper to taste
- 1 **tablespoon Dijon-style mustard**
- ¼ **cup minced shallots**
- ½ **cup olive oil**

Drop the orzo into a large saucepan of lightly salted boiling water. Return to a boil and cook until just tender, about 8 minutes. Drain, but do not rinse.

Whisk together the other ingredients. Pour the vinaigrette over the drained, still-warm orzo. Allow to cool, stirring several times.

Serves 6 to 8

Layered Fresh Fruit with Raspberry Sauce

Charlotte Combe doesn't actually have a recipe when she makes this, instead using any fruits that might be handy. So use this recipe simply as a guide.

- 2 **oranges, juiced**
- ½ **fresh pineapple, peeled and cut into medium cubes**
- 1 **medium banana, sliced**
- 2 **or 3 purple plums, pitted and sliced**
- 1 **pint strawberries, hulled and thickly sliced**
- 1 **large nectarine, thickly sliced**
- 1 **large peach, peeled, pitted, and thickly sliced**
- 1 **small bunch red or green seedless grapes (about ⅓ pound)**
- 1 **basket red raspberries (or 10-ounce box of frozen berries)**
  Superfine sugar and kirsch (optional)

Place orange juice in a medium bowl. Select a large glass jar with a wide mouth in which to layer fruit. Alternating various fruits according to color, dip the fruit into the orange juice and place in the jar. After using all the fruit, pour any leftover orange juice over all. Cover and refrigerate.

To make the raspberry sauce, puree the berries and strain out seeds. If desired, sweeten berry sauce to taste with a little superfine sugar and add a tablespoon or two of kirsch.

Serves 6 to 8

❧

About the Wines

Charlotte Combe, well-known cooking instructor and friend of the Sullivan family who descended from de Latour, prepared this meal for us. Following are her thoughts on the wines served at lunch:

Referring to the 1987 Reserve Chardonnay: "Because this wine is neither buttery and fat, nor tart and austere, it is a natural choice to marry with the Chicken in Tuna Sauce. Together, both wine and food are allowed to star individually and also to support each other as a team, bringing out the best in both."

Of the 1987 Carneros Reserve Pinot Noir: "Aged ten months in French oak, this Pinot Noir is intensely varietal—spicy, fresh, and minty. The wine, evidencing the versatility of Pinot Noir in marrying with so many foods, serves as catalyst for the salads. It gently cushioned the transitions among the three—artichokes, fresh beets, and baby green beans."

Of the 1982 Brut Champagne: "This made a perfect match with the layered fruit salad dessert, adding yet another dimension to the sweet naturalness of the fruit flavors."

A Balloon Ride Breakfast

BUENA VISTA WINERY & VINEYARDS

⤔

WHEN A. RACKE bought it in 1979, Buena Vista Winery & Vineyards was billed as California's oldest premium winery. However, what was equally true was that Buena Vista's reputation in the industry and with most wine lovers was as musty as its historic caves.

So it was fortunate that the German Racke family, with a wine-making and marketing history going back more than six generations, sent young Marcus Moller-Racke to Buena Vista in the fall of 1981 to

expanded the Domaine Buena Vista propriety line, with David Rosenthal as its winemaker, and introduced new white wines. Then, to ensure an uninterrupted supply of high-quality grapes that would enable him to reach his long-term goal of producing only estate wines, he encouraged the purchase of what is now Buena Vista's Carneros II vineyard estate.

By the time he became Buena Vista's president in May of 1983, Marcus was well on the way to creating a state-of-the-art winery. But knowing land acquisitions and all the machinery and equipment in the world can't alone produce the quality of wines on which he was convinced the winery's future success depended, he promoted Jill Davis, whom he had hired as assistant winemaker, to winemaker; he put Anna in charge of vineyard operations; and his talented team was complete. Marcus is proudest today to be able

LEFT: **Breakfast in the field.**
ABOVE: **Entrance to the winery.**

to say that "Buena Vista has joined the ranks of California's most illustrious wineries and now enjoys a reputation as a pacesetter in the world of fine premium wines."

And, I might add, in a very short number of years, too!

But if you think all this dedication to excellence and progress has dimmed Marcus and Anna's sense of fun, you're wrong. To entertain friends they are apt to host anything from a relaxed swimming party by the pool overlooking the vineyards, to the surprise they treated us to—an early morning balloon ride followed by a hearty breakfast-lunch devised by Sonoma Mission Inn's well-known chef, Charles Saunders (more on Saunders on page 157).

This is California entertaining par excellence.

become the Director of Vineyard Operations. For it was he, along with his attractive and energetic wife, Anna (also from a renowned German wine-producing family), who have cleared out the cobwebs and developed Buena Vista into one of the premiere estate vineyards in the Carneros region of Sonoma.

Early on, Marcus decided to streamline Buena Vista's line. He eliminated some wines and focused the company's resources on their strengths: the premium Carneros Chardonnay, Pinot Noir, Merlot, and Cabernet varietals. At the same time, he also

Bricout Carte or Champagne
Sauvignon Blanc–Lake Country
Private Reserve Chardonnay
Private Reserve Pinot Noir
Late Harvest Johannisberg Riesling

White Corn and Oyster Chowder with Ancho Chile Cream

With its croutons and chili cream, this silky soup is almost a meal it itself.

- 1 ½ cups dry white wine
- 18 oysters, shucked with liquor reserved
- 2 tablespoons unsalted butter
- ½ cup roughly chopped onion
- ½ cup roughly chopped celery
- 6 medium ears white corn, kernels cut from cobs and milk scraped out, cobs reserved
- 2 quarts fish stock
- 1 cup heavy cream
- 1 medium garlic head, roasted (page 65)
- 1 tablespoon roughly chopped fresh sage
- 6 tablespoons dry sherry
  Salt and pepper to taste
- 6 to 8 toasted rounds of French or Italian bread
  Ancho Chile Cream (recipe follows)

Bring the wine to a boil in a medium pot and add the oysters. Remove from the heat and let oysters cool in the wine. When cool, remove oysters and set aside, covered. Reduce wine by half over high heat, 5 minutes or more. Set aside.

In a soup pot, melt the butter over medium heat. Add the onions and celery and sauté until wilted, about 5 minutes. Add the reserved corn cobs, fish stock, oyster liquor, and reduced wine to the vegetables. Bring to a low boil and simmer for 30 minutes.

Add three-fourths of the corn kernels (saving the balance for garnish), the cream, garlic pulp squeezed from the roasted head, and sage. Continue to simmer for 20 minutes more.

Remove cobs and discard. Puree soup in a food processor or blender and strain through a medium strainer. Stir in sherry and add salt and pepper.

To serve, ladle the soup into heated soup bowls. Float a crouton in each and top with oysters. Drizzle Ancho Chile Cream over each portion.

Serves 6 to 8

LEFT: **White Corn and Oyster Chowder with Ancho Chile Cream.**

ANCHO CHILE CREAM

- ¼ cup ancho chiles (2 ounces)
- 4 sun-dried tomatoes
- 1 cup dry white wine or water, warmed
- 1 cup heavy cream, reduced to ½ cup
- 2 tablespoons dry sherry
- Pinch each of chili powder, ground cumin, and dried oregano
- Salt, black pepper, and cayenne pepper to taste

Place chiles and tomatoes in separate bowls and pour ½ cup warm wine or water over each. Allow to soak for 10 minutes. When reconstituted, drain and discard the liquid from both. Carefully remove and discard the stems and seeds from chiles. Scrape the chiles and tomatoes to remove the pulp and reserve. Discard skins. Place all ingredients in a blender and puree until smooth.

Makes about 1½ cups

Grilled Chicken Apple Sausage

Be sure to make this enough in advance —at least a day—so that the flavors will have time to blend together in the refrigerator.

- 1 pound skinless chicken meat, from the leg and thigh only, chilled and cut into large dice
- 4 ounces pork fat, chilled and cut into large dice

- 4 ounces pork meat (butt), chilled and cut into large dice
- 1 ½ tart apples (Pippin or Granny Smith), peeled, cored, and cut into large dice
- 1 small onion, cut into medium dice
- 1 tablespoon coarse salt
- ¼ teaspoon white pepper
- 1 teaspoon dried sage
- 2 tablespoons Calvados (apple brandy)

Toss all ingredients together and put through a grinder fitted with a medium-hole plate or place in a food processor and pulse until medium chopped. Do not overprocess. Divide into 8 patties and refrigerate overnight.

Grill until cooked through but not dry, about 5 minutes or less on each side. Serve with Braised Leek and Herb Custard (recipe follows) and slices of sourdough bread brushed lightly with olive oil and grilled along with the sausage.

Serves 6 to 8

ABOVE: **Braised Leek and Herb Custard, and Grilled Chicken Apple Sausage.**
LEFT: **Post-flight celebratory champagne.**
BELOW: **Marcus and Anna Moller-Racke.**

Braised Leek and Herb Custard

This luscious custard is like a crustless quiche.

- 2 tablespoons unsalted butter, plus additional for molds
- 1 cup finely diced (well-washed) leek, mostly white part
- ½ cup finely diced onion
- 4 eggs
- 1 cup half-and-half
- 2 tablespoons grated Parmesan cheese
- 1 teaspoon mixed minced fresh Italian parsley and fresh rosemary
- Salt and pepper to taste

Preheat the oven to 325 degrees and butter six 4-ounce molds. Set aside.

Place butter in a small skillet and sauté leek and onion over medium heat until wilted, 3 to 5 minutes. In another bowl, combine eggs, half-and-half, cheese, herbs, and seasonings. Stir in leek and onion mixture. Pour into molds. Place molds in a larger pan and surround with boiling water. Bake until firm, 15 or 20 minutes, or until a knife inserted in the center comes out clean.

Serves 6

Oak-Grilled Steelhead Trout Wrapped in Vine Leaves

If vine leaves are not handy, you can substitute romaine or savoy cabbage leaves.

- 6 whole boned steelhead trout (12 ounces each) with heads and tails left on
- 6 tablespoons olive oil
  Salt and pepper to taste
- 24 slices lemon, cut ⅛-inch thick
- 1 bunch fresh thyme
- 24 blanched vine leaves

Prepare grill to have ash-covered coals (see Note).

Place trout skin side down on a cutting board. Drizzle l tablespoon of the olive oil in the cavity of each, sprinkle with salt and pepper, then lay 4 lemon slices and several sprigs of thyme in each cavity. Close the fish and wrap them individually in vine leaves. Use wooden skewers to hold fish closed.

Place on a moderately hot grill for about 3 minutes per side, then remove fish to the edge of the grill to finish cooking more slowly. This will take several minutes, depending on how hot the fire is. Flesh should be flaky. Remove skewers before serving.

Serves 6

Note: If you don't have a grill or would rather sauté these, first preheat the oven to 350 degrees. Place a slick of olive oil in 2 large skillets and place over high heat. Sear fish on both sides and place pans in the oven for 6 to 8 minutes.

❧

Mesclun with Pears, Blue Cheese, and Port Vinaigrette

Port vinaigrette works well with any sort of fruit-and-cheese combination salad.

- ½ cup mayonnaise
- ½ cup plain yogurt
- 1 teaspoon minced fresh tarragon
- 1 tablespoon minced fresh chives
- 1 tablespoon minced red onion
- 2 tablespoons Tawny Port
- 1 tablespoon fresh lemon juice

- Salt and pepper to taste
- ¾ pound mixed mesclun (see Note), washed and dried
- 3 ripe pears, peeled, cored, sliced thick, and rubbed with lemon juice
- 6 ounces blue cheese

Whisk together the mayonnaise and yogurt, sprinkle the tarragon over, along with the chives, onion, port, and lemon juice. Mix well. Add salt and pepper and set aside.

Toss the greens with just enough vinaigrette to coat them well. Serve on individual plates garnished with pear slices and crumbled blue cheese.

Serves 6 or more

Note: Mesclun is the name given to a combination of salad greens, made up of different textures and flavor, which may often by purchased already mixed from specialty green grocers.

Three Peach Pie

As if one kind of peach weren't enough, here we have three. However, as wonderful and subtle as this may be, you could make it with all one variety.

PASTRY

- 2 cups all-purpose flour
- 1/2 teaspoon salt
- 1/2 teaspoon sugar
- 1/2 teaspoon grated lemon rind
- 3/4 cup (1 1/2 sticks) plus 2 tablespoons chilled unsalted butter, cut into walnut-size pieces
- 1/4 cup ice water

FILLING

- 1/3 cup toasted, roughly chopped unsalted pistachios or almonds
- 3 pounds mixed varieties of peaches (white, yellow, and aromatic), peeled, pitted, and sliced
- 1/2 cup sun-dried cherries (see Note), plumped in brandy and drained
- 1 cup light brown sugar
- 1 teaspoon ground cinnamon
- 2 3/4 tablespoons quick-cooking tapioca
- 2 tablespoons fresh lemon juice
- 3 tablespoons unsalted butter
- 2 tablespoons milk
- 2 tablespoons granulated sugar and 1 teaspoon cinnamon (optional)
- Whipped cream or ice cream

Make the pastry. Sift the dry ingredients together; stir in lemon rind. Quickly cut in butter with 2 knives or a pastry blender until it is the size of small peas. Sprinkle with ice water and mix with as few strokes as possible. Form into a long, flat disk, wrap in plastic wrap, and refrigerate for at least an hour, more if possible. (This may also be done in a food processor.)

Preheat the oven to 400 degrees and lightly butter a deep 9-inch pie tin. Set aside.

Fill the pie. Divide the dough into 2 parts, roll out one on a floured surface to approximately 1/8-inch thickness, and line the prepared pan. Sprinkle the nuts over the bottom. Toss the peaches, cherries, brown sugar, 1 teaspoon cinnamon, tapioca, and lemon juice together in a bowl, then heap into the pie pan. Dot with butter. Cover the top with the re-

maining pastry, sealing carefully and brushing lightly with milk. You might also combine the sugar and cinnamon and sprinkle this over the top crust.

Bake for 10 minutes, lower heat to 350 degrees, and bake for another 35 to 40 minutes, until golden. Allow to cool completely before removing from the pan.

Serve pie from the pan if it does not come out easily. Top each portion with lightly whipped cream or ice cream.

Serves 8 or more

Note: Sun-dried cherries are available at specialty food stores.

❦

ABOUT THE WINES

When the Moller-Rackes decide to entertain and ask chef Charles Saunders to suggest menus, they invariably start by discussing how certain of their wines and the suggested dishes will enhance one another, and together they come up with the final selection. Here are comments excerpted from the session that produced this delicious breakfast.

It's interesting that Marcus's comments not only illuminate his reasons but give you a glimpse into the qualities he sees in his wines:

"Our Bricout Carte or a champagne from France matches the festive mood. Either will refresh your palates and awaken your appetite.

"With its light grassy aftertaste and ripe summer-melon aroma, our Sauvignon Blanc–Lake Country provides

OPPOSITE TOP: **The trout served with Mesclun with Pears, Blue Cheese, and Port Vinaigrette;** BOTTOM: **Oak-Grilled Steelhead Trout Wrapped in Vine Leaves.** ABOVE: **Three Peach Pie.**

a wonderful beginning to meals featuring salads or seafood.

"To take the challenge of a hearty sausage and baked egg dish, a wine with firm structure and a strong backbone is needed. Our Private Reserve Chardonnay, with its rich and full flavor, balances and completes the dish.

"Grilled steelhead trout, surrounded by grape leaves, thyme, and lemon, is perfectly complemented by the fresh fruit flavor of our Private Reserve Pinot Noir. Pinot Noir is the most versatile of all red wines, often finding a perfect match with firmly textured fish.

"One of the secrets to pairing desserts with wines is to find the aromas and flavors common to both. One of the most often used descriptions for late-harvest Riesling is peaches. What better combination than this, our Late Harvest Johannisberg Riesling and the ripe summer peaches in the Three Peach Pie?"

A California-Mexican Feast

MATANZAS CREEK WINERY

❧

IN 1971 SANDRA STERN, a transplanted South-
ern belle, purchased the old LaFranconi Dairy
in Bennett Valley. It is situated in a lovely spot,
with Bennett Peak rising at its back and in front a
view of Mount Taylor in the distance. I suppose
that's not so unusual, but Sandra, with no previous
experience in wine making or production, had already decided to "make the best wine in California." Obviously, she can't be accused of thinking
small. And on top of having had no previous experience, she was entering what had been mostly a
man's game.

But she was so fixed on her goal that probably
none of this even crossed her mind. And by 1974
Sandra had managed to start working her land and
had twenty-two acres planted to Chardonnay and
Merlot grapes.

Her plans progressed apace and only three years
later she was ready to convert the old milking shed
into the winery. Matanzas Creek Winery was born—
and Sandra had met her husband-to-be, Bill
MacIver. Together, a year later, they released the
winery's first 3,000 cases.

A string of successes followed, beginning with
the MacIvers' early Chardonnays, which won awards
and accolades. Recognition from wine enthusiasts
was so swift that within only a few months after
their 1979 release the inventory was gone.

There followed other varietals in those early days,
but it turned out to be another white, the Sauvignon Blanc, that caught the public's attention with
its rich, classic style.

So it isn't surprising that by 1984 the original
facility was hard pressed to keep up with its own
success. It became all too evident to the MacIvers
that attempting to supply a national distribution
network with an inventory that could never be
guaranteed to last more than a few months after
release would have to be corrected. Consequently,
plans were made to expand, with a vast two-story
winery building and a state-of-the-art laboratory.

Miraculously, by fall of 1985 the expansion was
finished. These new facilities allowed important
changes in their wine-making methods. With the
new laboratory, cellar treatment of wines "in mini-
ature" could actually be simulated, tasted, and studied before being committed to on a larger scale.

Red wine production also gained. Early focus on
Pinot Noir and Cabernet Sauvignon was shifted to a
single red, Merlot. Style changes influenced by the
wines of Pomerol were introduced, making their
red wine "softer and rounder, with more supple
tannins." And in a few short years, Matanzas was to
became known for its Merlots.

Our meal with the MacIvers was one of their
special favorites—California Mexican. And what a
feast it was. Read on!

M E N U

LEMON CHICKEN SOUP
MARINATED SHRIMP WITH GREEN CHILE
POLENTA AND CORN SALSA
SEVICHE SALAD WITH ORANGE-
OREGANO VINAIGRETTE
CHICKEN AND WALNUT ENCHILADAS WITH
ROASTED GREEN CHILE SAUCE
SONORAN TUILE BASKETS
COCONUT CARAMEL FLAN

Matanzas Creek Chardonnay
Matanzas Creek Sauvignon Blanc

The table in the garden, set with the
meal starting with Lemon Chicken Soup
and ending with Coconut Caramel Flan.

Lemon Chicken Soup

This soup has a light hint of Mexico.

6 chicken thighs (about 1½ pounds), skin removed

7 cups chicken stock, canned or fresh

Juice and grated rind of 1 large lemon (about ¼ cup lemon juice)

2 tablespoons unsalted butter

1 large yellow onion, coarsely chopped

2 medium garlic cloves, crushed

5 medium ears fresh corn, kernels cut off with milk scraped out, or 2 cups frozen corn kernels

2 large red tomatoes (about 1 pound), coarsely chopped

1 bunch scallions, coarsely chopped

1 bunch cilantro, or to taste, coarsely chopped with a few sprigs reserved for garnish

Salt and pepper to taste

5 corn tortillas, cut into bite-size pieces

6 thin slices of lemon, for garnish

Place thighs in a saucepan and cover with a generous amount of cold water. Bring to a boil and simmer until meat is very tender, about 45 minutes. Remove chicken and allow to cool. Reserve the cooking liquid and shred the chicken.

Measure 4 cups of cooking liquid (add more water if you don't have enough to make that amount) and combine it with the chicken stock in a large saucepan. Bring to a simmer and add the chicken meat, lemon juice, and grated rind.

Meanwhile, melt the butter in a medium skillet over medium heat and sauté the onion and garlic until lightly golden, about 5 minutes. Add this and the corn with its pulp to the simmering stock. Simmer a few more minutes. Add tomatoes, scallions, cilantro, and salt and pepper. Simmer 15 minutes longer. Skim fat.

To serve, place some of the tortilla triangles in each of the soup bowls before ladling in soup. Let stand 2 or 3 minutes for the hot soup to soften tortillas. Garnish with lemon slices and cilantro sprigs.

Serves 6 to 8

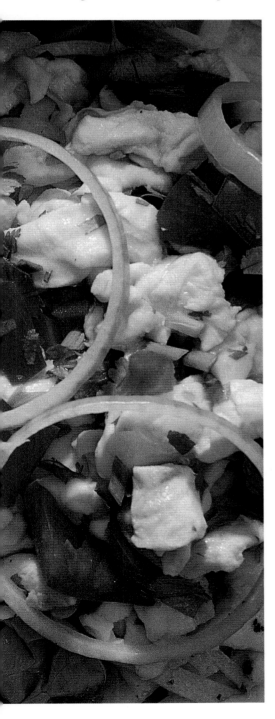

ᘒ

Marinated Shrimp with Green Chile Polenta and Corn Salsa

What a tempting combination of flavors this is.

- 18 **large prawns or shrimp, peeled and deveined with tails left on**
  Grated rind of ½ medium lemon
- 5 **medium garlic cloves, minced**
- 1 **medium serrano chile, seeded and minced**
- ¼ **cup loosely packed cilantro**
- ¼ **cup olive oil**
  Salt and pepper to taste
  Green Chile Polenta (recipe follows)
  Fresh Corn Salsa (recipe follows)

Toss shrimp, lemon rind, chile, cilantro, oil, and seasonings together in a glass bowl. Cover tightly with plastic wrap and marinate for at least 1 hour. Drain the shrimp and grill until opaque, about 3 minutes per side, sprinkling with more salt and pepper. (Shrimp may also be cooked under a preheated broiler.)

Serve with Green Chile Polenta and Fresh Corn Salsa.

Serves 6 to 8

GREEN CHILE POLENTA

- 7 **to 8 tablespoons (1 stick) unsalted butter**
- 5 **cups chicken stock**
- 2 **cups coarse polenta (Golden Pheasant, if available)**
- 1 **8-ounce can roasted and diced green chiles, drained**

Butter a large baking sheet with a short lip with 2 to 3 tablespoons of the butter. Set aside.

Combine another 4 tablespoons butter with the chicken stock and bring to a boil in a large pot. Over medium heat, pour in the polenta in a steady stream, stirring constantly to prevent lumps from forming. Add the chiles, stirring, and continue to cook for 5 minutes, until thick and sticky. Quickly spoon mixture out onto baking sheet, spreading to a thickness of about ½ inch, using a buttered spatula. Rub more butter all over the top. As the polenta cools, it will become firm. Cut into triangles.

Serves 8 to 10

FRESH CORN SALSA

- 1 **large white onion (about 10 ounces), chopped**
- 2 **large red tomatoes (about 1 pound), chopped**
- ¼ **cup loosely packed, coarsely chopped cilantro**
- 1 **medium ear of corn, kernels cut from cob**
- ½ **serrano chile (about 2½ inches), seeded and minced**
- 1 **tablespoon fresh lemon juice**
  Salt and white pepper to taste

Combine all ingredients and macerate for 1 hour or so before serving.

Makes approximately 1½ cups

OPPOSITE TOP: **Lemon Chicken Soup.**
LEFT: **Marinated Shrimp with Green Chile Polenta and Corn Salsa, and Seviche Salad with Orange-Oregano Vinaigrette.**
ABOVE: **Bill and Sandra MacIvers.**

Seviche Salad with Orange-Oregano Vinaigrette

Orange-Oregano Vinaigrette would also be very good on a fruit and green salad.

- 1 ½ pounds fresh white fish filets (preferably halibut or cod)
- 1 cup fresh lime juice
- ½ cup olive oil
- 1 medium shallot, minced
- ½ teaspoon dried oregano
- 1 ½ cups fresh sweet orange juice
- ¼ cup loosely packed, coarsely chopped cilantro
- 1 large tomato (about ½ pound), diced
- 2 small to medium jicama, peeled and thinly sliced
- 2 heads butter lettuce, leaves separated, washed, and dried
- 1 medium red onion, thinly sliced and separated into rings, tossed with 3 tablespoons of rice vinegar, and marinated for several hours
- 2 medium ripe avocados, peeled, pitted, sliced, and rubbed with lemon juice

Cut fish filets into very thin, small slices. Place in a glass bowl and toss with the lime juice. Cover and marinate for 1½ hours in the refrigerator.

Meanwhile, combine the olive oil, shallot, oregano, and orange juice and shake together. Set aside.

To serve, drain the fish and combine with the cilantro and tomato. Toss the jicama with the vinaigrette. Place a small amount of jicama on a bed of butter lettuce, top with the fish, and add the drained, marinated onion rings. Garnish with a "fan" of avocado slices.

Serves 6 to 8

⤳

Chicken and Walnut Enchiladas with Roasted Green Chile Sauce

The sauce is rather mild, so if you like yours hot, add more jalapeño. Serve these as the centerpiece of any supper.

SAUCE

- 20 to 25 tomatillos (3 to 3¼ pounds)
- 2 tablespoons olive oil
- 2 cups coarsely chopped onions
- 2 7-ounce cans diced roasted green chiles, drained and diced
- 3 medium garlic cloves, minced
- 2 teaspoons dried oregano
- 2 cups chicken stock
- 2 medium bay leaves
- 1 tablespoon sugar
- Salt and pepper to taste

FILLING

- 1 chicken, about 3 to 4 pounds
- 1 cup shredded mild cheddar cheese
- 1 ½ cups shredded Monterey Jack cheese
- 1 cup shelled walnuts, roasted and chopped
- 1 tablespoon dried oregano
- Salt and pepper to taste

ASSEMBLY

- 1 cup vegetable oil
- 12 corn tortillas
- 2 cups shredded Monterey Jack cheese
- 2 large tomatoes (about 1 pound), coarsely diced
- 2 medium avocados, peeled, pitted, sliced, and rubbed with lemon juice
- 1 cup sour cream
- 6 ounces black olives packed in brine, drained
- 12 sprigs cilantro, chopped
- 1 cup shelled, roasted pumpkin seeds (see Note)

Make the sauce. Remove the husks and stems from the tomatillos. Place in a saucepan and cover with water. Bring

rapidly to a boil and cook over medium-high heat until tender, about 5 minutes. Drain and rinse. Set aside. Place olive oil in a medium skillet over medium-high heat, add onions, and sauté until translucent, about 3 minutes, stirring. Transfer to a food processor with the tomatillos, chiles, garlic, oregano, and 1 cup of the chicken stock. Process a few seconds until coarse. Return to the saucepan and stir in remaining stock, bay leaves, sugar, salt, and pepper. Bring to a boil and simmer for 30 minutes. Remove bay leaves and discard. Set sauce aside.

Make the filling. Place the chicken in a large pot and cover with water. Bring quickly to a boil, cover, reduce heat, and simmer until very tender,

1¹/₂ to 2 hours. Cool chicken in liquid. Discard skin and bones and shred meat. Combine shredded chicken with the cheeses, walnuts, oregano, salt, and pepper. Set aside.

Preheat the oven to 350 degrees.

Heat the oil in a large skillet over medium heat and quickly cook the tortillas, one at the time, for a few seconds. Drain as you remove them from the oil. Dip each into the green chile sauce and lay flat in a large baking dish. Spoon ¹/₂ cup chicken filling onto tortillas and roll, placing seam side down. Continue until all tortillas are used. Spoon remainder of the sauce over the top. Cover with foil and bake until heated through, 15 to 20 minutes. Remove the foil and sprinkle

OPPOSITE: **Chicken and Walnut Enchiladas with Roasted Green Chile Sauce.** ABOVE: **Dramatic front window of the winery.**

with Monterey Jack cheese. Return dish to oven and bake until cheese melts, 5 to 10 minutes.

Serve 2 enchiladas on a warm plate, garnished with diced tomatoes, avocado slices, sour cream, olives, and cilantro. Sprinkle roasted pumpkin seeds over the top.

Serves 6

Note: To roast pumpkin seeds, spread them on a baking sheet and place in a moderate oven until golden, 5 to 8 minutes.

Sonoran Tuile Baskets

Here are the classic almond cookies filled with lemon-lime curd.

CURD

    3   whole eggs plus 3 egg yolks
    ¼   cup fresh lime juice
    ¼   cup fresh lemon juice
    5   tablespoons unsalted butter
    ¼   cup sugar
    1   tablespoons grated lemon
        rind

TUILES

    1   cup sliced, blanched, toasted
        almonds
    ¼   cup sugar
    ¼   cup egg whites, at room
        temperature
    2   tablespoons flour
  1 ½   tablespoons unsalted butter,
        melted and cooled slightly

ASSEMBLY

        Fresh berries to taste
        Crème fraîche or whipped
        cream to taste
        Mint sprigs, for garnish

Make the curd. Place the ingredients into the top of a double boiler. Cook, whisking, until mixture thickens and leaves a ribbon on the surface, 3 to 5 minutes. Strain into a bowl and press a sheet of plastic wrap onto the mixture. Cool completely and refrigerate.

Preheat the oven to 350 degrees.

Make the tuiles. Mix the almonds, sugar, egg whites, and flour in a small bowl. Blend in melted butter. Generously butter 2 cookie sheets. Drop the batter by 2 tablespoonfuls onto the sheets, spacing cookies 5 inches apart. Use the back of a fork to flatten batter into thin 4-inch rounds. Bake until centers are golden brown, 7 or 8 minutes. Working quickly, shape the cookies by placing them over a rolling pin or bottle to form a shell. Let cookies stand in place until cool. (If cookies become hard before shaping, return them to the oven for a minute or so to soften them.)

To serve, place tuiles on individual plates, fill each with a spoonful of curd, sprinkle with fresh berries, and top with a teaspoon of crème fraîche or whipped cream and a sprig of mint.

Serves 6

Coconut Caramel Flan

Flans are always a welcome treat after a spicy meal. This one is very rich but especially nice.

> 2 **cups sugar**
> 2 **tablespoons water**
> ½ **teaspoon fresh lemon juice**
> 4 ⅓ **cups milk**
> 1 **vanilla bean, split lengthwise**
> 4 **whole eggs plus 8 egg yolks**
> 7 **ounces shredded unsweet-ened coconut, toasted**

Preheat the oven to 325 degrees.

In a small saucepan, combine 1 cup of the sugar with the water and lemon juice. Over low heat, bring to a boil, then raise heat to medium and cook without stirring for 8 to 10 minutes, until golden. Quickly pour into an ungreased 8-cup mold. Using a pot holder, swirl caramel around until it cools, coating the bottom and sides of the mold.

Bring milk and vanilla bean to a boil. Remove bean and set pan off the heat. In a large mixing bowl, beat the eggs, yolks, and remaining cup of sugar until well blended. Stirring constantly, add the hot milk and coconut. Pour into the prepared mold and place in larger ovenproof pan. Surround with hot water. Bake approximately 1 hour, until a knife inserted in the center comes out clean. Remove from the hot water bath and let cool.

To serve, run a sharp knife around the mold and turn out onto a dish with a lip, being careful not to spill melted caramel as you do. Cool slightly before serving.

Serves 6

ABOVE: **Chef Matthew D. Gipson.** OPPOSITE TOP: **The lush flower garden;** BOTTOM: **Sonoran Tuile Baskets.**

About the Wines

Chef Matthew Gipson, best known for his California-Mexican food so enjoyed by the MacIvers, often prepares his specialties for them. Because these meals have flavors that reappear in almost all the dishes, you may serve a single wine or offer several throughout the meal.

"Matanzas Creek Chardonnay goes quite well with this entire menu. The citrus characteristics of the wine are enhanced greatly by these dishes.

"However the Sauvignon Blanc accents the Lemon Chicken Soup and the Seviche nicely. And Matanzas's famous Merlot would also be perfect with the enchiladas. You have lots of choices."

Dinner in the Gallery

HESS COLLECTION WINERY

❧

THE Hess Collection Winery has two things that make it distinct in the wine country. The most visible is, of course, the gallery-museum that occupies part of the renovated turn-of-the-century winery at Mt. Veeder. This space is given over to house a portion of Donald Hess's extensive personal collection of American and European art, and it is open to the public.

The other is what some around here have dubbed "one of the best-kept secrets in the Napa Valley." They are referring to the fact that Hess has been quietly following a plan that began with the purchase of his first parcels of mountain property in 1970. This is difficult land to work; but Hess believes in the special quality that mountain grapes have, and he accepted the challange of developing such unforgiving terrain.

Hess has been proved right, since for the next decade Hess grapes were sold to some of the best

wineries in the region. But out of each season's crop some grapes were set aside for the future—to experiment with and to analyze.

By 1983 the land under cultivation had grown to 280 acres, with an additional 160 acres acquired for future development. So, with the results of his years of analysis completed, finally in 1986 the actual wine-making operations were established in the renovated winery building (which was the original Napa Valley home of Christian Brothers, called Mt. La Salle).

The first Hess Collection wines were released in 1987, with another in 1989. About then their 1987 Chardonnay became available, as did the 1986 Cabernet Sauvignon; the 1986 Cabernet Sauvignon Reserve was released in 1990.

TOP: **The stylishly restored winery buildings.** ABOVE: **Donald and Joanna Hess.** RIGHT: **The front façade of the winery.**

Donald Hess himself has an interesting background. Born of a Swiss father and an American mother in Bern, Switzerland (where he still resides for part of the year), he was trained as a ninth-generation brewmaster and assumed responsibility for the family's brewery and hotel businesses.

Shortly thereafter Hess began diversifying the family holdings by bottling and distributing a natural mineral water from a source high in the Swiss Alps, at St. Peter's Spring, situated in the valley of Valais.

From the initial success of Valser, the mineral water distribution company, Hess established an umbrella organization, Hess Holdings, Ltd. Over the years it has grown to include agricultural products and real estate. And now Hess Winery and Vineyards.

For our dinner at Hess, a table was set up in the gallery among the pictures and sculpture, making the occasion a triple treat: Chef Carisio's superb food, Donald Hess's superb art, and the winery's superb wine.

MENU

Grilled Prawns with Papaya Salsa

Roasted Garlic Mashed Potatoes

Thin Onion Rings

Grilled Pork Tenderloin with Cabernet Mustard Sauce

Walnut Bread

Frozen Lime Souffle with Boysenbery Sauce

Chardonnay
1986 Cabernet

Grilled Prawns with Papaya Salsa

Papaya salsa makes an interesting complement to the grilled prawns.

18 jumbo prawns, peeled except for the tail, and deveined

MARINADE

¼ cup vegetable oil

Juice of 1 medium lime

½ cup chopped cilantro

4 scallions, coarsely chopped with some greens

SALSA

1 medium papaya, peeled, seeded, and finely diced

1 medium red bell pepper, finely diced

6 scallions, finely diced with some greens

½ cup chopped cilantro

1 to 2 small jalapeño peppers, seeded and minced

Juice of 2 medium limes

½ teaspoon coarse salt

GARNISH

3 small avocados, peeled, pitted, and thinly sliced

Place prawns in a glass bowl, whisk together the marinade ingredients, and pour over them. Cover and marinate for 1 hour, unrefrigerated.

Combine salsa ingredients in a bowl and toss to mix.

Prepare grill so coals are ash-covered. Grill prawns 4 inches from coals until opaque, approximately 2 minutes per side.

To serve, fan out avocado slices on individual plates, add a line of prawns, and garnish with salsa.

Serves 6

ABOVE: **Grilled Prawns with Papaya Salsa.**
BELOW: **The table set for dinner.**
OPPOSITE: **Grilled Pork Tenderloin with Cabernet Mustard Sauce, Roasted Garlic Mashed Potatoes, Thin Onion Rings, and in the background, Walnut Bread.**

Roasted Garlic Mashed Potatoes

These are sinfully good!

- 2 medium garlic heads
- 2 tablespoons olive oil
- 4 large baking potatoes (about 3½ pounds), peeled
- 6 tablespoons (¾ stick) unsalted butter
- ¼ cup heavy cream
- ½ teaspoon coarse salt
  Freshly ground white pepper to taste

Preheat the oven to 375 degrees.

Cut the bottoms off the heads of garlic, place each head on a square of aluminum foil, and drizzle the olive oil over them. Wrap and bake for 1 to 1½ hours, until the garlic is very soft. Squeeze the pulp out of each garlic head. Set aside. Cut potatoes into large cubes, place in a medium saucepan and cover with cold water. Over medium heat, bring quickly to a boil and reduce to a simmer. Simmer until potatoes are very soft, about 20 minutes. Drain and place in a large mixer bowl with the garlic pulp, butter, cream, salt, and pepper. Mash briefly, just until smooth. Do not overbeat.

Serves 6 to 8

Thin Onion Rings

These are absolutely no trouble to make. You'll serve them often.

- 4 medium red onions, very thinly sliced
  Flour
- 4 cups vegetable oil

Separate the rings and sprinkle flour over all, tossing until coated.

Heat the oil in a deep saucepan to 375 degrees. Shake any excess flour off the onion rings and fry in batches until crisp, approximately 3 minutes.

Serves 6 to 8

Grilled Pork Tenderloin with Cabernet Mustard Sauce

Pork is being served slightly pink these days. If this doesn't appeal to you, cook the pork a bit longer, but be careful not to dry it out.

- 2 cups Cabernet Sauvignon
- 1 cup veal or chicken stock
- 2 tablespoons whole-grain mustard
- 3 pork tenderloins, approximately 12 ounces each
  Salt and black pepper to taste

To make the sauce, place the wine in a small saucepan and reduce by half over high heat, about 10 minutes. Add the stock and reduce by about one-third over high heat, about 8 minutes. Whisk in the mustard and keep warm.

Preheat the broiler or prepare the grill. Rub the tenderloins well with salt and pepper. Grill meat about 4 inches from heat source about 12 minutes per side, or until just slightly pink inside. Allow to rest a few minutes before slicing ¼ inch thick. Serve with the sauce.

Serves 6 to 8

Walnut Bread

Walnut bread is very popular in the valleys here, and Chef Renee Carisio's is among the best.

- **1 tablespoon active dry yeast**
- **1½ cups warm water (110° to 115° F)**
- **3 tablespoons honey**
- **3 tablesoons olive oil**
- **1 teaspoon coarse salt**
- **4 cups unbleached all-purpose flour**
- **2 cups toasted walnuts, ground or chopped very fine (to just before a paste is formed) in a food processor**

Place a baking stone in the oven and preheat oven to 375 degrees.

Combine the yeast, warm water, and 1 tablespoon of honey in a 2-cup measure; let stand until foamy, about 10 minutes. Combine the yeast mixture, remaining honey, olive oil, and salt in the bowl of a heavy-duty mixer fitted with the paddle attachment. Beat mixture, gradually adding 3 cups of flour, until a soft dough forms. Add the walnuts and beat in remaining flour. Change the paddle to a dough hook and knead until dough is smooth and elastic, about 5 minutes.

Place dough in a lightly oiled bowl, cover, and let rise in a warm place until doubled in size. Punch down, divide in half, and shape into 2 round loaves. Let rise until almost doubled in size again. Place loaves on stone and score top with a knife or razor blade. Bake for 40 to 45 minutes, or until loaves sound hollow when tapped on the bottom.

Makes 2 loaves

Tie baking paper collars around six ½-cup ramekins to extend 1 inch above the rim. Combine the sugar and water in a small saucepan. Stir to dissolve and place over high heat until mixture boils. Do not stir. (It might crystallize.) Continue to boil until mixture reaches 240 degrees or the soft-ball stage. Remove from heat.

Meanwhile, with a heavy-duty mixer, beat egg yolks until pale and thick. With mixer running, add the hot sugar syrup in a steady stream. Continue to beat until bowl reaches room temperature, about 15 minutes. Beat in lemon and lime juices. Separately, beat cream to soft peaks and gently fold into the yolk mixture. Divide among the ramekins and freeze for at least 4 hours. Serve with sauce and garnish with mint and candied lime peel, if you have it.

Serves 6

BERRY SAUCE

- ½ **cup sugar**
- ½ **cup water**
- 1 **package frozen boysenberries, thawed**

Combine the sugar and water in a small saucepan and bring quickly to a boil. Remove from heat and cool. Puree the berries in a blender or food processor and add the syrup to them. Strain out seeds.

Makes about 2 cups

✻

Frozen Lime Soufflé with Boysenberry Sauce

Blackberries or raspberries could be substituted for the boysenberries here.

- 1 **cup sugar**
- ¼ **cup water**
- 6 **egg yolks**
  Juice of 3 medium lemons
  Juice of 4 medium limes
- 2 **cups heavy cream**
  Berry Sauce (recipe follows)
  Mint leaves and candied lime peel, for garnish (optional)

ABOVE LEFT: **Frozen Lime Soufflé with Boysenberry Sauce, served with a palmier.**
ABOVE: **Winery chef Renee Carisio.**

ABOUT THE WINES

Renee Carisio, Hess's resident chef, planned this updated version of an old-fashioned hearty meal. She knows her wines and very succinctly explains what qualities the particular wines chosen for her meal have to make them work so well with the food:

"Shellfish and Chardonnay are a classic combination since the acid in the wine's structure underscores the richness of the fish. Our Chardonnay has tropical nuances of pineapple and guava that are complemented by the papaya salsa.

"The 1986 Cabernet is a refined, elegant wine whose spicy, brambly character goes especially well with pork (and lamb). The Cabernet holds up well to strong flavors such as mustard and herbs."

Lunch and an Afternoon of Croquet

SONOMA-CUTRER VINEYARDS

✌

Wᴴᴇɴ ʏᴏᴜ sᴇᴇ the complex of modern buildings, gleaming equipment, and busy staff—not to mention the unexpected genteel, manicured croquet fields at the entrance to Sonoma-Cutrer Vineyards—it is immediately obvious that there had to be a person of rare vision and purpose to create such an establishment. That person is Canal Zone–born, West Point graduate, and ex-fighter pilot Brice Cutrer Jones.

There wasn't much in his background to foreshadow an interest in wines and their production, except for a year spent posted to NATO, during

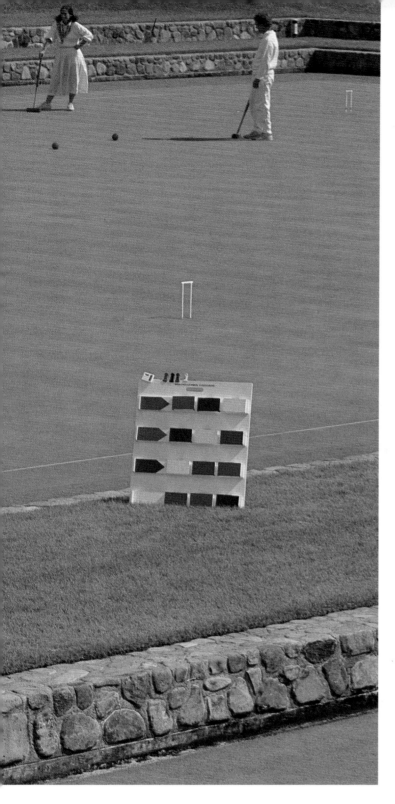

LEFT: **Lunch aside the croquet lawn.**
BELOW: **Brice Cutrer Jones.**

sive research led him to the difficult conclusion that those grapes best suited to his new land were all of the white wine variety, especially Chardonnay. I say "difficult" because this was at a time when red wine, not white, was increasingly in demand.

But fate had a nice surprise in store to reward Brice for his unwavering commitment to quality. By the time those vineyards came into production, white wines had gained in popularity and it didn't take long before Sonoma-Cutrer's grapes were in demand by many premium wineries.

In 1981 Brice and his partners broke ground for the winery, which was to be devoted exclusively to the production of Chardonnay wine made only from the grapes of their vineyards. The final part of the team was also added that year: Bill Bonetti came aboard as winemaker and vice-president. Bonetti's desire to preserve the beneficial aspects of traditional wine-making practices neatly complemented Brice's engineering background and familiarity with technology.

Today, Brice Jones has seen his "no compromise" dream realized, but insists characteristically that much work is yet to be done: "To reach our goal will require unwavering dedication and a mountain of hard work. Even then, we will have to redouble our commitment as we continue to push out the frontiers of knowledge and discover new ways to enhance the inherent character of the wine." It looks as if Brice Jones has an exciting twenty or thirty years ahead of him.

On a lighter side, how about an afternoon of croquet on those pristine courts, accompanied by one of chef Mark Malicki's special lunches (more on Malicki on page 152) and toasted by Sonoma-Cutrer's remarkable Chardonnays?

which he had the opportunity to sample some of Europe's best wines. However, apparently that year was all he needed, and in 1970 Jones resigned his commission to enter Harvard Business School. With typical efficiency, by the time he graduated he had secured the informal financial backing to found Sonoma-Cutrer in January 1973.

In the early 1970s, "good" vineyard land had become practically impossible to come by. Undaunted, he turned to the marginal bench lands, hillsides, and rocky foothills in the cool climate of the Russian River Valley and Carneros Creek regions. Exten-

M E N U

FRESH PORCINI MUSHROOMS BAKED WITH BACON
LOBSTER FRUIT SALAD
FRENCH CREAM WITH BERRIES

Sonoma-Cutrer Russian River Ranches Chardonnay
Sonoma-Cutrer Vineyard Chardonnay

Fresh Porcini Mushrooms Baked with Bacon

Fresh porcini mushrooms are so delicious they don't require much doing. Here they are combined with bacon to create a first course as tasty as it is easy to prepare.

  4 **very large, fresh porcini mushrooms (about ¾-pound each), brushed, trimmed, and split in half**
      Olive oil
 16 **slices thick-cut lean bacon (about ½ pound or more), each cut in half lengthwise**
      Freshly ground black pepper

Preheat the oven to 450 degrees.

Generously brush mushroom halves on all sides with olive oil. Wrap each in bacon and place on a baking sheet. Bake until bacon crisps, about 8 to 10 minutes. Remove to warmed serving plates and top with a generous grind of black pepper.

Serves 8

Lobster Fruit Salad

Chef Mark Malicki's interest in Thai food is evident in this beautiful hot, spicy, and cool dish.

  8 **medium lobsters (1¼ pounds each)**
  1 **tablespoon plus 1 teaspoon salt**
  1 **tablespoon plus 1 teaspoon sugar**
 ½ **cup fresh lime juice**
  2 **cups mixed red and green seedless grapes, halved**
  2 **cups orange sections, seeded and cut into chunks**
  2 **cups peeled and cored apples, cut into medium dice**
  2 **cups peeled fresh whole water chestnuts or peeled and diced jicama**
  2 **cups halved fresh strawberries**
  2 **cups thick-sliced fresh lychees or drained canned ones**
  2 **tablespoons peanut oil**
 ½ **cup thinly sliced garlic**
 ½ **cup thinly sliced shallots**
 ½ **cup raw peanuts, boiled to remove skins and thinly sliced**
  1 **fresh red chile, sliced into very thin julienne strips (optional)**
      Coriander leaves, for garnish

Place 2 lobsters at the time in a steamer over rapidly boiling water and steam, covered, for 13 to 14 minutes. Immediately plunge into ice water. Allow to remain in the water until completely cooled, about 10 minutes. Drain and remove meat, reserving head and tail shells (see photograph). Set aside.

Dissolve the salt and sugar in the lime juice and place all the fruits in a large bowl. Toss with the lime juice mixture. Set aside.

Heat the oil in a small skillet and fry the garlic, shallots, and peanuts separately until lightly browned. Drain and when cool, sprinkle half of each over the fruit along with the julienned chile. Toss.

To assemble the salad, place the heads and tails of each lobster on individual plates, leaving a space between. Toss the lobster meat with the fruit and divide among the 8 plates, mounding in the space left. Sprinkle with the remaining fried garlic, shallots, and peanuts. Garnish with coriander leaves.

Serves 8

❧

French Cream with Berries

Here is an elegant "little" dessert that is sinfully rich, but irresistible.

  1 **tablespoon plus 2¼ teaspoons unflavored gelatin**
  2 **cups heavy cream**
  1 **cup sugar**
  2 **cups sour cream**
  2 **teaspoons vanilla extract**
      Strawberry Syrup (recipe follows)
      Mixed berries and pomegranate seeds, for garnish (optional)

Dissolve the gelatin in 6 tablespoons of the cream and let stand for 10 minutes. Combine the remaining cream and sugar in a heavy saucepan and

ABOUT THE WINES

Since Sonoma-Cutrer specializes in white wines, Chef Mark Malicki created a menu to show off the individual characteristics of two different ones:

"The porcini with smoked bacon represents a sampling of the very high-quality, regional specialty foods that I like to use. The earthy, smoky character of this dish contrasts nicely with the fresh, lively quality of Sonoma-Cutrer Russian River Ranches Chardonnay. You could also pair this wine with any dish that features fresh, vibrant flavors. For instance, many of my preparations are centered on Thai cuisine and these exotic flavors play off the youthfulness of the wine.

"The lobster dish, on the other hand, complements the Sonoma-Cutrer Vineyard Chardonnay as opposed to contrasting to it. The similarities between the lobster and wine—that is, the elegant, rich character that the two share—provide for an appealing match. Seafood dishes in general will probably show off this wine nicely."

warm, but do not simmer, over the lowest possible heat for about 5 minutes, stirring once or twice until sugar is melted. Add the gelatin mixture and stir until completely dissolved, about 5 minutes.

Mix sour cream and vanilla. Whisk in the warmed mixture, then strain into a 4-cup loaf pan. Allow to chill in the refrigerator, covered, until set, at least 6 hours.

To serve, unmold and cut into ½-inch slices. Place on a slick of Strawberry Syrup and sprinkle with berries and pomegranate seeds.

Serves 8 or more

STRAWBERRY SYRUP

3 **cups hulled and thickly sliced strawberries**

1 **cup sugar**

2 **cups water**

2 **tablespoons rose water**

Combine all ingredients in a heavy saucepan and bring quickly to a boil over high heat. Turn back immediately to a simmer and cook for 20 minutes. Place in a blender or food processor and give it a few whirls. Put through a fine sieve and chill.

Makes about 3 cups

OPPOSITE: **Fresh Porcini Mushrooms Baked with Bacon.** ABOVE LEFT: **Lobster Fruit Salad.** ABOVE: **French Cream with Berries.**

An Elegant Dinner at the Winery

MONTICELLO CELLARS

~

MONTICELLO CELLARS was founded in 1970 by Jay Corley and his wife, Marilyn, in part of an area know locally as Big Ranch–Oak Knoll. Because of its cooler climate, the region is ideally suited to growing the white varietals from which Chardonnay is made.

For ten years after its founding, all energies were concentrated on creating a modern facility and preparing the extensive vineyards to produce the kind and quantity of grapes needed. To ensure that their requirements could be met while the vineyards were being established, new and innovative farming techniques were used, including an underground sprinkler system and heat-treated and bench-grafted root stock.

As a matter of fact, as a further safeguard, Monticello's vineyard manager, Walt Chavoor, lives right on the vineyard site so he can keep a 24-hour watch on things during frost and harvest season.

Jay Corley's family has roots that run deep in Virginia. Lore has it that his ancestors were among the first settlers of the state, with substantial holdings near one of Thomas Jefferson's plantations. And since Jefferson was among America's first viticulturalists and a renowned wine enthusiast, it seemed fitting to honor his memory with a winery named after his residence in Charlottesville, Virginia, and a winery building called Jefferson House, inspired by Jefferson's actual home. After all, it was Jefferson who purportedly said "Good wine is a necessity of life."

Further following Jefferson's example, all of Monticello's wines are made using French oak for aging. And all are estate bottled, with the exception of its Cabernet Sauvignon, which is made from the fruit of selected vineyards in upper Napa Valley, noted for such grapes.

Although the winery is comparatively new—Jefferson House was only completed in 1984—it has already begun to win its share of awards in competitions all over the state of California. So obviously all this effort, planning, and hard work is just now starting to pay off; and with their quickening pace, the Corleys and their staff are sure to do the memory of Mr. Jefferson proud for a long time to come.

Since Jay and Marilyn are so devoted to the idea of wine marrying well with food, they hired a full-time winery chef, whose job it is to create meals that complement Monticello's wines. Of course, this is good news for friends and acquaintances because the Corleys like nothing better than having a group in for a lunch or dinner prepared and served in the small elegant dining room of Jefferson House.

The meal here is typical of the food guests enjoy on these festive occasions, and of course it is served and complemented by their own "necessity of life."

ABOVE: **The Monticello-inspired winery.**
OPPOSITE: **The dining room set for dinner.**

pan, boil the wine over highest heat until reduced to ½ cup, about 10 minutes. Meanwhile, puree the peppers in a food processor. Add to the wine and cook over medium heat for 2 to 3 minutes. Stir in the cream and bring to a boil. Lower the heat and simmer gently for 4 or 5 minutes. Add the basil, salt, and pepper.

To serve, cook pasta in a large pot of lightly salted water until al dente, about 1 to 3 minutes for fresh pasta. Drain and toss with the sauce, then sprinkle with the Parmesan. Garnish with basil and strips of roasted red pepper, if desired.

Serves 6 as a first course

۶۶

Marinated Roast Loin of Veal in Port Wine and Orange

This unusual method calls for marinating the loin and placing the tenderloin inside it.

2 to 3 pounds loin and tenderloin of veal

1 bottle Port wine

3 medium oranges, juiced, with the zest finely chopped

1 cup coarsely chopped fresh basil

1 tablespoon ground black pepper

Salt to taste

1 cup veal or chicken stock

Trim the loin of all fat and sinew. In a deep roasting pan, combine wine, orange juice and zest, basil, pepper, and salt. Add the loin, cover, and marinate in the refrigerator for 24 hours.

Preheat the oven to 350 degrees.

Remove the loin from the marinade, make a cut three-fourths through the width of the loin, spread out, and place the tenderloin in the center of the loin. Close to form a cylinder and tie securely with kitchen string.

Roast the meat on a rack until a meat thermometer inserted in the center of the roast registers between 135 to 140 degrees, about 1¼ hours. Let rest for 10 minutes with a foil tent loosely over it.

While roast is in the oven, strain 3 cups of the marinade into a nonreactive pan. Boil over high heat until reduced to 1½ cups, about 20 min-

MENU

SAFFRON PASTA WITH CHARDONNAY RED PEPPER SAUCE

MARINATED ROAST LOIN OF VEAL IN PORT WINE AND ORANGE

CRISPY ROSEMARY POTATOES WITH PARMESAN

BRAISED APPLES AND RED ONIONS

ENDIVE, MIXED GREEN, AND NEW POTATO SALAD WITH LEMON-DILL CHARDONNAY VINAIGRETTE

ALMOND TART WITH APRICOT ICE CREAM

1987 Corley Reserve Chardonnay
1987 Pinot Noir
1985 Chateau "M" Late Harvest Sauvignon Blanc

Saffron Pasta with Chardonnay Red Pepper Sauce

For those ambitious souls, I'm including Chef Ned Gill's recipe for saffron pasta. But don't feel guilty if you buy it ready made; I wouldn't. You'll need about 12 ounces of store-bought pasta for this course.

Incidentally, served with the simple salad here and finished by the apricot ice cream, this pasta would make a delightful lunch.

PASTA

½ teaspoon saffron threads

¼ cup warm water

4 eggs

3 cups all-purpose flour

SAUCE

2 cups Chardonnay

2 large red bell peppers, roasted, seeded, and peeled (page 104)

1 cup heavy cream

¼ cup coarsely chopped fresh basil

Salt and pepper to taste

½ cup finely grated Parmesan cheese

Basil leaves cut in strips, and strips of roasted red pepper, for garnish (optional)

Make the pasta. Crush the saffron and let it sit in warm water until water turns deep gold, about 5 minutes.

Place the eggs in a food processor along with the flour and saffron water. Process until a ball forms. Knead on a lightly floured surface for a few minutes, then cover with a tea towel and let sit for 1 hour. (This can be made the day before.)

Roll out dough until very thin and cut into fettuccini strips. Dough should be deep gold color with specks of saffron visible. Set aside.

Make the sauce. In a nonreactive

utes. Add the stock and cook over medium-high heat until sauce is reduced to about 1 cup and is just slightly thickened, about 12 minutes. Add pepper and salt to taste if necessary. Reheat, if necessary, before serving.

To serve, slice roast about ½ inch thick and drizzle sauce over all.

Serves 6

❧

Crispy Rosemary Potatoes with Parmesan

Since these are served at room temperature, you should cook them before the roast.

   3 pounds baking potatoes (about 6 large), peeled and sliced ⅛ inch thick
   ⅓ cup olive oil

   ¼ cup coarsely chopped fresh rosemary
   1 teaspoon salt
   1 teaspoon pepper
   1 cup grated Parmesan cheese

Preheat the oven to 400 degrees.

Oil the ring of a 9½-inch springform pan and place it on a well-oiled baking sheet with a rim. Toss the potatoes in all the remaining oil and the rosemary, salt, and pepper. Beginning with the potatoes, alternate layers of potatoes and cheese, finishing with potatoes. Bake 1 hour or until top potatoes turn medium brown and crispy. Let cool before running a knife around rim and removing ring. Cut into wedges to serve.

Serves 6

❧

Braised Apples and Red Onions

Of course, this would be perfect served with ham or some other kind of pork.

   3 tablespoons olive oil
   3 large red onions, peeled and chopped into 1-inch pieces
   3 large Granny Smith or Pippin apples, peeled, cored, and cut into 1-inch slices

   3 cups dry red wine, preferably Pinot Noir
   Salt and pepper to taste

Place the oil in a large, nonreactive sauté pan, add the onions and sauté over medium-low heat until wilted and translucent, about 7 minutes. Add the apples and continue cooking over medium-low heat until softened, about 5 minutes. Add the wine and raise heat to medium-high, cover, and cook approximately 5 minutes or until wine is completely reduced and apples and onions are completely soft. Add salt and pepper to taste.

Serves 6

OPPOSITE: **The view of the gardens from the dining room window.** LEFT: **Crispy Rosemary Potatoes with Parmesan.** ABOVE: **Marinated Roast Loin of Veal in Port Wine and Orange with Braised Apples and Red Onions.** BELOW: **Saffron Pasta with Chardonnay Red Pepper Sauce.**

Endive, Mixed Green, and New Potato Salad with Lemon-Dill Chardonnay Vinaigrette

This salad has potatoes in it, but they taste so different from the crispy rosemary ones you would think they were a different vegetable.

- 2 pounds new red potatoes, scrubbed
- ¼ cup fresh lemon juice
- 2 tablespoons Chardonnay
- 3 tablespoons chopped fresh dill
- 1 teaspoon Dijon-style mustard
  Salt and pepper to taste
- ½ cup olive oil
  Assorted mixed greens—red leaf, bibb, butter, and the like—torn into pieces
- 2 to 3 heads of endive, leaves separated, washed and dried, and rubbed with a little lemon juice

Boil the potatoes in a large pot of lightly salted water until tender enough to pierce through with a fork. Drain and cool. Set aside.

Combine the lemon juice, wine, dill, and mustard in a small bowl and whisk. Add salt and pepper to taste. Whisking, pour in oil in a steady stream.

Halve the potatoes and toss with some of the vinaigrette. Make a bed of the assorted greens and endive on individual salad plates. Arrange 3 or 4 leaves on top and divide potato halves among the plates.

Drizzle balance of the vinaigrette over all and top with a grinding of fresh pepper.

Serves 6

Almond Tart with Apricot Ice Cream

This tart would be delicious with simple whipped cream, but the ice cream sends it over the top.

PASTRY

- 2 ½ cups all-purpose flour
- ½ cup sugar
  Pinch of salt
- 14 tablespoons (1¾ sticks) frozen unsalted butter, cut into small pieces
- 1 whole egg plus 1 egg yolk
- 1 teaspoon vanilla extract
- ½ teaspoon grated lemon zest

ALMOND FILLING

- ⅔ cup unpeeled almonds
- ½ cup plus 2 tablespoons sugar
- 1 cup (2 sticks) plus 1 tablespoon unsalted butter
- 1 whole egg plus 1 egg yolk
- 1 teaspoon vanilla extract
- ¼ teaspoon almond extract
- 1 cup sliced, toasted almonds

Make the pastry. Mix the flour, sugar, and salt in a food processor fitted with a steel blade. Add butter and process until mixture is the texture of meal.

In a small bowl, beat together the egg, egg yolk, vanilla, and zest. With the motor running, pour this mixture through the feed tube. Process just until dough begins to cling together. Remove dough and knead lightly on a sparsely floured board until dough is no longer sticky and forms a ball. Divide in half; flatten, wrap in plastic, and refrigerate for at least an hour.

Remove one-half of the dough and allow it to stand for 30 minutes at room temperature, then knead again lightly. Roll it out on a floured surface to a thickness of ¼ to ⅜ inch. Roll it onto the pin, then unroll over a 10-inch tart pan and line, building up the edges with the excess. If the dough should come apart, piece it and press together in the pan. You can also simply pat the dough into the pan.

Preheat the oven to 350 degrees.

Make the filling. Place unpeeled almonds and sugar in a food processor with a steel blade. Grind to a coarse powder, then transfer to a mixer with a heavy-duty paddle. Add butter and beat until light and fluffy, about 5 minutes. (You can use a hand mixer.) Exchange paddle for a whisk attach-

ment and add egg and yolk, whisking until well mixed. Add the vanilla and almond extracts and continue whisking for another 5 minutes.

Spread the mixture in the tart shell and sprinkle top with the almonds. Bake until shell is golden and filling is set, about 40 minutes. Cool on a rack.

Serves 8

APRICOT ICE CREAM

- 12 ripe medium apricots
- 1 ½ cups milk
- ½ cup heavy cream
- ½ cup sugar

Peel and pit the apricots. The easiest way to peel the apricots is to bring a pot of water to a boil. Cut an X in the bottom of each apricot—just through the skin and not too deep. Place half the apricots in the boiling water and

when water returns to a boil, leave them in for 1 minute or until skins begin to peel back from the Xs. Remove apricots and place in cold water. Skins should come off easily. Repeat with remaining apricots.

Puree apricots in a blender; mix in milk, cream, and sugar. Freeze in an ice cream maker according to manufacturer's directions.

Makes 1¹/₂ pints

ABOUT THE WINES

Because there are many different flavors working together in resident chef Ned Gill's menu, he has lots to say about the reasoning behind his choices, to wit:

"The Saffron Pasta with Chardonnay Red Pepper Sauce is a natural with the 1987 Corley Reserve Chardonnay. This wine was barrel fermented, so the wood of the wine and the smoky characteristics of the roasted bell peppers mingle comfortably in the back of the mouth. The reduced Chardonnay in the sauce provides a nice, compatible foundation for the food and wine to play off of. In essence the reduced wine in the sauce acts first as a link between the food and wine and then as a springboard for the other flavors in the food. Finally, the texture of the wine is what I consider smooth, because the barrel fermenting seems to take some of the edge off the wine. This smooth texture matches up well with the creamy consistency of the sauce.

"The winemaker here at Monticello, Alan Phillips, has said, 'Pinot Noir is a crazy varietal. If it were a person, it would be committed.' Well, in 1987 Alan hand selected just twelve tons of fruit from our vineyards and produced a traditional Burgundian-style Pinot Noir, and judging from the results, this fruit was as sane as you and I. The depth of color and flavor make the 1987 Pinot Noir a wonderful accompaniment to veal. Again, the wine, in this case Port, provides the foundation for the other flavors. The Pinot Noir is perfect for this since it is hearty enough to stand up to the dense flavors of the Port and the veal, but not so overpowering as to destroy the slightly sweet flavors from the basil and orange. This is a classic example of contrasting flavors creating a unique harmony.

"The Almond Tart with Apricot Ice Cream served with the Late Harvest Sauvignon Blanc (1985 Chateau "M") is the exact opposite of the food-and-wine pairing of the main course. The flavors in the tart and ice cream are nearly identical to the characteristics of the wine. The slightly caramel flavor of the tart is there quite clearly in the finish of the wine. The apricot flavor is quite apparent in the nose of this wine and the initial flavor as it enters your mouth. Serving this dessert without this wine is a sin. Period."

Well now, Ned has strong feelings about his reasons for pairing wines and foods, which I think give you an insight into what some professionals consider when doing such things. Of course, some of this might seem rather arcane, and quite frankly many such subtleties would probably zoom right past the average palate. But even such a deluge of information helps to make us more comfortable with wine—doing so by giving us clues as to what we might look for in wines to increase our pleasure in drinking them.

Sunday Supper

FETZER VINEYARDS

I F YOU want to see a real family business, this is it! There are eleven Fetzer offspring in all, so buying a historic 750-acre Redwood Valley ranch in 1958 was almost a necessity for Bernard and Kathleen Fetzer—the kids needed some place to spread out. And their timing was great because the property was bought a crucial few years before things starting booming in the California north coast wine region.

Nebraska-born Bernard was a Mendocino County lumber executive, and for the first decade, after getting the eighty-year-old vineyard on their property back in working order, the Fetzers sold their grapes to home winemakers—and made wine for themselves just for fun.

But little by little they got the bug to improve their wine-making techniques and equipment. Finally, in 1968 they had their first commercial vintage. Over the years, the Fetzer clan has built a nationwide reputation for producing award-winning varietal wines at reasonable prices. An unbeatable combination.

ABOVE: **Kathleen Fetzer.**
RIGHT: **Dining on the front terrace.**

Although Bernard died in 1981, Kathleen and ten of the children have carried on what began in the '60s. Today the statistics alone are rather staggering, especially when you consider that the Fetzers didn't intend to go into the wine business when the ranch was purchased back in 1958. The Fetzer family currently owns and operates five ranches totaling nearly 4,000 acres. First was Redwood Valley, which grew to 780 acres planted to Cabernet Sauvignon, Sauvignon Blanc, and Zinfandel.

Next, 1,130 acres are planted to Chardonnay and Pinot Noir at Sundial Ranch in Hopland. At Valley Oaks Ranch, also in Hopland, 1,700 acres are planted to Cabernet Sauvignon, Sauvignon Blanc, Chenin Blanc, Zinfandel, and Chardonnay.

Kircher Ranch in northeast Ukiah, along the Russian River, has 160 acres planted in Chardonnay. And last, Chalfant Ranch in the Ukiah Valley has 100 acres planted in 1990. But, that's not all.

In April 1989, the Fetzer Valley Oaks Food and Wine Center opened in Mendocino County; it includes a four-acre organic garden with 2,000 varieties of fresh fruits, vegetables, herbs, and ornamental and edible flowers throughout the growing season.

There is also a dining pavilion with both commercial and demonstration kitchens; a conference facility fully equipped for food-and-beverage ex-

ecutive training programs; a bed-and-breakfast facility with swimming pool and tennis courts; an
exhibition area; and an outdoor amphitheater to be
used for concerts, theater, and other special events.

From the looks of all this, it will *take* the whole
family to manage this operation.

For our dinner at Fetzer, Kathleen thought it
would be fun to do a meal that was the sort the kids
favored when they were growing up. It was delicious—sweet retro.

And just look at her sweet smiling face—the
quintessential Mom.

M E N U

COUNTRY-STYLE BARBECUED RIBS
COLE SLAW
BAKED ACORN SQUASH
STONE-GROUND WHEAT BREAD
PINEAPPLE UPSIDE DOWN CAKE

1985 Barrel Select Cabernet
1988 Red Zinfandel
1988 Gewürztraminer

Country-Style Barbecued Ribs

I'm not saying these are low-cal, but the fact that they are simmered before they are grilled (or broiled) does take some of the fat out of these delicious morsels.

- 4 pounds country-style pork ribs
- ¼ cup vegetable oil
- ½ cup coarsely chopped onion
- ½ medium garlic clove, minced
- 1 8-ounce can tomato sauce
- ¼ cup light brown sugar, packed
- ¼ cup fresh lemon juice
- 2 tablespoons Worcestershire sauce
- 2 tablespoons prepared mustard
- 1 tablespoon chopped fresh parsley
- 1½ teaspoons grated lemon rind
- ½ cup Cabernet

Place ribs in a deep saucepan and cover with lightly salted water. Bring to a boil over high heat, then turn heat to low; simmer until tender, about 50 minutes. Drain and discard liquid.

Meanwhile, heat the oil in a large skillet and sauté the onion and garlic over medium heat until tender, about 5 minutes. Stir in the tomato sauce and the balance of the ingredients. Simmer, uncovered, for 20 minutes.

To finish the ribs, grill them over ash-covered coals or place them under a preheated broiler. Brush often with the sauce and cook until ribs are well coated and browned, 5 to 8 minutes to a side. Grilling too long will cause the sugar in the sauce to burn.

Serves 6

❧

Cole Slaw

This is referred to by the Fetzer clan as Mom's Justifiably Famous Cole Slaw. They got the name right, as you'll realize when you taste this.

- ½ cup mayonnaise
- 1 tablespoon wine vinegar
- 2 teaspoons sugar
- ¼ teaspoon salt
- ¼ cup sweet pickle juice
- 2 cups shredded green cabbage
- 2 cups shredded red cabbage
- ½ cup shredded carrot
- ¼ cup finely chopped green bell pepper
- 2 tablespoons minced onion

Whisk together the mayonnaise, vinegar, sugar, salt, and pickle juice. Chill.

To finish the salad, toss remaining ingredients together in a large bowl and combine with the dressing.

Serves 6 to 8

Baked Acorn Squash

Of course these may be cooked in a regular oven, but here they were done much quicker in a microwave. Take your pick.

- 3 medium acorn squash, split and seeded
- 3 tablespoons unsalted butter
  Lawry's Lemon Pepper to taste
  Salt to taste

Place split squash halves in a covered dish and dot with the butter. Season with pepper and salt to taste.

To bake in a microwave oven, cover and place in microwave set at 100% power. Cook for about 18 minutes in a full-wattage oven or longer in a smaller oven, checking every 6 minutes for doneness.

To bake squash in a conventional oven, preheat oven to 350 degrees. Place squash cut side down on a baking dish and bake for 30 minutes. Turn the squash over and dot with butter, pepper, and salt. Bake for approximately another 30 minutes, or until fork tender.

Serves 6

❧

Stone-Ground Wheat Bread

Kathleen Fetzer, who has been making bread for years, says that you have to try bread making a few times to get the hang of it. So if at first you get less than spectacular results, don't be discouraged. The rewards are worth the effort once you gain the necessary know-how.

> 3 tablespoons (or 3 packages) dry active yeast
> 1 ½ cups warm water (110° to 115°F)
> ¼ cup sugar
> 1 5-ounce can evaporated milk
> ⅓ cup vegetable oil
> ⅓ cup molasses
> 1 teaspoon salt
> 4 cups stone-ground wheat flour
> 5 ½ cups all-purpose flour, approximately

Combine yeast, warm water, and sugar in a large mixing bowl. Stir and let stand for 15 minutes, until frothy.

Add the evaporated milk, then fill milk can with warm water and stir in. Mix in oil, molasses, and salt.

With a hand mixer, beat some of each flour into the bowl, enough to make a heavy dough that can still be beaten easily with the mixer. Continue beating for 3 minutes.

Using a wooden spoon, mix in more of each flour until dough is very stiff. Turn out onto a floured board and knead until dough is easy to handle, about 3 to 4 minutes. Use as much flour as it takes to create an elastic, shiny, and slightly sticky dough.

Clean out bowl well and oil it. Put in dough and turn it over once to coat with oil. Let rise in a warm draft-free spot for 1 to 1½ hours. It should double in bulk, but not be risen fully.

Turn out dough onto a lightly floured board and punch down. Divide into 4 balls and knead each into a loaf shape.

Grease four 8 by 4-inch loaf pans, place dough in, and allow to rise until double in size again, about 1 hour.

Preheat oven to 350 degrees. Bake for 45 minutes or until nicely browned. Cover the tops with foil for the last 15 or 20 minutes to prevent tops from becoming too brown.

Makes 4 loaves

Pineapple Upside Down Cake

What could be more of a family favorite—especially for the kids—than this? Maybe only apple pie.

> 1 8-ounce can pineapple rings
> 2 tablespoons unsalted butter
> ½ cup dark brown sugar, packed
> Maraschino cherries, cut into halves
> ⅓ cup vegetable shortening
> ¾ cup granulated sugar
> 1 egg
> 1 ¾ cups all-purpose flour
> 2 ½ teaspoons baking powder
> ¼ teaspoon salt
> 1 ½ teaspoons vanilla extract
> Ice cream or whipped cream

Preheat the oven to 350 degrees.

Drain the pineapple, reserving the liquid. Melt the butter in a deep 9-inch ovenproof skillet. Stir in the brown sugar and 1 tablespoon of the reserved pineapple juice. Arrange pineapple rings in the pan, filling all centers with cherry halves. Set aside.

Beat the shortening, granulated sugar, and egg together until well blended, about 3 to 4 minutes. Combine the flour, baking powder, and salt. Measure the remaining pineapple juice and add water if necessary to make ⅔ cup. Add the dry mixture and pineapple juice to the shortening mixture alternately and beat. Pour over pineapple rings and place in oven. Bake for 45 minutes or until done in the middle (see Note). Cool for 5 minutes before running a knife around the edge and inverting cake onto a plate.

Serve with ice cream or whipped cream.

Serves 6 to 8

Note: This cake can be a bit deceptive, looking done on top while being uncooked in the middle, so test center with a wooden pick before removing cake from the oven.

❦

About the Wines

I think you will find Kathleen Fetzer's remarks about the wines served at lunch as accessible and straightforward as her food. All is in harmony here.

Of the 1985 Barrel Select Cabernet: "Always use a nice (not poor quality) wine in the sauce, and if you're serving a red with the meal, then you could use the same wine in the sauce. But we like a fuller-bodied red in the sauce and the lighter red on the table."

The 1988 Red Zinfandel is a "lighter, fruity red especially great with outdoor meals. We like to offer two different wines with each course for variety, so we also offer the Barrel Select Chardonnay, which is particularily good with the buttery squash and the cole slaw."

And the 1988 Gewürztraminer is a "fruity, floral, and slightly sweet white that matches perfectly with simpler fruit desserts. This is a favorite of mine and I usually pair it with everything—there's just enough sweetness in the wine, and plenty of flavor to suit it to all sorts of different dishes."

OPPOSITE: **Country-Style Barbecued Ribs and Baked Acorn Squash.**
LEFT: **Pineapple Upside Down Cake.**

A Seasonal Dinner

STAG'S LEAP WINE CELLARS

ᔧ

IT REALLY all began in 1964, when Warren Winiarski, a young professor at the University of Chicago, and his artist wife, Barbara, settled on the idea of leaving the Windy City and moving to the Napa Valley. Winiarski was interested in home wine making as his father had been, and by 1964 he'd decided professional wine making was for him—full time. However, it was not until six years after their move that the vineyards, which are now known as Stag's Leap Wine Cellars, were actually purchased.

At the beginning of those intervening years, with recommendations from many of the people whom

Entrance to the winery.

nity presented itself, he knew where he wanted his winery to be.

He began with the purchase of a tract of land next to the Fay Vineyard. It was this vineyard, which incidentally he ultimately purchased, that was producing wine in the late sixties that inspired him.

It wasn't until 1972, however, after the old vines and trees on his new land were torn out and planted with Cabernet grapes, that Stag's Leap Wine Cellars would be able to harvest its first modest crop. But each new year brought growth in quantity and quality and by 1976, at a blind tasting in Paris, his Cabernet won out over all others in its class, including the then seemingly invincible French wines. This startling win was such news that *Time* magazine saw fit to tell the world what Warren Winiarski had accomplished.

While the winery grew, so did the Winiarski family, which includes wife, Barbara, now an accomplished cook as well as an artist, and their daughters, Kasia and Julia, and son, Stephen.

Like most families, favorite menus have evolved over the years, and this is one all its members (and friends) like and look forward to. The meal celebrates the annual arrival of the magnificent king salmon, which also happens to coincide with the time when luscious black cherries come into season. Here the fish is served cold and the cherries are marinated in wine and spices.

he had met and worked with during his amateur wine-making days, Warren Winiarski started with Souverain. There he did anything and everything, from laying out hose for the irrigation system to cleaning wine tanks. Then, when the new Robert Mondavi Winery began hiring, he signed on as one of its first employees.

During this time Winiarski also took the opportunity to sample wines from various locations in the valley and decided that grapes grown on its eastern side, hard against the Stag's Leap Ridge, were best suited to his tastes. So in 1970, when the opportu-

M E N U

ENDIVE AND GOLDEN CAVIAR
COLD KING SALMON WITH ASPIC AND HERB SAUCE
COLD VEGETABLES WITH MUSTARD SAUCE
CAMBAZOLA CHEESE AND ASIAN PEARS
BLACK CHERRIES IN WINE

Sauvignon Blanc 1987
Merlot 1986
White Riesling 1986
Chardonnay 1987 Reserve

Endive and Golden Caviar

As you can see from the photograph, this simple-to-prepare first course makes a smashing presentation.

> 2 medium shallots
> 1 large scallion, with some green
> 8 ounces cream cheese, at room temperature
> 2 tablespoons fresh lemon juice
> 1/2 cup sour cream or plain yogurt
> 4 to 5 whole endive
> 2 ounces fresh golden caviar (see Note)
>   Chives, for garnish

Mince the shallots and scallion in a food processor. Add the cream cheese

Cold King Salmon with Aspic and Herb Sauce

This is a dish for a special occasion because it takes a bit of doing, but the result is well worth it. However, when you look over the menu and recipes you will see that everything else is quite simple so it all balances out.

and lemon juice and blend well. Add the sour cream and pulse a few times, just enough to mix.

Separate the endive leaves and select 24 of the best ones, trim them and place in ice water. Reserve the balance of the leaves for another use.

To serve, dry the endive leaves and arrange 3 each on individual plates. Put a tablespoon of the cream cheese mixture in the lower part of each leaf and then 1/2 teaspoon of caviar above and slightly overlapping the cream. Sprinkle with chives.

Serves 8

Note: Do not use prepackaged caviar, which is too salty and metallic tasting.

🦎

ABOVE: **Cold King Salmon with Aspic.** BELOW LEFT: **Endive and Golden Caviar.** OPPOSITE TOP: **Herb Sauce for the salmon;** BOTTOM: **The dining room overlooking the surrounding hills.**

Barbara Winiarski tells me she learned this poaching technique from Joe Hyde, whose book Love, Time and Butter, *unfortunately now out of print, she calls "one of the best cookbooks ever written."*

You will need a deep 24-inch lidded fish poacher with a rack with handles. In a pinch you could improvise with a deep roasting pan, wrapping the fish in several layers of cheesecloth in order to lift it out.

This dish should be made a day ahead to give the fish time to chill thoroughly.

FISH

> 2 cups Chardonnay or other dry white wine
> 2 medium onions, finely sliced
> 2 medium carrots, thickly sliced
> 1 large celery rib, thickly sliced
> 2 tablespoons black peppercorns
> 2 tablespoons salt
> 3 large bay leaves
> 1 cleaned king salmon with head, tail, and skin intact, but with gills removed (5 to 7 pounds)

ASPIC

- 5 envelopes unflavored gelatin
- ½ cup cold water
- 3 cups poaching liquid
  Ice cubes

ASSEMBLY

- 1 medium carrot, cut into thin rings
- 1 pitted black olive
  Fresh tarragon, blanched for 15 seconds and dried
  Fresh dill, blanched for 5 seconds and dried
- 1 medium leek, cut into julienne, blanched for 40 seconds, and dried

Poach the fish. Make a court bouillon by combining all the ingredients except fish in the poacher and bringing it to a boil over 2 heating units at high heat. Turn back heat and simmer for 1 hour.

The cooking time for the fish is calculated by its thickness (not weight), so measure the salmon at its widest point. Rinse salmon carefully and be sure the red vein along the inner backbone is removed (this is actually the fish's kidney). Slide the fish into the poacher on its side. Add boiling water to court bouillon so that the fish is just covered by the poaching liquid. Return heat to high and when boiling, lower heat so that liquid barely moves in the covered poacher. Poach for 13 minutes for each inch of thickness (see Note).

Allow the fish to cool in the liquid, uncovered at room temperature. Then cover it and refrigerate overnight.

Carefully lift the fish out of the poaching liquid and allow to drain. Slide gently onto a serving platter. With the point of a sharp knife, cut through the skin along the sides of the gill plates and along the backbone. Peel the skin away, cutting a neat curve where it joins the tail. Gently scrape away any brown meat on the sides until only pink is showing. Clean the platter around the fish.

Make the aspic. Soften the gelatin in the water for several minutes. Strain the poaching liquid through a thickness or two of cheesecloth and add to the gelatin. Bring to a simmer, stirring constantly, then remove from heat.

Prepare the garnish. Dip a carrot round in warm aspic and place over fish's eye. Cut a slice of black olive, dip it in the aspic, and place on the carrot as the "pupil." Decorate the sides of the fish with the blanched dill, tarragon, and leeks, again dipping them into the warm aspic first.

Place the pot with the remaining aspic into a large bowl filled with ice cubes. Stir the aspic as it thickens. When it is somewhat thicker than heavy cream ladle it on the fish in long, smooth strokes from head to tail. Work very rapidly since aspic will continue to thicken and get lumpy. If you do have a few lumps, heat the blade of a wooden-handled knife over a flame and smooth them out.

Finish the decoration by cutting a dorsal fin from a length of cucumber and "gluing" it along the backbone with aspic.

Serve with Herb Sauce.

Serves 8 to 12

HERB SAUCE

Make this the day you'll serve it.

- ½ cup mayonnaise
  Juice of 1 large lemon
- 1 medium shallot, minced
- ½ cup plain yogurt
- ½ cup sour cream
- ¼ cup finely chopped fresh parsley
- ¼ cup finely chopped fresh tarragon or dill

Combine the mayonnaise, lemon juice, and shallot and beat well. Stir in yogurt and sour cream. Fold in herbs. Chill until ready to use.

Makes approximately 1 pint

Note: To serve the salmon hot, poach it 15 minutes to the inch. This extra time is because it will be lifted from the poaching liquid as soon as it is done.

Variation: You can also bake the salmon, which was how the fish pictured here was done.

To do so, tear off a large sheet of foil and place it in a deep poacher with enough extra to seal it on top. Put the fish on its stomach on a bed of finely sliced onion, curving it in the foil and against the sides of the pan so it has a graceful shape. You could prop the fish's mouth open with a broken off toothpick.

Dot with 3 tablespoons of unsalted butter and tuck sprigs of dill, sorrel, or tarragon along and around the sides of the salmon. Squeeze a lemon over, pour on a cup of dry white wine, and carefully seal foil, making sure entire fish is enclosed. Cook in a preheated 325-degree oven.

Allow fish to cool and then refrigerate. To serve, gently slide fish onto the platter and carefully peel away the foil and cooked vegetables. Continue with instructions for cleaning and decorating.

Cold Vegetables with Mustard Sauce

This is another one of those very easy and eye-catching combinations.

BELOW: **A bouquet of roses, poppies, and wildflowers.** BOTTOM: **Cold Vegetables with Mustard Sauce.** BOTTOM RIGHT: **Black Cherries in Wine.**

4 **medium carrots, scraped and cut into thin julienne**

4 **medium zucchini, cut into thin julienne**

4 **medium yellow summer squash, cut into thin julienne**

1 ½ **pounds small green beans, tipped and stemmed**

1½ **pounds very small new red potatoes**

Salt

1 **tablespoon minced shallot**

2 **tablespoons Dijon-style mustard**

3 **tablespoons boiling water**

½ **cup olive oil**

Freshly ground pepper

Fresh lemon juice

2 **tablespoons minced parsley or other herb of your choice**

Steam the carrots, zucchini, and yellow squash separately until just crisp-tender, 2 to 3 minutes or less. Refresh with cold water. Drain well and dry in paper towels. Place in plastic bags and store in refrigerator.

Steam the beans for 4 to 8 minutes, refresh, and place in a plastic bag and refrigerate.

Drop the unpeeled potatoes in lightly salted boiling water and cook until just tender, 5 to 8 minutes depending on size. Refresh in cold water and store, whole, in the refrigerator.

Rinse a mixing bowl in hot water, then dry. Place shallot and mustard in bowl and whisk in boiling water a few drops at the time. Whisk in olive oil in a steady stream. Add salt, pepper, and lemon juice to taste, mixing well. Mix in herbs.

To serve, toss the carrots, zucchini, and yellow squash lightly with 3 table-spoons of the sauce. Thinly slice the potatoes and arrange vegetables on a cold serving platter. Drizzle remaining sauce over potatoes and green beans.

Serves 8

About the Wines

Cambazola Cheese and Asian Pears

Barbara Winiarski says she likes this in place of the traditional salad course.

- ¾ **pound Cambazola cheese, thinly sliced and at room temperature**
- 1 **Asian pear (see Note), thinly sliced and slices rubbed with lemon juice**
- ¼ **pound assorted small lettuce leaves, if desired**
  Light dressing of good olive oil and lemon juice in a 4-to-1 combination with salt and pepper to taste
  French bread, thinly sliced and toasted

Place a thin slice of cheese on individual plates along with 2 slices of Asian pear. Add a few lettuce leaves for garnish, and drizzle with dressing.

Serve this with thin slices of toasted French bread.

Serves 8

Note: Asian pear tastes like a smooth-textured cross between a pear and an apple. If not available, use firm Bosc pears or jicama.

Black Cherries in Wine

Barbara traditionally makes this with their Merlot.

- 2 **cups Merlot or other dry red wine**
- 1 **cup sugar**
- 1 **cinnamon stick**
  Peel of 1 medium lemon
  Juice of ½ medium lemon
- 2 **tablespoons brandy**
- 2 **pounds black cherries, pitted**

Combine all ingredients except the cherries in a small saucepan and simmer for 20 minutes. Cool.

Macerate cherries for ½ to 2 hours in the cooled syrup, turning several times. If you like, serve with a dab of whipped cream or crème fraîche.

Serves 8

Barbara Winiarski, who prepared these favorite family dishes for us, has a pleasingly relaxed and flexible approach to combining wines and food, which I find at once helpful and reassuring.

To go with the Endive and Golden Caviar course she suggests their Sauvignon Blanc because "it is crisp and restrained and not herbaceous or otherwise too overpowering for the delicate caviar." She says, however, that you might serve the same Chardonnay as is served with the salmon. "This Chardonnay is not overly oaked and is well balanced and fresh—a perfect foil for the fish."

As for the dessert, she feels Merlot is too dry and recommends their Late Harvest Johannisberg Riesling. But, as as she puts it, this dessert would be fine without *any* wine.

A Family
Reunion Lunch

ALEXANDER VALLEY VINEYARDS

LEXANDER VALLEY VINEYARDS had its beginning in the early 1960s when Maggie and Harry Wetzel of Palo Verdes, California, bought a summer place on the Russian River for themselves and their four young children.

The house itself was an old tumble-down Victorian, resting at a rakish angle in a stand of five-foot-high weeds. Constructed in 1842 by Cyrus Alexander—an early European immigrant who made his fortune selling produce in San Francisco—the original adobe structure was dressed up later with the kind of fancy woodwork fashionable in the valleys around 1906, the year of the great earthquake.

But by the time the property was acquired by the Wetzels, the house had, almost literally, fallen on hard times.

Since its purchase, however, the house has been carefully restored and refurnished. New vegetable and flower gardens were laid out, orchards were pruned and cultivated—and the vineyards were planted. Along the way, an 1868 one-room schoolhouse was reclaimed and moved to the compound to add more space for weekend guests and the grow-

ing family. Finally, in 1975 construction on the winery was begun at the urging of the Wetzel children, particularly Hank Wetzel III, who had just taken his degree at the renowned oenology department of the University of California, Davis. Today he is the winemaker and general manager, and his younger sister, Katie Wetzel Murphy, is the national sales manager. Presently the whole place is undergoing an extensive expansion.

The elder Wetzels are very active in the cultural life of Los Angeles and over the years have served on many boards and councils having to do with art

and music. Harry Wetzel is the chairman of the board of Garrett Corporation, a manufacturer of aircraft equipment.

But when the bustling and burgeoning family is in residence at the valley house, picnics and outdoor lunches are the order of the day with everyone pitching in to help. Tasty, abundant food and the family seem to go together naturally. Add to this wine produced from your own grapes and you have California vibes about as good as they can get.

OPPOSITE: **The house glimpsed through the vineyards.** ABOVE LEFT: **Hank and Linda Wetzel are standing at left, Lori Wetzel is sitting behind Harry and Maggie Wetzel, and Katie Wetzel Murphy is standing at right. Seated on the bottom step are, from left, Susan Kirkpatrick, John Wetzel, and Dennis Murphy.** TOP: **John's daughter Blair.** ABOVE: **Sally Wetzel Fallon's son James.** LEFT: **The doors to the winery.**

CONFIT OF GARDEN VEGETABLES
BREAD AND SWEET BUTTER
TWO KINDS OF DUCK SAUSAGES, GRILLED
CORN PANCAKES
FRESH APPLESAUCE WITH SAUTEED APPLES
BOYSENBERRY COBBLER WITH CREAM

1987 Chardonnay
1986 Pinot Noir
Gewürztraminer

TOP: **Confit of Garden Vegetables.** ABOVE:
The grown-ups' table. OPPOSITE TOP: **The
younger members of the Wetzel clan;**
BOTTOM: **Harry Wetzel at the grill.**

Confit of Garden Vegetables

This recipe was given to the Wetzels by Randi Middleton.

1 pound eggplant, cut into 1-inch cubes

1 ½ pounds tomatoes, peeled, seeded, and cut into 1-inch dice

1 teaspoon salt

1 pound red bell peppers, quartered lengthwise, roasted and peeled (page 104), and cut into 1-inch dice

1 pound red onions, cut into 1-inch dice

1 pound zucchini, cut into quarters lengthwise, then into 1-inch sections

About 1 cup olive oil

About 2 tablespoons coarse salt

1 large garlic head

¼ cup chicken stock

½ cup mixed chopped fresh parsley, basil, marjoram, and thyme

Preheat the oven to 375 degrees.

Sprinkle eggplant and tomatoes with regular salt, then let drain about 30 minutes. Rinse eggplant and pat it dry.

Place one vegetable at a time in individual mixing bowls and toss with just enough olive oil to coat. As you finish spread the vegetables in single layers on separate sheet pans lined with baking parchment. Sprinkle with coarse salt.

Bake until the vegetables caramelize. They should still be tender and a bit chewy but not obliterated. The eggplant, zucchini, and onions will take about 40 minutes, the peppers about 30. As each vegetable is finished, remove to a large bowl for a communal toss while still warm.

Meanwhile, break apart the head of garlic, removing the paper but leaving skins on the whole cloves. In a small saucepan, toss the garlic with olive oil to just coat. Sprinkle with regular salt. Add chicken stock, cover, and simmer over a low heat until tender, 30 to 45 minutes. Push through a sieve to remove the skins. Add garlic puree to the vegetables. Toss.

When confit has cooled somewhat, add herbs and toss again. Serve at room temperature with garnish (recipe follows).

Makes 4 cups, plus garnish

GARNISH

1 to 2 tablespoons oil

1 to 2 tablespoons unsalted butter

2 large red onions, peeled and cut into ¼-inch rings

2 pounds eggplant, sliced ½ inch thick, salted, and drained for 30 minutes, washed and dried

1 pound medium zucchini, split lengthwise

Combine the oil and butter in a large skillet and fry the vegetables, turning as necessary, over medium heat until brown, about 10 minutes.

Two Kinds of Duck Sausages, Grilled

These two kinds of duck sausage came from master California sausage maker Bruce Aidells, who very generously gave us the recipes you see here. Be on the lookout for his new book, Hot Links and Country Flavors, *published by Knopf, as well as his sausages from the Aidells Sausage Company, headquartered in Kensington, California (see page 173).*

SMOKED DUCK AND FENNEL SAUSAGE

2 ½ **pounds duck meat, cut into 2-inch pieces (see Note)**
1 **pound salt pork, cut into 1- by 5-inch strips**
¼ **teaspoon dried sage**
¼ **teaspoon dried thyme**
½ **teaspoon fennel seed**
⅛ **teaspoon ground bay leaf**
½ **teaspoon paprika**
  Pinch of allspice
1 ½ **teaspoons black pepper**
1 **tablespoon coarse salt**
½ **teaspoon minced garlic**
2 **tablespoons Drambuie**
8 **to 10 feet medium hog casing, rinsed**

Grind meat and fat in a meat grinder using the ⅛-inch plate. Transfer to a large mixing bowl and add the spices, salt, garlic, and Drambuie. Mix well with your hands until all ingredients are combined. Stuff mixture into hog casing and tie off in 6-inch links. Follow instructions for smoking.

Makes approximately 4 pounds, or 20 to 25 sausages

Note: Use the duck carcass and scraps to make a flavorful duck stock, which is perfect for cooking lentils or white beans.

SMOKING METHOD

Soak 3 to 4 cups of wood chips or 6 to 8 wood chunks in water for at least 30 minutes. Mound 10 to 15 briquettes to one side of a barbecue kettle with cover. Once the coals are hot, allow them to burn down to medium-low. This takes about 30 minutes and they should be covered with gray ash. Spread the coals in a single layer to one side of the barbecue. Sprinkle the chips or chunks over the coals. Place a pan half full of hot water next to the coals. Replace grill rack and spread sausages on the grill on the side opposite from the coals and over the pan of water. Cover the grill, making sure the vent in the lid is directly over the sausages. Open the top and bottom vents about ¼ inch. Smoke the sausages at 180 to 280 degrees. This temperature can be measured by inserting an instant thermometer into the partially opened top vent. Add more wood or charcoal if needed. Smoke the sausages for 1½ to 2 hours, turning every 30 minutes, until the internal temperature of the sausages is 160 degrees.

❧

DUCK AND ORANGE SAUSAGE

- 1 pound duck breast meat, including skin, cut into 2-inch pieces
- 1 pound (approximately) duck meat from 2 deboned duck legs, including skin, cut into 2-inch pieces
- ¼ pound smoky bacon, chilled in the freezer for 30 minutes, then cut into 2-inch cubes
- 2 teaspoons coarse salt
- 2 teaspoons coarsely ground black pepper
- 1 teaspoon finely chopped garlic
- 1 teaspoon Hungarian sweet paprika
- ¼ teaspoon ground dried sage
- ½ teaspoon whole dried thyme
- ¼ teaspoon whole dried savory
- ½ teaspoon cayenne pepper
  Pinch of ground allspice
- 1 teaspoon sugar
- ¼ cup orange-flavored liqueur, such as Grand Marnier or Curaçao
- ¼ cup water
- 5 to 6 feet medium hog casing, rinsed

Place duck meat, skin, and bacon in a grinder fitted with a ¼-inch plate and grind. Place in a bowl and sprinkle other ingredients over all. Blend well with your hands, kneading and squeezing as you mix, but do not overmix because the fat will begin to melt and the sausage will turn white. Stuff into hog casings and tie off in 5-inch links. (Sausages will keep 3 days refrigerated or 2 months frozen.)

To cook, prick casings and place links in a cold skillet over medium heat. Cook 15 to 18 minutes, turning occasionally, until evenly browned.

Makes 2½ pounds, or 12 to 15 links

TOP: **The view from the porch.** OPPOSITE TOP: **A sampling of fruits and vegetables grown on the grounds;** BOTTOM: **The kids' table.** RIGHT: **Katie's son Matthew (making a face) and John's son Kirk.**

Corn Pancakes

Keep these warm in the oven until you finish making the whole batch. Serve them warm.

1 ½ **cups all-purpose flour**
½ **cup yellow cornmeal**
1 **teaspoon baking powder**
½ **teaspoon salt**
1 **17-ounce can creamed corn**
2 **eggs**
1 **cup milk**
2 **large ears fresh corn, kernels cut from the cob**
¼ **cup chopped fresh chives**

Mix the dry ingredients in a large bowl and then add the creamed corn. Beat the eggs with the milk and stir into the dry ingredients, mixing quickly and lightly. Refrigerate for an hour before using, or overnight.

Just before cooking, stir in the fresh corn and chives. Fry quickly in a lightly oiled pan or grill until golden brown, turning once.

Makes 5 dozen small pancakes

Fresh Applesauce with Sautéed Apples

The combination of sautéed apples with the sauce gives this old standby a marvelous texture. Incidentally, the sauce freezes quite well. The method is rather inexact, but it is easy and you can make it to your own taste.

22 to 26 large apples, peeled, quartered, and seeded
1 cup water
 Honey to taste
 Nutmeg and cinnamon to taste
3 to 4 tablespoons unsalted butter, or to taste

Place 16 to 20 of the prepared apples in a 6-quart pot. Add the water and cover. Place over low heat. In about 20 to 30 minutes, give the apples a stir and repeat at intervals until applesauce reaches the desired consistency, which may take an hour or more. If a smooth sauce is desired, put through a potato ricer or food mill. Sweeten with honey and sprinkle with cinnamon and nutmeg to taste.

To serve, cut remaining apples into eighths and sauté in butter until translucent. Dust with cinnamon and arrange on top of the bowl of sauce.

Makes about 3 quarts

Boysenberry Cobbler with Cream

This is equally good with wild blackberries. For the reunion party, three of these were made.

2 cups all-purpose flour
1 teaspoon salt
1 tablespoon granulated sugar
5 tablespoons chilled unsalted butter, cut into small pieces
5 tablespoons chilled vegetable shortening, cut into small pieces
5 tablespoons ice water
6 or more cups fresh boysenberries
½ to 1 cup raw or granulated sugar
2 tablespoons quick-cooking tapioca (optional)
4 tablespoons (½ stick) unsalted butter in thin slices
2 cups heavy cream

Mix the flour, salt, and sugar in a large bowl. Add the cold butter and vegetable shortening. Cut in with 2 knives or a pastry blender. When the mixture resembles coarse meal, sprinkle with water and mix quickly until dough can be lightly pressed together. You can add more water, but do this sparingly. Place the dough in a plastic bag and press it together. Flatten into a rectangle and refrigerate for 1 hour.

Preheat the oven to 350 degrees.

Roll out the dough into a large rectangle, about 17 by 21 inches, on a floured surface. Transfer to a 9 by 15-inch baking dish and leave the excess draped over the sides.

The measurement of berries is a bit imprecise and depends on their size and ripeness, but the cobbler should be plump. Start with 6 cups of berries, and toss with sugar to taste. If the berries are very ripe and soft, sprinkle with the tapioca before tossing. Heap

that no one component of the wine would stand out or be out of balance. I like to be able to taste each vegetable in that dish, and the wine should blend with them and help to meld them harmoniously rather than accentuate any one particular taste. The balance of fruit, acid, oak, and alcohol in this wine achieves this, while an older Chardonnay with less fruit or more wood overtones might overpower the hearty vegetable tastes in this dish.

"The 1986 Pinot Noir is a very nice match with meats or entree dishes that have several flavors working off of each other. The combinations of duck, herbs, and other meats are nicely offset by the changing flavor of the Pinot Noir. By this I mean that I find that the wine changes in the glass as I drink it, first being fruity, almost berrylike, then herbal overtones, then earthy and woody. This makes an interesting match with the varying tastes of the different sausages. In contrast, a Cabernet Sauvignon that tastes very much the same from one sip to the next is more appropriate with food that is more straightforward, such as grilled steak or roast.

"I have always liked the combination of Gewürztraminer and berries; they bring out the best in each other. And there is no better taste than fresh boysenberry cobbler. I don't have much of a sweet tooth, and both the berries and the wine have enough acid to make them interesting when offset with a little whipping cream. This is a perfect way to end any family meal."

the berries in the center of the dough and randomly put 6 to 8 thin slices of butter on the berries. Fold over the excess pastry. Sprinkle the top with additional sugar and bake on the middle shelf of the oven for 45 minutes to 1 hour, until bubbly and golden. Cool before serving, but do not refrigerate.

Whip the cream until thickened but still pourable, and pass it with the cobbler.

Serves 8 or more

❧

OPPOSITE TOP: **Hank's daughter Margaret Ellen;** BOTTOM: **Fresh Applesauce with Sautéed Apples.** ABOVE: **Boysenberry Cobbler with Cream.**

ABOUT THE WINES

Katie Wetzel Murphy and brother Hank III often make the decisions about what wines are best suited to these family celebrations, although on such occasions with the whole clan gathered, it can also be a time for tasting special reserve wines, which are not yet marketed to the general public.

Here are Katie's comments about this particular meal:

"We all have different reasons for choosing a particular wine to go with a dish we are preparing, but I feel it is especially important to try to reach a balance between the food ingredients and the components of the wine. I chose the 1987 Chardonnay to accompany the mixed baked vegetables because I felt the Chardonnay could stand up to the strong vegetable flavors, and

Lunch in the Vineyard

LOUIS M. MARTINI WINERY

⁂

THE LOUIS M. MARTINI for whom Martini winery is named came by his interest in wine making by helping his father, Agostino. As did many other Italians, Agostino made wine for his family and friends. Young Louis's interest was sufficiently piqued for him to be sent to Italy for six months to study wine making at the school in Alba. When he got back to California, he and his father took to wine making in a more serious and businesslike manner. However, the venture was not profitable and they gave it up.

But Louis had got the bug, so at the beginning of Prohibition he audaciously built the Louis M. Martini Grape Products Company. Louis sensed something that others had missed: if wine could not be sold, grape juice surely could. One who remembers the times facetiously observes, "Never was grape juice so popular as in those days!" As a matter of

fact, Martini's company once sold 100,000 gallons of the stuff to home winemakers in one day.

By 1933, when Prohibition ended, Martini had bought the old Greystone Cellars north of St. Helena. Characteristically, he chose to invest all his capital in equipment and the nuts and bolts of a winery instead of in a fine winery building. And ultimately, Louis M. established an identity for himself as a winemaker and for his wines when California was not generally known for quality.

By the time Louis M.'s son, Louis P.—with his young wife, Elizabeth—joined the family business, the vineyards were producing more and better grapes. Over the years, father and son developed new vineyard lands slowly, with careful testing right up to 1974, when Louis M. died.

This slow, sure approach was, and is, the hallmark of everything they did in the past and are

OPPOSITE: **Lunch under the trees by the vineyard.**
ABOVE: **Crab Gazpacho and a hearty loaf of bread.**

doing now. Not for them the big splash. The Martinis are interested in quality and reliability, not razzle-dazzle. Now with the third generation—Carolyn, Michael, and Patricia—working in the business, they have the great advantage of five very well understood vineyards to build and rely upon.

As someone who has known the family over the years says, "Point by point, the three winemakers in the three generations have varied enough in feeling to stamp their wines with individual traits. They are in perfect agreement about the character that must underlie all Martini wines, almost as if it were stamped in their genetic codes." And as Louis P. himself put it, "We want to make wine that is enjoyable when it leaves the winery and still is age-worthy. We are very conservative in following this goal. We grow slowly. We stick with techniques that have worked down through the years."

So it should come as no surprise that when Louis and "Liz" Martini entertain it is with the same no-nonsense gusto that informs their whole background and way of doing business. Simple food is plentiful and so is the wine.

I'm sure that if I were to come back in the middle of the next century, I'd find the same unassuming devotion to quality and consistency as I see today. That's reassuring indeed!

M E N U

CRAB GAZPACHO
TABASCO HONEY-GLAZED CHICKEN
**POTATO, CORN, AND WHITE BUTTER
BEAN SALAD**
VINE-RIPENED TOMATOES
CRUSTY BREAD WITH SWEET BUTTER
FRESH CHERRIES
COCONUT MACADAMIA BISCOTTI

1988 Louis M. Martini Johannisberg Riesling
1988 Louis M. Martini Chardonnay
1986 Louis M. Martini Zinfandel
Louis M. Martini Cream Sherry

Crab Gazpacho

Made with Dungeness crab, this gazpacho has a definite California twist.

¼ cup olive oil

¼ cup dry white wine

1 tablespoon red wine vinegar

1 tablespoon fresh lime juice

3 medium tomatoes, peeled and seeded

1 medium red bell pepper, seeded and coarsely chopped

1 medium green bell pepper, seeded and coarsely chopped

1 medium cucumber, seeded and coarsely chopped

2 cups tomato juice

½ medium sweet onion, diced

2 tablespoons chopped chives or scallions

2 tablespoons chopped cilantro

¼ to ½ medium jalapeño pepper, minced

1 teaspoon salt, or to taste

1 to 2 teaspoons Tabasco sauce, or to taste

Freshly ground pepper to taste

1 cooked Dungeness crab

Plain yogurt (optional)

Cilantro sprigs (optional)

Whisk together the oil, wine, vinegar, and lime juice and set aside. In a food processor, combine tomatoes, bell peppers, and cucumber. Add tomato juice and pulse several times until mixture is fine but not pureed. Pour into a large bowl and stir in onion, chives or scallions, cilantro, and jalapeño. Mix and add salt, Tabasco, and pepper.

Crack and clean the crab. Remove the meat and reserve the whole claws for garnish. Flake the balance of the meat and stir into the soup. Chill in a covered bowl for at least 4 hours.

Serve in chilled bowls each garnished with a dab of yogurt and a sprig of cilantro.

Serves 6

LEFT: **A bouquet of summer flowers on the table.** BELOW: **Vine-ripened tomatoes; Tabasco Honey-Glazed Chicken; and Potato, Corn, and White Butter Bean Salad.**

Tabasco Honey-Glazed Chicken

This chicken can be cooked under the broiler instead of on the grill.

6 small chicken breasts, split and skinned

6 small chicken thighs, skinned

MARINADE

⅓ cup olive oil

2 tablespoons chopped fresh sage

2 tablespoons fresh lemon juice

3 tablespoons honey

GLAZE

⅓ cup honey

2 tablespoons lemon juice

6 dashes Tabasco sauce

Place chicken in a bowl. Mix marinade ingredients. Pour over chicken, cover, and refrigerate for at least 3 hours.

Prepare grill so coals are ash-covered. Drain and discard marinade. Grill chicken over charcoal for 5 minutes per side. Meanwhile, whisk together ingredients for the glaze, remove chicken pieces, and paint tops. Grill for 2 minutes, turn and paint other side, and grill another 2 minutes.

Serves 6 to 8

Note: You can bake both on one cookie sheet; just be sure to space them evenly apart from the edge and from each other to allow for spreading. However, 2 sheets make it easier when you cut and lay out the cookies on their sides.

ABOUT THE WINES

Liz Martini and her son Michael agreed that for this picnic they would probably follow their usual habit of putting a selection of wines out for guests to taste. Below are descriptions of some of the qualities you might find in the particular wines they selected to be served that day:

"The 1988 Johannisberg Riesling was chosen for its floral-apple qualities, slightly sweet flavors, and crisp finish. The sweetness balances the tang of the gazpacho and chicken while the floral aroma marries well with the salad.

"In a picnic setting it is often desirable to mix and match. This 1988 Chardonnay, a blend of Napa and Sonoma fruit, may serve to achieve the same ends as the Riesling but in a drier style. The butter-honey tones of the Chardonnay show off the Tabasco honey sauce of the chicken.

"The 1986 Zinfandel has always been one of our favorite wines because it goes with everything: the chicken, the tomatoes, the fresh bread, and even the potato and bean salad. Its medium body and very berry flavor offer an alternative for interest.

"Cream Sherry has been in the family for decades and lends the warm, rounded caramel flavor to the slightly drier biscotti. The crisp crunch of this dessert and the richness of a time-honored wine are a wonderful match."

Potato, Corn, and White Butter Bean Salad

To use it uncooked, the corn in this salad must be very fresh. If it's not, steam it briefly.

 3 medium waxy potatoes (about 2 pounds), cooked, peeled, and cubed
 1 15-ounce can white butter beans or lima beans, drained and rinsed lightly
 3 ears fresh young corn, kernels cut off
 1/3 cup olive oil
 1 1/2 tablespoons lemon juice
 1/4 cup mayonnaise
 1/2 teaspoon sugar
 Salt and pepper to taste
 2 tablespoons chopped chives

Toss together the potatoes, beans, and corn. Set aside. Whisk together the olive oil, lemon juice, mayonnaise, sugar, salt, and pepper. Fold into potato mixture.

Sprinkle salad with chives and mix. Refrigerate for 1 hour, covered, before serving.

Serves 6 to 8

Coconut Macadamia Biscotti

Here is a strictly California version of the classic biscotti.

 1 whole egg plus 1 egg white
 1/2 cup vegetable oil
 3/4 cup sugar
 1 teaspoon vanilla extract
 1/2 teaspoon salt
 1/2 to 3/4 cup coarsely chopped macadamia nuts
 1/2 cup flaked, sweetened coconut
 2 tablespoons anise seed
 1 1/2 cups all-purpose flour
 1 1/2 teaspoons baking powder

Whisk together the egg, egg white, and oil. Add the sugar, vanilla, salt, nuts, coconut, and anise seeds. Mix well. Set aside. Sift the flour with baking powder, then add gradually to the wet mixture and mix until well blended. Cover and chill overnight.

Preheat the oven to 325 degrees and coat 2 cookie sheets (see Note) with vegetable spray. Divide dough into 2 parts and roll each into a log long enough to fit lengthwise on a cookie sheet. (The dough is sticky; you may want to coat your hands with vegetable oil to do this.)

Place 1 roll on each baking sheet and bake until lightly browned, 25 to 30 minutes. Remove from oven (logs will have flattened out) and cut each log at a diagonal into 1/2-inch thick strips. Arrange each strip on its side on the baking sheets and bake until lightly browned, 15 to 20 minutes.

Makes approximately 3 dozen

A Hearty Spring Dinner

ROBERT MONDAVI WINERY

❧

ROBERT MONDAVI always had faith in Napa Valley wines and was sure that ultimately they could compete in the world market. He knew the area was blessed with the right climate and soil. And having come from a wine-making family, he certainly had the basic know-

how. Also, his marketing talents had been amply displayed before 1966, when the winery that carries his name was founded.

Although it was Mondavi's vision that started the business, it is a family affair and all its members are active in formulating winery policy. Sons Mi-

chael and Tim are managing partners, daughter Marcia is vice-president, and wife, Margrit Biever, is busy with the activities to promote fine wine and food.

In the early sixties the local wine industry was just recovering from a long slump, and Robert Mondavi decided the time was right for an operation large enough in scale and well financed enough to do the sort of experimenting that would result in the truly superior wines he envisioned making. Together with a group of silent partners, whom he bought out in 1978, he began, and has never stopped

growing or innovating. Today the winery's holdings include not only the facilities at Oakville, where the winery buildings and management offices are, but more than 1,600 acres of vineyards in Napa and Carneros.

But this family fervently believes there is more to their business than simply producing the best wines possible. Consequently they sponsor wide-ranging educational programs where the public can learn about wines. These include tastings, extensive and comprehensive tours, and seminars on various aspects of wine making.

That would be enough for most, but not the Mondavis. Their commitment doesn't stop with wine education, for they feel "all arts emerge from the same wellspring, including the vinous ones." Accordingly, the winery started hosting art shows in 1967 right after the new buildings opened. Soon there followed literary presentations and concerts, as

LEFT: **Table by the terrace.**
ABOVE: **The striking entrance to the winery.**

well as an annual summer jazz festival. And their famous Great Chefs cooking courses have been in place since 1976.

Since Robert and Margrit both spend their days, and often their vacations, with winery business and myriad public service activities, they decided to build a retreat atop Wappo Hill in Oakville.

Here they balance their busy lives in a peaceful setting surrounded by splendid vistas, and relax by entertaining close friends with small dinners like this.

M E N U

LEEK AND GOAT CHEESE PIE
ROAST BEEF TENDERLOIN STEAK
PENNE WITH BROILED
RATATOUILLE VEGETABLES
PINEAPPLE BANANA SORBET
CITRUS LACE COOKIES

1986 Robert Mondavi Pinot Noir
1981 Robert Mondavi Cabernet Sauvignon

Leek and Goat Cheese Pie

Puff pastry may be bought ready made in most food specialty shops so there is no recipe for it included here. And frankly, unless you are a dedicated cook, I don't think it is worth making from scratch because it is so time consuming to do.

Incidentally, this pie with a crisp salad and a bit of fruit for dessert would make a perfect little lunch.

Chez Panisse's version of this classic pie was the inspiration for this variation.

6	medium leeks
6	tablespoons (¾ stick) unsalted butter
	Salt and pepper to taste
¼	pound pancetta or bacon, in 1 piece
1	egg
½	cup heavy cream
1	teaspoon Dijon-style mustard
¼	teaspoon curry powder
⅓	pound mild goat cheese
1	piece puff pastry, rolled into a 10-inch round about ⅛ inch thick
½	cup fresh bread crumbs

Preheat the oven to 400 degrees.

Trim the leeks, leaving just a small amount of the green. Julienne them and wash very carefully in several changes of water. Drain and pat dry.

Heat 4 tablespoons of the butter in a medium skillet over low heat. Add the leeks and cook for about 15 minutes, until wilted. Sprinkle with salt and pepper and cover. Continue cooking, shaking pan occasionally for another 10 minutes. Set aside to cool slightly.

TOP: **Leek and Goat Cheese Pie.**
ABOVE LEFT: **Robert Mondavi.**
ABOVE: **Margrit Biever Mondavi.**

Meanwhile, cut the pancetta into medium dice and fry in a separate pan over medium heat until crispy, about 3 minutes. Drain off fat.

Beat egg and cream together, then add mustard and curry powder. Crumble half of the cheese into the egg-cream mixture. Add the cooled leeks and pancetta. Mix well and set aside.

Place pastry on a baking sheet. Roll up around the edges to make a ½-inch-deep shell. Use a double thickness of folded foil around this edge to keep it in place. Fill shell with the leek mixture. Crumble remaining cheese over the top, sprinkle with the bread crumbs, and melt; then drizzle the 2 remaining tablespoon of butter over all.

Bake for 15 minutes to set pie. Remove foil and reduce heat to 350 degrees. Continue baking until nicely browned, about 30 minutes more.

Serves 8

ABOVE: **Roast Beef Tenderloin Steak.**
BELOW: **Table set for lunch.**

Roast Beef Tenderloin Steak

This cut of beef is referred to as a chateaubriand and should be about 1¼ inches thick.

> 1 beef tenderloin steak (3 to 4 pounds), trimmed of fat
> Salt and pepper to taste

Preheat the oven to 450 degrees.

Place a heavy skillet, large enough to accommodate the meat comforta-bly, onto high heat. Meanwhile, season the meat very well with salt and a generous amount of freshly ground pepper. When the skillet is very hot, put the steak in and brown quickly on both sides. Transfer to a sheet pan with low edges, and roast for about 20 minutes, or until 120 degrees in the center for rare.

Remove meat to a cutting board and allow to rest for 10 minutes before slicing and serving with juices.

Serves 8

Penne with Broiled Ratatouille Vegetables

Penne is the large tubular pasta.

- 1 **medium eggplant**
  Salt
- 2 **large red bell peppers, roasted (see Note)**
- 4 **medium tomatoes**
- ½ **cup olive oil**
- 8 **ounces penne, cooked until al dente**
- 3 **tablespoons red wine vinegar**
- 1 **tablespoon minced shallot**
- 1 **medium garlic clove, finely chopped**
  Freshly ground pepper to taste
- 1 **tablespoon minced fresh parsley**

Wash and dry the eggplant, cut off the top, and cut into ¼-inch slices. Sprinkle with salt and set in a colander over a plate. Allow to drain for 30 minutes.

Cut pepper in half lengthwise. Drain on paper towels.

Cut tomatoes in half horizontally and remove seeds. Put them on a baking sheet cut side up and broil until they begin to brown, about 5 minutes or less. Set aside.

Rinse or pat off salt from eggplant and brush with olive oil on both sides. Broil until golden on both sides, several minutes.

Cut cooked eggplant into strips and tomatoes into large chunks. Place in a mixing bowl. Add peppers and toss. Add vegetables to cooked penne. Pour vinegar, remaining olive oil, shallot, and garlic over all. Toss and season to taste with salt and freshly ground black pepper. Sprinkle with parsley before serving.

Serve this hot or at room temperature.

Serves 8

Note: To peel peppers, char them over a gas flame or under the broiler until blackened on all sides. Place the peppers in a paper bag and fold closed. Allow to sit for approximately 15 minutes, then peel and seed under running water. Drain well on paper towels.

Pineapple Banana Sorbet

The flavors of these two tropical fruits are delicious together, as you already undoubtedly know, so here they are in a luscious sorbet.

- 2 **cups sugar**
- 2 **cups water**
- 1 **large pineapple, peeled and cored**
- 2 **large ripe bananas, peeled**
- ¼ **cup fresh lemon juice**
- ¼ **cup fresh orange juice**

Dissolve the sugar in the water over medium heat. Set aside to cool.

Cut the pineapple and banana into chunks and process until almost smooth. Add the juices and process to mix. It is not necessary, but it makes a smoother consistency if this mixture is then passed through a strainer.

Add the reserved simple syrup to the fruit and mix. Pour into an ice cream maker and freeze according to manufacturer's directions.

Makes 1 quart

ABOUT THE WINES

I do like resident chef Annie Roberts no-nonsense approach to choosing wine to go with her delightful food. Her simple remarks are a perfect example of how personal (and minimal) this task can be:

"I chose the 1986 Pinot Noir for the leek pie because I like the complex balance between the sharp, rich flavor of the chèvre and the peppery flavor of the wine.

"The steeliness and full body of the 1981 Cabernet Sauvignon I find is a perfect match for beef. And the peppers and tomatoes in the pasta salad complement its fruitiness."

৵৫

Citrus Lace Cookies

The juice in these cookies gives them an unusual flavor, which is especially good when you serve the cookies with sorbets and ice creams.

1 ½ cups sugar
 1 cup slivered almonds
 ¾ cup all-purpose flour
 ½ cup citrus juice (grapefruit, orange, or lemon)
 ½ cup (1 stick) unsalted butter, melted

Preheat the oven to 400 degrees.

Combine the sugar, almonds, and flour in a bowl. Add juice and melted butter and stir well. If you have time, leave this in the refrigerator for sev-eral hours before using; it makes the dough easier to handle.

Drop the mixture by rounded tea-spoonfuls onto nonstick baking sheets, spreading the mounds into flat 2-inch circles with the back of a spoon which has been dipped into hot water. These cookies double in width, so leave enough space between them on the pan. Bake for about 5 minutes, or until golden brown. Watch them carefully since they burn easily.

Remove sheets from oven and al-low cookies to rest for about a minute to firm slightly. Remove the cookies with a spatula and drape them over a rolling pin or wine bottles to shape them. Cool and store in a cool dry spot or sealed in a cookie tin.

Makes about 3 dozen

Some Salads, Pastas, and Wines

INGLENOOK-NAPA VALLEY

ESTABLISHED IN 1879 by Captain Gustave Niebaum, a 37-year-old, recently married and retired sailor, at the site of Inglenook Spa, Inglenook Vineyards certainly qualifies as one of the longest lasting old-timers in the valley.

The venture was not taken up for profit but, rather, to satisfy the captain's great interest in wine and wine making. The fortune that made this possible came from the Alaska Commercial Company, which Gustave had formed when, at the age of 22, he successfully petitioned the czar for exclusive fur-trading rights in Alaska.

Over the years Niebaum had traveled extensively, learned to speak five languages (with a reading knowledge of several more), and already had considerable first-hand knowledge of European wineries and their techniques by the time he decided to enter the wine-producing business for his own pleasure. From the very beginning his first concern was excellence, and toward that end he not only continued to visit wineries but over the years amassed an extensive wine-related library.

ABOVE: **The winery viewed from across the courtyard.** RIGHT: **Oak wine casks in the cool winery building.**

By 1881, Niebaum had imported budwood of twenty-one grape varieties with cuttings from selected great vineyards (identified today as clones). Thus Inglenook became the source of many of the top varieties and clones utilized in Napa today.

So in 1884, after carefully studying the soil and weather conditions peculiar to his vineyards and finding them what he had hoped for, Inglenook's great winery building was started. Research, technique refinement, and awards continued until the captain's death in 1908.

Fortunately, Niebaum's dream did not die with him; the year before his death a nephew, John Daniel, was born, and it was to be he who would take up the reins in 1936. In the years between Niebaum's death and the arrival of Daniel, the winery, which had survived the great earthquake as well as the man-made disaster of Prohibition, continued to operate. Because the Niebaum family had never considered it a source of income, the winery was maintained even during Prohibition.

Then in 1964 Inglenook entered the world of big business; it was sold to United Vintners, which in turn was sold to Heublein. These were turbulent years for a comparatively small winery accustomed

to the benign ways of private ownership. However, during the transition new vineyards were purchased, old ones reworked, new equipment installed, and the great winery building restored. And finally in 1983, Inglenook-Napa Valley was quietly reestablished as an independent subsidiary with local management. They were once more on the track.

But the story doesn't end there. Daniel, who had died in 1970, had one last gift to the winery: his granddaughter, Jamie Morningstar, who was appointed resident chef. So a Daniel Niebaum descendent is once more on board.

When Jamie decides to entertain friends, it is usually on the weekends and on the spur of the moment. One of her favorite menus for large groups is a hearty warm salad for a start, then a pasta, and finish with a luscious dessert. Here are two each of her favorite salads, pastas, and desserts, from which she makes different combinations.

Incidentally, Jamie Morningstar's helpful do's and don'ts for combining particular wines and foods can be found beginning on page 170.

Zinfandel
Gravion
Sauvignon Blanc
Reserve Merlot
Muscat Blanc
Late Harvest Gewürztraminer

Warm Spicy Chicken with Bacon Molasses Dressing

This same salad can also be prepared with quail.

SALAD

- 1 teaspoon paprika
- 1 teaspoon ground cumin
- 1 teaspoon ground coriander
- ¾ teaspoon cayenne pepper
- 4 tablespoons olive oil
- 1 whole chicken breast, boned and skinned
- 1 medium head romaine or ruby lettuce, washed, dried, and torn into bite-size pieces
- 6 to 8 large white mushrooms, sliced
- 1 red or yellow bell pepper, seeded and sliced
- 1 bunch red radishes, tipped, stemmed, and cut into quarters lengthwise
- 1 medium carrot, grated
- ½ teaspoon toasted sesame seeds

DRESSING

- ½ pound bacon, finely diced
- 2 to 3 medium shallots, chopped
- ⅓ cup homemade or store-bought pesto
- ⅓ cup red wine vinegar
- 2 tablespoons molasses
- ¼ to ½ cup olive oil

Combine the paprika, cumin, coriander, and cayenne with 2 tablespoons of olive oil. Cut the chicken breast into ½-inch strips and coat with the spice mixture. Set aside. Place the lettuce, mushrooms, bell pepper, and radishes in a large salad bowl. Set aside.

Make the dressing by sautéing the bacon until golden brown. Remove to paper towels and reserve the fat in pan.

Combine the shallots, pesto, vinegar, and molasses in a blender and blend until pureed. Add enough olive oil to the bacon fat to measure 1 cup and add gradually to the blender. Blend well. Pour into a bowl and add bacon bits. Set aside.

Heat the remaining 2 tablespoons of olive oil in a medium sauté pan over high heat and sauté the chicken strips until golden brown, 2 to 3 minutes. Add ¼ cup of the dressing and cook for 30 seconds. Add the chicken strips to the salad, and toss. Pour dressing over all and toss again quickly. Garnish with grated carrot and sprinkle sesame seeds on top.

Serves 2 as an entree or 4 as a first course

Butterleaf Lettuce with Tomatoes and Squash Blossoms

If you just happen not to have squash blossoms handy, substitute yellow tomatoes for them. I see yellow tomatoes in my local markets all the time in the summer.

I don't think you should ever make a salad with anything but vine-ripened tomatoes. If they are not available, wait for the time when they are. To my way of thinking, there is nothing worse than those tasteless commercial tomatoes.

SALAD

- 2 medium heads butterleaf lettuce, inside leaves only
- 1 medium to large red tomato, sliced
- 12 squash blossoms

DRESSING

- ¼ cup fresh lemon juice (from 2 medium lemons)
- 1 teaspoon minced garlic
- 1 teaspoon each minced fresh dill, oregano, thyme, basil, rosemary, sage, and marjoram, or ¼ teaspoon each dried herbs
- ½ teaspoon salt
- 1 teaspoon freshly ground black pepper
- ½ cup olive oil

Wash and dry the lettuce carefully; divide evenly among 4 plates. Place tomato slices in the center and arrange blossoms at the outside.

Prepare the dressing by combining the lemon juice with all the remaining ingredients except the olive oil. Whisk oil in last to bind dressing. Ladle dressing over the salads and serve.

Serves 4

Orecchiette with Tomatoes, Cilantro, and Goat Cheese

This "little ear" pasta is also very good served with roasted meats.

- 1 cup dry white wine
- 4 large tomatoes, about 2½ pounds, peeled, seeded, and chopped, with juice reserved
- 1 cup scallions, roughly chopped with some greens
- 2 heaping tablespoons finely chopped cilantro
- 8 ounces orecchiette
- 6 ounces mild goat cheese
  Salt and pepper to taste
  Cilantro leaves, for garnish

In a large nonreactive skillet, combine the wine and tomato juice and bring to a boil. Cook over medium heat until reduced by half, about 5 minutes. Add the tomatoes, scallions, and cilantro and simmer for about 2 minutes. Set aside.

Meanwhile, cook the pasta in lightly salted water until al dente. Drain and add to the sauce. Reheat quickly if necessary. Crumble cheese and add; toss and adjust seasonings if necessary. Garnish with cilantro leaves.

Serves 6 as a first course, or 4 as a main course

OPPOSITE: **Warm Spicy Chicken with Bacon Molasses Dressing.** TOP: **Orecchiette with Tomatoes, Cilantro, and Goat Cheese.** ABOVE: **Butterleaf Lettuce with Tomatoes and Squash Blossoms.**

Bow Tie Pasta with Smoked Duck, Shiitake Mushrooms, and Bacon

Markets that sell smoked chicken breasts, ham, and fish often also sell smoked duck breast, too.

1 pound bacon, diced

10 large shiitake mushrooms (about ½ pound), sliced (large white mushrooms may be substituted)

8 ounces bow tie pasta

1 pint heavy cream

2 cups diced smoked duck breast (smoked ham may be substituted)

2 cups grated Gouda or Parmesan cheese

Salt and pepper to taste

Sauté the bacon in a large skillet over medium heat until brown and crisp. Drain on paper towels. Pour out the grease and add the mushrooms. Cook over medium heat, turning, until browned, about 5 minutes. Drain with the bacon. Cook the pasta in a large quantity of lightly salted water until al dente, drain, and put aside.

Meanwhile, in a separate large saucepan, reduce the cream by half over medium heat, 10 to 15 minutes; do not scorch. Mix in the bacon, mushrooms, and duck. Let ingredients cook together for a few minutes, then add the cheese. Stir until cheese is melted; keep an eye on this so it doesn't boil over. Toss in the pasta and cook just long enough to heat pasta through. Season with salt and pepper, then serve.

Serves 6 to 8 as an appetizer, or 4 as an entree

LEFT: **Bow Tie Pasta with Smoked Duck, Shiitake Mushrooms, and Bacon.** BELOW: **The vineyards.**

Perfect Poached Pears

This poaching liquid may be reused and is good for poaching peaches, apples, and apricots as well as pears.

POACHING LIQUID

- 3 bottles Muscat Blanc, or 1½ bottles plus 4¾ cups water
- 1 whole nutmeg
- 1 whole cinnamon stick
- 1 large bay leaf
- 1 vanilla bean, split lengthwise
- 1½ teaspoons whole cloves
- 1½ teaspoons whole cardamom seeds
- 1½ teaspoons whole allspice
- 1 tablespoon chopped fresh ginger

- 1 medium lemon, quartered
- 5 medium pears, peeled and cored with stems attached (see Note)

SPICED WHIPPED CREAM

- 1 cup heavy cream
- ½ teaspoon ground cinnamon
- ½ teaspoon ground allspice
- ½ teaspoon grated nutmeg
- ½ teaspoon ground cloves
- ½ teaspoon ground ginger
- ½ teaspoon vanilla extract
- 1 tablespoon sugar
  Mint leaves, for garnish (optional)

Combine the poaching ingredients in a nonreactive saucepan and simmer for 30 minutes. Strain out solids and set liquid aside. This liquid may be made any time and used over and over. Just strain it after each use and keep it refrigerated. Incidentally, at the end of its usefulness (when enough has been cooked away so you can't poach anymore), this liquid can be reduced and used as an ice cream topping.

Place poaching liquid and pears in a deep nonreactive saucepan and weight down with a saucer that can withstand high heat. (This is to keep pears submerged.) Bring to a simmer and poach until pears are tender but not falling apart, 10 to 20 minutes. Place entire pot in the refrigerator until pears are chilled.

Make whipped cream by combining ingredients and whipping to soft peaks.

To serve, make a bed of whipped cream on individual plates and add drained pears. Garnish near the stems with a mint leaf (held in place with a dab of cream), if you have mint handy.

Serves 4

Note: The extra pear is insurance in case you have an accident with one.

ABOVE: **Perfect Poached Pears.**
BELOW: **The garden porch set for lunch.**

Ginger Mousse with Grated Coconut

Because this mousse has to set and chill, plan to make it ahead of time.

1	cup milk
2	tablespoons grated fresh ginger
1	tablespoon orange zest
2	egg yolks
¹⁄₂	cup sugar
	Juice of 3 medium oranges
1	teaspoon unflavored gelatin
¹⁄₄	cup hot water
1¹⁄₂	cups heavy cream
¹⁄₄	cup grated coconut (fresh or packaged), toasted if desired

Combine milk, ginger, and orange zest in a small, nonreactive saucepan and bring to a boil over low heat. Mixture will curdle but that is okay. While waiting for milk to come to a boil, combine yolks and sugar in a medium mixing bowl. Beat at high speed with a hand mixer until mixture is pale yellow and falls in ribbons when beaters are lifted, 5 to 8 minutes.

When milk comes to a boil, slowly add it to the egg mixture in a steady stream, whisking constantly. Pour into the top of a double boiler and cook over hot water, stirring until mixture thickens, 10 to 20 minutes. When you can draw a line through the mixture with the back of a wooden spoon and it doesn't close, it has thickened properly. Set aside to cool.

Meanwhile, in a small pan, reduce orange juice to 2 tablespoons over medium heat, about 10 minutes. Set aside to cool, then add to the cooled custard mixture.

Combine the gelatin and hot water in a small bowl. Mix well, making sure gelatin is dissolved. Stir into cooled custard mixture. Mix well. Strain mixture and refrigerate, covered, until it sets. This will take 6 to 8 hours.

When mousse is set, briskly whip the mousse with a whisk for 2 minutes. Whip the cream and fold into the mousse. Allow to chill and set again, another 1 to 2 hours.

Scoop mousse into individual serving dishes and sprinkle tops with grated coconut.

Serves 8 or more

About the Wines

These are the comments Jamie Morningstar made when we asked her to explain what wines would go with her various dishes. Although all but four of them call for a different wine each, she is not suggesting that you necessarily have to serve such a variety. Rather, in understanding her reasoning you will be better able to choose wines for yourself:

"Warm Spicy Chicken with Bacon Molasses Dressing has many bold and spicy flavors and requires a very bold and spicy wine, such as Zinfandel. The spices used in the marinade would overpower most wines, but Zinfandel has spicy flavors to stand up to and complement this dish. Also, the mushrooms, bell peppers, and radishes bring out some of the earthy flavors found in the Zinfandel.

"Butterleaf Lettuce with Tomatoes and Squash Blossoms is composed

of tart flavors. There are acids found in the tomatoes and also the lemons in the dressing. Usually these acids work against a wine and make it taste sour. But Gravion is made from wines that are high in acid; it is a 50-50 Semillon and Sauvignon Blanc blend. These high-acid wines welcome other foods high in acid and complement the salad well, making the wine have a very long lemony finish. Also, the herbs in the dressing bring out the herbal flavors found in both of these wines.

"Orecchiette with Tomatoes, Cilantro, and Goat Cheese is paired with Sauvignon Blanc because once again we see a dish that has acidic components—tomatoes and goat cheese. Goat cheese is a low-butterfat and high-acid cheese. In the Sancerre region of France it has been paired with Sauvignon Blanc for hundreds of years. These tart flavors work well with Sauvignon Blanc, which is high in acid itself and make the wine taste very lemony. Cilantro is a great herb to use with Sauvignon Blanc; it really complements the herbal flavors found in the wine.

"Bow Tie Pasta with Smoked Duck, Shiitake Mushrooms, and Bacon is served with Reserve Merlot because this pasta dish is very rich, and this helps to cut the drying sensation (tannin) of the wine. The rich-

ness makes the wine taste softer and more pleasant. The smoked duck and bacon both bring out more fruit flavors in the wine and make it taste more cherrylike. I personally like mushrooms with Merlots, too. They bring out a rich, earthy character in the wine and make it taste very smooth.

"Perfect Poached Pears is served with Muscat Blanc. Desserts should always be less sweet than the dessert wine, but with a nice balance of acid and sugar. Not too tart and not too sweet! That way they do not cover up

the natural fruit flavors found in the wine and make the wine taste tart. This dessert poaches the pears in the same wine as is served with the dessert. It does not add any sugar to the poaching liquid and uses only a touch in the whipped cream. The pears have a very simple fruit flavor which complements the Muscat well. The additional spices in the poaching liquid and whipped cream make the combination of food and wine more flavorful and interesting.

"Ginger Mousse with Grated Coconut is served with Late Harvest Gewürztraminer because here again we must be careful about the sweetness of the dessert. It must be less sweet than the wine but not too tart, either. We have done this by using orange juice and relying on the spicy flavor of the ginger. These two flavors draw away from the sweet and work well with the fruit and spice that are found naturally in the wine."

&

OPPOSITE TOP: **Drive leading to the winery;** LEFT: **Ginger Mousse with Grated Coconut.** ABOVE: **Winery chef Jamie Morningstar.** BELOW: **A vintage photograph of Gustave Niebaum, founder of Inglenook, and Joseph Schram.**

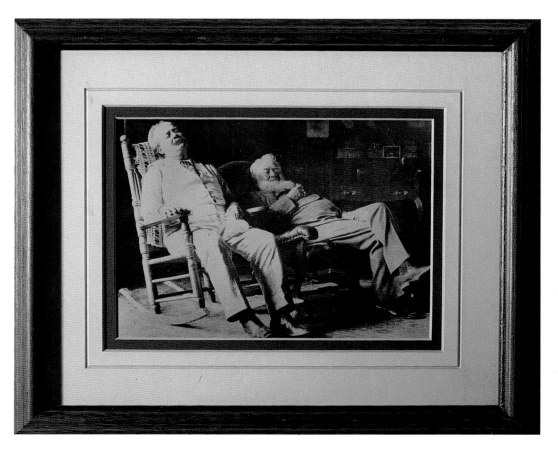

A Sunday Lunch on the Lawn

NEWTON VINEYARD

ᕤ

BRITISHER Peter Newton was one of an early group of winemakers who came to Napa as the industry started reviving in the sixties, ultimately planning the spectacular buildings that constitute Sterling Vineyards—a glistening white complex perched on a hillside between St. Helena and Calistoga.

But by 1977, Newton had decided that selling Sterling would make good business sense and allow him to move on. What he envisioned with this change was a smaller winery with special qualities that could make his wine truly distinctive.

Experience at Sterling had kindled in him an interest in hillside vineyards and lead him to land high in the hills west of St. Helena. Although this land had been planted in wine grapes over 100

years before, it was abandoned during Prohibition and allowed to return to its wild state. You can imagine what a task clearing and terracing these steep, erosion-prone hillsides presented. In doing this Newton was following the example of early Napa Valley settlers who, being predominately people from the Mediterranean, were accustomed to such vineyards.

However, it was not simply this historical use of land that interested him, but rather the conviction that such spartan conditions make vines struggle to thrive, forcing them to ingest minerals from the soil that can subtly influence and intensify the flavor of their fruit. Another intriguing aspect of this site, aside from its excellent drainage and absence of frost

hazard, was its volcanic nature, which is responsible for compressing many soil types in a small area. As a matter of fact, within the square mile of land on which sixty-two acres are now planted, there are seven really different types, each of which can contribute to the complexity of a finished wine's flavor.

Perhaps Peter Newton's English heritage is partly responsible for the love of gardens and interest in horticulture he has always had. Whatever its source, this interest obviously played an important part in the decision to build the winery underground with a formal garden on top. The result is a garden winery that, aside from being so very pleasing, seems particularly appropriate to the interests of its founder. This plan also honors his wish that the finished facility blend with, and enhance, its natural surroundings.

Newton's wife, Su Hua, is a doctor and professor at the University of San Francisco as well as one of the two founders of the Wine Marketing Center there. Because of their varied and demanding schedules, the Newtons have devised an easy way of entertaining with Sunday luncheons that are both informal and festive.

Su Hua delights in the presentation of flowers and food—something for which she shows considerable flair. All the dishes you see pictured on these pages are really simple to prepare; but if they are carefully and artfully arranged, they belie their ease of preparation. (She also loves a bit of whimsy, as you can see in what she refers to as chef Sean's "bread mice.")

OPPOSITE: **Newton's beautiful formal gardens, and beyond, the vineyards.**
ABOVE: **The winemaker's aerie.**

MENU

CRUDITES WITH HERB MAYONNAISE
CRAYFISH WITH SPICY TOMATO SAUCE
GLAZED ASPARAGUS
SMOKED STURGEON
SEAN'S BREAD MICE
PISTACHIO AND PECAN MERINGUES WITH
STRAWBERRY FILLING

Newton Chardonnay
Newton Merlot

Crudités with Herb Mayonnaise

You may include any selection of fresh vegetables you like here—jicama, green onions, red and white radishes, cucumbers, carrots, cauliflower, broccoli, small mushrooms, small turnips, or red, yellow, and green bell peppers. Simply wash and clean them carefully and cut them neatly into strips and slices.

For mushrooms, peel and stalk them (save stalks for another use) and marinate overnight in olive oil and lime juice, mixed in a proportion of 1 cup mild olive oil to the juice and zest of 1 large lime. Add salt and pepper to taste.

To serve, dry all vegetables well, drain mushrooms, and arrange neatly on individual plates. Serve with Herb Mayonnaise.

HERB MAYONNAISE

- 2　egg yolks
- 1 ½ to 2 teaspoons Dijon-style mustard
- 2　cups corn oil
  Salt and pepper to taste
- ¼ to ½ cup chopped fresh herbs, using mostly basil and tarragon with smaller quantities of thyme, oregano, and mint
- 2　teaspoons Dijon-style mustard

Mix yolks and mustard in a blender. With the motor running, slowly add oil until mayonnaise consistency is reached. Add salt and pepper.

Add herbs and additional mustard, and refrigerate until ready to use.
Makes 2¼ cups

Crayfish with Spicy Tomato Sauce

Since all you eat of these delicious little crustaceans is their tails, it takes a fairly large quantity to serve 12 guests as part of a meal.

- 3　quarts chicken stock (fresh or canned)
- 3　large bay leaves
- 1　large sweet red onion, cut in quarters
- 1　tablespoon black peppercorns
- 1　teaspoon salt
- 2　large celery ribs with leaves
- 5　pounds live crayfish
  Fresh dill, for garnish
  Lemon wedges, for garnish
  Spicy Tomato Sauce (recipe follows)

Place stock and all other ingredients except crayfish and garnish into a large pot. Bring to a hard boil and add one-fourth of the crayfish. Cook until bright red, only a few minutes. Remove with a wire sieve and allow to cool. Repeat until all are cooked.

Arrange neatly on a long serving platter garnished around the edges with the fresh dill and lemon slices; serve with Spicy Tomato Sauce.
Serves 12 or more

SPICY TOMATO SAUCE

- 2　cups thick ketchup
- ½　cup freshly grated (fine) horseradish
- 2　teaspoons Worcestershire sauce
  Dash of Tabasco sauce

Combine all ingredients and refrigerate until ready to use.
Makes 2½ cups

ABOVE: **Glazed Asparagus.**
BELOW: **Crudités.**

Glazed Asparagus

What a feast for the eyes these are.

- 2 quarts chicken stock
- ½ cup olive oil
- 5 pounds fresh asparagus, trimmed and peeled
- 1 large red bell pepper, cut into thin strips
  Zest of 1 large lemon

Place chicken stock and olive oil in a large pot and bring to a hard boil. Add asparagus, and when the liquid returns to a boil, cook for 2 or 3 minutes or until barely cooked and crisp.

Remove with a wire strainer and allow to cool. (Incidentally, this stock/ oil may be used in soup.)

To serve, arrange neatly on a platter interspersed with strips of pepper and sprinkled with the lemon zest.

Serves 12 or more

Smoked Sturgeon

Other smoked fish may be substituted for the sturgeon.

- 5 pounds smoked sturgeon, thinly sliced
- 1 each of 2 different colors of bell pepper, cut into slices or long pieces
  Lemon wedges

Arrange smoked sturgeon on a serving platter and surround with mixed pepper pieces and lemon wedges.

Serves 12 or more

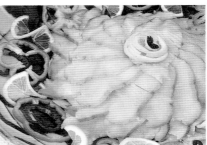

TOP: **Crayfish with Spicy Tomato Sauce.**
ABOVE: **Smoked Sturgeon.**
BELOW: **Peter Newton.**

Pistachio and Pecan Meringues with Strawberry Filling

This recipe is enough for 2 meringue cakes, but you can halve it easily. Sean's unconventional cooking method makes a moist and tender meringue.

MERINGUES

  12 **egg whites, at room temperature**
    1 **teaspoon cream of tartar**
3 ⅓ **cups sugar**
  ½ **cup chopped pecans**
  ½ **cup chopped pistachios**

ASSEMBLY

    1 **pint heavy cream**
    2 **pints fresh strawberries, hulled and sliced**
        Raspberry Sauce (recipe follows)
        Mint leaves (optional)

Make the meringues. Preheat oven to 375 degrees. Line four 9-inch cake pans with foil and butter generously or spray with vegetable spray. Set aside.

Sean's Bread Mice

These amusing little fellows are easy to make.

    1 **package active dry yeast**
    1 **cup lukewarm milk (110° to 115°F)**
1 ½ **tablespoons sugar**
2 ½ **cups all-purpose (or bread) flour, plus additional for kneading**
    4 **tablespoons soft cream cheese**
    1 **teaspoon salt**
    1 **egg, lightly beaten**
  24 **shelled almonds, unskinned**
  24 **whole cloves**
  12 **toothpicks**

Sprinkle the yeast into ½ cup of the milk. Stir in 1 teaspoon of the sugar. Place in a warm, draft-free spot, such as an unlit oven with pilot light. Leave 5 to 8 minutes, until mixture has begun to bubble and almost double in volume.

Pour the yeast mixture into a large bowl and add the remaining ½ cup milk. Stir to mix and dissolve yeast. Slowly beat 1 cup of flour into mixture. Beat until smooth. While beating, add cream cheese, remaining sugar, salt, and remaining flour.

Transfer dough to a lightly floured surface and knead for at least 10 minutes, sprinkling dough lightly with flour now and again to prevent dough from sticking to board (this can be done in a mixer with a dough hook).

When dough is smooth and elastic, place it in a large, lightly greased bowl. Sprinkle lightly with flour and cover loosely with a kitchen towel.

Place dough in a warm, draft-free spot for 45 minutes to 1 hour, or until it has doubled in bulk and springs back to the touch. Punch dough down to its original volume. Let it rise again for 30 to 40 minutes until it again doubles in size.

Preheat the oven to 375 degrees.

Divide dough into 12 equal balls. Lightly grease a baking sheet and shape each ball into a mouse's body with head (see photograph). Place on the baking sheet, cover with a towel, and let rise for 15 to 25 minutes.

Thoroughly brush mice with the beaten egg, then bake in the lower part of the oven for 15 minutes or until golden brown and a toothpick comes out clean.

Transfer mice to a cooling rack and while still warm, put in 2 almonds for ears and the cloves for eyes. Add a toothpick for the tail.

Makes 12 mice

In the bowl of a large mixer, beat egg whites until foamy. Add cream of tartar. Continue beating until soft peaks form. Add the sugar gradually while beating at high speed until all the sugar is incorporated and stiff peaks form, 8 to 10 minutes. Divide among the 4 pans, smooth the tops, and sprinkle the chopped nuts evenly over each.

Bake for approximately 25 minutes, until brown and rather firm to the touch. Allow to cool in the pans. Meanwhile, whip the cream.

Assemble. Carefully remove meringue layers from the foil—they are very fragile—and divide whipped cream between 2 of the layers, smoothing the top of each. Place a layer of sliced strawberries over cream and top each with the remaining layers.

Slice with a serrated knife and serve individual slices on a slick of raspberry sauce. Garnish with mint.

Serves 12 or more

RASPBERRY SAUCE

1 **pound fresh or frozen raspberries**
1 **cup fresh orange juice**
   Sweetener (optional)

Combine the berries and juice in a food processor and blend until smooth. Add sweetener if desired and strain out seeds with a fine sieve.

Makes about 3 cups

❧

OPPOSITE: **Sean's Bread Mice.**
LEFT: **Pistachio and Pecan Meringues with Strawberry Filling.**
BELOW: **Su Hua Newton.**

ABOUT THE WINES

Su Hua Newton, who chose the wines for this lunch prepared by resident chef Sean Ennis, is characteristically meticulous and articulate about her choices:

"We began our lunch with Glazed Asparagus and Smoked Sturgeon. The young asparagus was barely cooked, as it gets a rather strong vegetable odor when well cooked. The sturgeon is rich in texture and taste, hence it is important to serve a wine that is essentially fruity in character and quite complex; Newton Chardonnay is a good complement. It has hints of lemon, pineapple, and apricot.

"We then moved on to the crayfish and crudités. The crayfish have a spicy sauce and the crudités have an herb mayonnaise. A white wine would not be able to handle this multiplicity of odors. It needs something that is light with a bit of tannin to cut through the richness of the food and create a counterbalance. Our Merlot is ideal for such a situation because it is light with a bit of tannin, and yet it has so much character of its own, it gives one that certain lingering feeling of well-being."

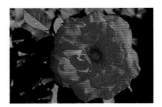

A Little Formal Outdoor Dinner

FERRARI-CARANO VINEYARDS AND WINERY

ᘐ

Don and Rhonda Carano, who own and operate Ferrari-Carano Vineyards and Winery, are both originally from the fabled gambling town of Reno, Nevada. Interestingly, they also both come from traditional Italian-American stock and Rhonda's ancestors emigrated from a small town in northern Italy only thirty kilometers from Don's. That makes them seem almost fated to be together.

In addition to the wine business, the two operate the Eldorado Hotel-Casino with the Carano children—four sons and a daughter, all active members

1981. And even then he took a circuitous route to wine making by becoming not only a hotel-casino operator and land developer along the way but a member of a respected Reno law firm.

For her part, Rhonda—with a degree in nutrition and an interest in food handed down from both grandmothers and mother—was perfectly suited to oversee the Eldorado's restaurants. So the partner-ship in their wine-making venture, dedicated to pro-ducing quality wines, was as natural and exciting for her as the hotel-restaurant experience.

At its founding, Ferrari-Carano comprised 250 acres of vineyards in Alex-ander and Dry Creek valleys, both known for their differing soils and microclimates. From the start, in the traditional estate manner, first priority was given to the winemakers' objective of finding the best conditions to grow various types of grapes from which to create the most distinctive wines possible. The economics of farming had to take a back seat. Today the vineyards are planted primarily in Cab-ernet Sauvignon, Merlot, Chardonnay, and Sauvi-gnon Blanc, the four classic varietals selected to be the signature wines produced by Ferrari-Carano. Petite Verdot, Malbec, Cabernet Franc, and Sémil-lon have also been planted to make additional choices available.

The wine-making facility itself allows separate lots of wine to be maintained so the winemaker is able to introduce many fermentation and aging vari-ables, all of which contribute to the complexity of the final blend.

So what began as a wine-buying trip has now become a flourishing business—and the Caranos have really only just begun.

I think you will agree that Rhonda's imaginative approach to food is especially evident in this menu for a little formal outdoor dinner. In it she manages to marry both their families' food traditions to California's abundant variety, which in turn makes an excellent complement to their distinctive wines.

of the management team. And it was the hotel-casino, with its eight dining rooms, that actually brought Don and Rhonda to Sonoma in the first place; they came to buy wine for all those dining rooms. As it turned out, the Caranos liked the valley so well they decided to put down roots and produce their own wines. I know that sounds rather whimsi-cal, but it was anything but. Don had grown up with his grandfathers' tradition of wine making and had pursued this interest with classes at the Univer-sity of California, Davis. But he didn't continue in that direction until Ferrari-Carano's founding in

MENU

FRESH OYSTERS WITH ORANGE BASIL-GINGER SAUCE

ANGEL HAIR WITH TOMATOES, SPINACH, AND THREE CHEESES

CHICKEN WITH CHARDONNAY

POACHED PEARS WITH ELDORADO GOLD RASPBERRY-CARAMEL SAUCE

1988 Fumé Blanc
1987 Alexander Valley Chardonnay
1986 Eldorado Gold, Late Harvest Sauvignon Blanc

Fresh Oysters with Orange Basil-Ginger Sauce

Some of the best oysters out this way come from a place called Hog Island.

- 6 tablespoons orange juice
- 4 tablespoons lemon juice
- 1 medium shallot, finely minced
- 1 teaspoon finely minced fresh ginger
  Pinch of cayenne pepper
- 12 medium fresh basil leaves, coarsely chopped
  Dash of soy sauce
- 2 drops sesame oil
- 36 Hog Island oysters, shucked and shells reserved

Whisk together all the ingredients except the oysters. Set aside.

Wash 36 half shells thoroughly and place on a plate of ice. Put an oyster in each half shell and serve the sauce on the side.

Serves 6

Angel Hair with Tomatoes, Spinach, and Three Cheeses

Pasta is always a delightful main course for a simple supper. Here is another great one for your files. The only thing you must be sure of is that the tomatoes are really fresh and ripe, otherwise it is better to used canned.

- 6 tablespoons olive oil
- 3 medium garlic cloves, chopped
- 3 pounds fresh spinach, washed, stemmed, drained, and coarsely chopped
- ¾ cup grated Asiago cheese (Parmesan cheese may be substituted)
- ¾ pound ricotta cheese
- ¾ pound mascarpone cheese
- 1½ cups coarsely chopped walnuts
- ¼ teaspoon grated nutmeg
- ¾ teaspoon salt
- ¼ teaspoon pepper
- 3 cups fresh tomato sauce (see Note)
  Generous ¼ cup coarsely chopped fresh basil
- 1½ pounds angel hair pasta

Place olive oil in a large frying pan. Sauté the garlic over medium-high heat for about 2 minutes, until golden brown. Add the spinach and cook until limp, tossing, about 5 minutes. Remove from heat and place in a large bowl. Toss with the Asaigo cheese and set aside.

In another bowl, combine the ricotta, mascarpone, walnuts, nutmeg, salt, and pepper. Bring a large pot of salted water to a boil. Meanwhile, in a medium saucepan, heat the tomato sauce, adding the basil. Cook about 5 minutes, to completely incorporate basil flavor.

Place pasta in boiling water and cook only 1 minute if fresh, according to package instructions if dried. Drain pasta and immediately toss with the tomato sauce.

Place pasta in 6 warmed serving bowls. Top each with a scoop of the spinach mixture and one of the cheese mixture. Toss lightly.

Serves 6

Note: To make fresh tomato sauce, peel and seed 3 pounds of plum tomatoes and add salt to taste. Simmer over low heat to reduce liquid by half, 45 minutes to 1 hour.

The table, with Angel Hair with Tomatoes, Spinach, and Three Cheeses being served.

Chicken with Chardonnay

The way I see it, you can't have too many chicken recipes.

- 6 boned medium chicken breasts, about 1 ½ pounds
- 3 cups Chardonnay
- 3 medium leeks, washed carefully and coarsely diced
- 3 medium carrots, coarsely diced
- 3 celery ribs, coarsely diced
- 3 ounces pancetta, coarsely chopped
- 2 small garlic heads, roasted (page 65)
- ¾ pound golden chanterelle mushrooms, coarsely chopped
- 2 teaspoons minced fresh thyme, or 1 teaspoon dried

  Salt and pepper to taste
- 3 tablespoons olive oil

  Sautéed mixed julienned peppers and sautéed mushroom caps, for garnish (optional)

Place chicken breasts in a marinade of the Chardonnay and half the leeks, carrots, and celery. Cover and marinate for a couple of hours.

Heat the pancetta in a medium skillet, covered, over low heat, for 1 minute. Squeeze the pulp from the roasted garlic into the pan and add the remaining leeks, carrots, and celery. Toss, add mushrooms, thyme, salt, and pepper, and toss again. Cover and cook over medium heat until the liquid evaporates, about 20 minutes. Reserve.

Remove the chicken breasts from the marinade and stuff the breasts with the cooled pancetta mixture, filling space between the meat and skin and making sure skin covers entire breast. Hold skin in place with toothpicks inserted on the underside of each breast. Clip off any protruding toothpicks.

Preheat the oven to 350 degrees.

Heat the olive oil in a large skillet over medium heat, place chicken breasts in skin side down, and brown on all sides. Place in the oven and cook until just done, about 20 minutes.

If desired, chicken may be served with sautéed peppers and garnished with a few sautéed mushroom caps.

Serves 6

TOP: **Fresh Oysters with Orange Basil-Ginger Sauce.**
ABOVE: **Chicken with Chardonnay.**

Poached Pears with Eldorado Gold Raspberry-Caramel Sauce

I think this raspberry sauce also would be great on other poached fruits or on ice cream.

    3 cups water
    1 bottle Fumé Blanc or other
       dry white wine
       Rinds of 4 lemons
    2 teaspoon vanilla extract
    2 cups sugar
  ¼ to ⅓ cup raspberry honey
       (plain honey may be
       substituted)
    6 medium pears, carefully
       peeled with stem on and
       bottoms cut off so they will
       sit flat on the plate, then
       rubbed with lemon juice
       Eldorado Gold Raspberry-
       Caramel Sauce (recipe
       follows)
       Fresh berries, mint leaves,
       whipped cream, for garnish
       (optional)

Place water, wine, lemon rind, vanilla, sugar, and honey in a deep saucepan and bring quickly to a boil. Turn back to a simmer and lower pears in carefully. Poach, uncovered, until pears are tender, about 15 minutes. Cool in the poaching liquid, then drain.

Serve individually on plates slicked with sauce. Garnish with fresh berries, mint leaves, and a dab of whipped cream, if desired.

Serves 6

ELDORADO GOLD
RASPBERRY-CARAMEL SAUCE

    1 pint golden or red rasp-
       berries
  ½ cup water
  1 ½ cups sugar
  ½ cup Ferrari-Carano Eldorado
       Gold (Sauternes may be
       substituted)
    1 tablespoon fresh lemon juice
       Kirsch to taste (optional)

Puree the berries and strain to remove seeds. Measure 1 cup puree. Set aside.

Place 4 tablespoons of water and the sugar in a heavy saucepan. Let stand until sugar is moist. Cook over medium-high heat until sugar is light golden in color, stirring constantly. Sugar will begin to smell caramelized.

Remove from heat and set pan in sink. Carefully stir in remaining water. Return pan to stove over medium heat and add wine. Cook, stirring constantly, until caramel has completely dissolved. Remove from heat and add puree, a tablespoon at a time. Add lemon juice and a few drops of Kirsch, if desired.

Makes about 1½ cups

❧

ABOUT THE WINES

Rhonda Carano, who created the menu for us from her extensive recipe file, is particularly aware of how the flavors of her food are enhanced by the vineyard's wines, over the years keenly customizing her recipes to suit the wines:

"I consider our 1988 Fumé Blanc and fresh oysters on the half shell a natural food-and-wine combination. So simple, yet exquisite—the faint nutty flavors of the oyster blend wonderfully with the melon and fig flavors present in this wine, [making] a very well-balanced match.

"The pasta and the chicken were chosen to complement our 1987 Alexander Valley Chardonnay. I call the

OPPOSITE: **Poached Pears with Eldorado Gold Raspberry-Caramel Sauce.** TOP: **Yellow tomatoes.** ABOVE: **Apricots.**

pasta dish *Pastprella*, which in Italian literally means the "shepherdess." Its simple ingredients make *Pastprella* as fresh as the morning dew.

"Our 1987 Chardonnay's toasty oak, spice flavors and the crisp, lemon-citrus quality of the wine add extra flavor to these unadorned, delicate foods.

"The slightly fruity pear flavors of our 1986 Eldorado Gold, Late Harvest Sauvignon Blanc, with its characteristic honey and caramel taste, makes a perfect marriage with the wine and poached pears. Raspberries maintain the balance of flavors and create a wonderful combination."

❧

Indian Summer Supper

QUIVIRA VINEYARDS

꒰

HENRY AND HOLLY Wendt, who founded Quivira Vineyards in 1981, have a romantic as well as a practical sense of history. The romantic part is expressed in the very name they chose for their winery. You see, in the sixteenth and seventeenth centuries, maps of the New World showed "The Kingdom of Quivira," and according to legend this kingdom had a sophisticated culture and great wealth, derived at least in part from their thriving trade with China. Of course, Europeans of the period had more compelling proof of China's existence and cultural life than they did of Quivira. However, this small lapse didn't dampen the enthusiasm created by the notion of this unseen

land and appears to have stimulated exploration of the North American continent for over two hundred years. Pretty potent stuff.

The clincher for the Wendts was that the great mapmakers of three centuries ago placed the kingdom right in the middle of Sonoma County's Dry Creek Valley, where their property is located. And to tell the truth, from the ridge where their upper vineyards begin and their residence stands, gazing down at the winery below and the splendid peaceful hills in the distance makes you think those ancient cartographers might have been on to something after all. This certainly looks to be a blessed spot.

On a more mundane level, agricultural history of the valley told the Wendts that several of the most important varieties of wine grapes excel here, which fit in with their anything-but-mundane goal: to produce the highest-quality wines from only estate-grown grapes that thrive in this region.

In addition to Sauvignon Blanc, Zinfandel, and Cabernet Sauvignon grapes—the proven varieties—over the intervening years small quantities of blending grapes have been planted. Sémillon, Petit Sirah, Cabernet Franc, and Merlot have expanded their planted acreage to 72.5 of their total 90 acres.

There is another aspect to the Quivira operation that makes it different from most others in the area: Henry Wendt is the chairman of the board of SmithKline Beecham, a multibillion-dollar transnational health care company. When asked how an executive with his obvious responsibilities can manage a wine business thousands of miles from his offices in Philadelphia and London, he explains: "The key is good people. The essence of long-distance management is finding the right people and giving them clear and proper guidance and authority. The Quivira team consists of energetic and committed professionals."

As well thought out as Wendt's operating technique is, there remains another nagging question. "Why?" Why bother with this added responsibility? Not surprisingly, Henry Wendt's response is as reasonable and as carefully conceived as his management plans. The point is that although he has no immediate thoughts of retirement, he and Holly realize that obviously they will ultimately want to make some changes. As he explains, "Partly in preparation for our next life stage when I will be less engaged in the international health care business, we wanted to create and develop a dynamic and interesting way of life and business—so we decided upon the wine business."

The meal we had on that bright fall afternoon—prepared by Holly in the kitchen and Henry at the grill—was as generous and delightful as these two are together, with plentiful food to choose from and all accompanied by their superb wines.

Chilled Buttermilk Vegetable Soup with chopped red peppers and Cheese Toasts.

MENU

CHILLED BUTTERMILK VEGETABLE SOUP
CHEESE TOASTS
BONED TURKEY BREAST WITH PEANUT SAUCE
RED POTATO SALAD
CORN CHIVE MUFFINS
AVOCADO AND MELON SALAD
LIME ICE CREAM WITH BLACKBERRY SAUCE
CHOCOLATE SQUARES

Quivira Sauvignon Blanc
Quivira Zinfandel
Quivira Cabernet Sauvignon

Chilled Buttermilk Vegetable Soup

I think you will love this tangy soup. You could even experiment by adding a few other kinds of vegetables after you have made this the first time.

2 tablespoons unsalted butter
1 large onion
3 medium apples, peeled, cored, and coarsely chopped
3 cups water

1 tablespoon chicken broth granules
2 ½ cups buttermilk
1 cup peeled, seeded, and finely diced cucumber
1 cup peeled, seeded, and finely diced tomato
1 cup corn cut from the cob (about 3 ears), steamed
1 ½ teaspoons salt
¼ cup finely chopped fresh dill, for garnish
2 tablespoons chopped red bell pepper, for garnish

Place the butter in a skillet and sauté the onion over medium heat until wilted but not browned, about 5 minutes. Add the apples, water, and chicken broth granules. Simmer until apples are soft, about 5 to 10 minutes. Puree in a blender or food processor. (May be frozen at this point.)

Add the buttermilk, vegetables, and salt. Refrigerate, covered, until well chilled. Serve garnished with dill and red pepper.

Serves 6 to 8

❧

ABOVE: **Holly and Henry Wendt.**
BELOW: **The vineyards in Indian summer colors.**

Cheese Toasts

These are so good you will serve them with many other soups as well.

- 1 cup freshly grated Parmesan cheese
- ½ cup commercial mayonnaise
- 1 baguette, sliced into ¼-inch rounds

Combine the cheese and mayonnaise and spread on the bread slices. Place under the broiler until browned and bubbly, about 1 to 2 minutes. Serve immediately.

Makes 18 or more

Boned Turkey Breast with Peanut Sauce

Grilled turkey breast can also be done under a broiler, about 6 inches from the heat.

- ½ cup chunky peanut butter
- ¼ cup soy sauce
- ¼ cup sesame oil
- 1 large garlic clove, minced
- 2 teaspoons sugar
- ¼ cup cider vinegar
- 1 ½ tablespoons oriental hot pepper oil
- 1 cup sour cream
  Milk as needed
- ½ turkey breast (about 3 pounds), boned

Combine all the ingredients except the milk and turkey breast and mix well. Thin with a little milk if necessary to make the consistency of softly whipped cream. Set aside.

Gently loosen and remove skin and any fat from the turkey breast. Cover with plastic wrap and flatten with a mallet or rolling pin to approximately 1-inch thick. Spread with half the peanut sauce and refrigerate, covered, for several hours or overnight.

Prepare outdoor grill. Grill turkey breast over a moderately hot fire for 15 minutes per side or until a slit in the middle reveals opaque meat. Slice and serve immediately with the remaining peanut sauce.

Serves 6 to 8

Note: This may also be made in advance and refrigerated, along with the sauce, and served cold (or at room temperature).

Red Potato Salad

Yet another delicious version of everyone's favorite.

- 2 ½ pounds small red potatoes
  Salt
- 1 tablespoon lemon juice
- ½ cup sour cream
- ½ cup mayonnaise
- ¼ cup fresh basil, cut into thin strips
- ¼ cup minced fresh parsley, no stems
- 1 medium garlic clove, minced
- 2 tablespoons vinegar
- 1 teaspoon Worchestershire sauce
- ½ teaspoon Dijon-style mustard
- ¼ teaspoon freshly ground pepper
- ½ teaspoon salt

Cover the potatoes with lightly salted water and add lemon juice. Bring rapidly to a boil and turn heat down to just a rolling boil. Cook potatoes until tender when pierced with the point of a knife, about 12 minutes or more. Drain and cool.

Meanwhile, whisk together all other ingredients to make a dressing.

Cut cooled potatoes into small chunks, leaving the skins on, and toss with the dressing. Refrigerate until time to serve.

Serves 6 to 8

TOP LEFT: **The vineyards.** CENTER: **Red Potato Salad.** ABOVE: **Boned Turkey Breast with Peanut Sauce.**

Corn Chive Muffins

Chives give these a nice twist.

1 cup all-purpose flour
½ teaspoon baking soda
1 ½ teaspoons baking powder
1 tablespoon sugar
¼ teaspoon salt
¾ cup stone-ground yellow cornmeal
2 tablespoons minced fresh chives
1 cup buttermilk
2 eggs, lightly beaten
4 tablespoons (½ stick) butter, melted

Preheat the oven to 425 degrees and grease 12 medium muffin tins. Set aside.

Combine the dry ingredients, plus chives. Combine buttermilk, eggs, and butter and stir into the dry ingredients quickly. Do not overmix. Divide batter among the 12 muffin tins and bake for 18 to 20 minutes, until lightly browned.

Makes 12 muffins

Avocado and Melon Salad

Here you have a typical California combination.

1 medium avocado, peeled, pitted, sliced thin, and rubbed with lemon juice
1 small to medium melon, peeled, seeded, sliced thin, and rubbed with lemon juice

¼ cup raspberry vinegar
½ teaspoon salt
½ teaspoon Dijon-style mustard
½ cup walnut oil
Several grinds of black pepper
1 tablespoon minced fresh tarragon

Arrange the avocado and melon slices on serving plates. Whisk together remaining ingredients and spoon a bit of vinaigrette over each plate.

Serves 6 to 8

Lime Ice Cream with Blackberry Sauce

This is actually called Laura's Lime Ice Cream because the recipe came from the Wendts' daughter, Laura. According to her mother, she's a marvelous cook. From the taste of this ice cream that's not just parental pride speaking.

ICE CREAM

1 cup heavy cream
1 egg
1 cup sugar
Grated rind of 1 medium to large lime
⅓ cup fresh lime juice
Pinch of salt
1 ⅓ cups milk
1 drop green food coloring (optional)

SAUCE

1 cup fresh or frozen blackberries, pureed with seeds strained out

1 tablespoon unsalted butter
1 tablespoon fresh lime juice
⅓ cup sugar
¾ cup dry white wine
¼ cup crème de cassis (black currant liqueur)
1 tablespoon cornstarch

Make the ice cream. Beat the cream and egg. Add sugar gradually and beat until almost stiff. Add the lime peel and juice, salt, milk, and food coloring. Freeze in an ice cream maker according to manufacturer's directions.

Make the sauce. In a saucepan blend the blackberry puree, butter, lime juice, sugar, and wine. Mix the cassis and cornstarch and stir in. Cook over medium heat, stirring, until the sauce thickens, 3 to 5 minutes or less. Chill completely.

This sauce may be made in advance and frozen. Allow to melt in the refrigerator before using.

Serves 6 to 8

TOP LEFT: **The ingredients for Avocado and Melon Salad.** ABOVE: **Corn Chive Muffins.** OPPOSITE: **Lime Ice Cream with Blackberry Sauce, and Chocolate Squares.**

Since all the recipes Holly Wendt used for our lunch were devised by her over a period of time, she is very well acquainted with the subtleties of her food, making it easy for her to match the various dishes to Quivira's wines:

"Sauvignon Blanc can carry the first and second course well—and the Zinfandel tastes delicious with the entrée and dessert. The Cabernet Sauvignon creates a nice finale with the chocolate squares.

"The tangy buttermilk and fresh vegetables in the soup are complemented by the citrus notes and silk texture of the Sauvignon Blanc.

"The robust ripe berry flavors of Zinfandel enhance any grilled meat, but they particularly suit the grilled turkey and the spicy nutty flavors of the peanut sauce.

"The cherry and currant flavors of Cabernet Sauvignon are a classic combination with chocolate. These flavors are brought to life when our Cabernet Sauvignon is paired with our chocolate.

"It's nice to linger after supper with both in hand."

Amen.

Chocolate Squares

These are known as "legendary chocolate squares" in the Wendt household. When you taste them, you'll know why.

1 **cup (2 sticks) plus 2 tablespoons unsalted butter or margarine, slightly softened**

½ **cup firmly packed light brown sugar**

½ **cup granulated sugar**

2 **egg yolks**

1 **cup all-purpose flour**

1 **cup quick oatmeal**

12 **ounces milk chocolate**

¾ **cup finely chopped walnuts**

Preheat the oven to 350 degrees.

Cream 1 cup of the butter and the sugars. Beat in the egg yolks, then add the flour and oatmeal. Press into a lightly greased 11 by 17-inch low-sided pan. Bake 20 minutes, until set. Meanwhile, melt the chocolate and butter together.

When a sheet of cookies are done, spread top with the chocolate mixture and sprinkle with nuts. Cut into squares.

Makes about 40 cookies

A Formal Dinner at Home

JORDAN VINEYARD & WINERY

EVERYONE you talk to about Jordan Winery remarks on the glorious buildings and manicured grounds surrounding it. There is literally nothing to rival this lovely chateaulike complex in all of the northern California wine country.

Of course, the buildings, the grounds, the splendid setting would simply be a pleasing treat for the eyes if there were not the quality wines to give this impressive background meaning. Never fear, the wines are there—subtle, supple, and distinctive. The picture is complete and real.

But where did this all come from? Did some

As it turns out, his ship did come in—in the form of a spectacular series of oil and gas discoveries in western New Guinea. That was in the early 1970s, and with it came the very real probability that Tom and Sally would be able to achieve their goal. And so the search began.

But the Jordans hadn't reckoned with the French government's not taking kindly to the prospect of foreigners purchasing a premier grand cru chateau. The alternative, a lesser chateau, would not satisfy.

Then fate led them to a well-known San Francisco restaurant. Here they were served a bottle of 1968

LEFT AND ABOVE: **The lovely vine-traced facade of the winery.**

Cabernet Sauvignon, Beaulieu Vineyards, Georges de Latour Private Reserve. That did it. Tom realized that what he and Sally were looking for was possible here in California. In short order, land was located—over 1,000 acres of it over time—and Tom sold his interest in the oil and gas business, and the task of creating a world-class winery—buildings and all—was begun.

The results speak for themselves.

The story could end right there and it would still be a remarkable dream come true, but there is more. That more is Judy Jordan, daughter of Tom and Sally. She originally planned to be a geologist and join her father in oil and gas exploration; she completed her studies at Stanford, her mother's alma mater, in preparation for her career. But, as Tom puts it, "It didn't take Judy long to realize it would be years before she would be as knowledgeable as the senior geologists in my office. And she told me she thought she could make a better contribution to the winery. Which she has—and besides, it's more fun."

Over time Judy has become an increasingly knowledgeable and articulate member of the operation, ensuring that what Tom and Sally began will go on into the next generation—just as many great French wineries have done.

Entertaining at Jordan fits the surroundings: impressive food, though in the simpler California manner, served in wide candlelit rooms filled with flowers gathered from the winery gardens, and, of course, that wonderful wine.

titled Frenchman forsake Bordeaux for Sonoma? Well, yes and no. There is no nobleman, but Bordeaux is in the equation.

To begin at the beginning, Tom and Sally Jordan, Francophiles to the core, were living in Denver. For years they had been dining on French food, drinking French wine, and developing what seemed a remote dream: to own a French winery. As Tom Jordan, a geologist and former oil and gas prospecter, says today, "I thought if my ship ever came in, I'd buy a vineyard in France."

a small, nonreactive saucepan and bring to a boil over high heat. Reduce to about 2 tablespoons, about 8 minutes. Add mussel cooking liquid and herbs, and reduce for another 5 minutes over medium-high heat, to about 2 tablespoons. Over low heat, gradually whisk in the pieces of butter, one at a time. When all butter has been incorporated, remove sauce from heat and pass through a sieve. Add the pea puree and stir until well mixed and light green. Press a sheet of wax paper or plastic wrap onto the surface of the puree and set aside.

M E N U

PASTA AND MUSSELS WITH YOUNG PEAS IN BUTTER SAUCE
ROASTED LAMB LOIN WITH CABERNET WINE SAUCE
ROASTED GARLIC CUSTARD
MARINATED GOAT CHEESE
FRESH FIGS WITH WILD STRAWBERRY SAUCE

1986 Jordan Chardonnay
1985 Jordan Cabernet Sauvignon

Pasta and Mussels with Young Peas in Butter Sauce

When preparing this dish, do the mussels first, then the peas, and finally the pasta if you are using the commercially prepared kind. Should you decide to make fresh pasta, prepare it earlier in the day.

STEAMED MUSSELS

2 tablespoons unsalted butter
2 tablespoons olive oil
3 medium shallots, minced
3 medium garlic cloves, minced
¼ cup minced celery
2 pounds mussels, scrubbed and trimmed
1 ½ cups Chardonnay

PEAS IN BUTTER SAUCE

1 ½ cups shelled fresh, small green peas
2 medium shallots, minced
1 cup Chardonnay

2 sprigs fresh thyme, or 1 scant teaspoon dried
6 fresh basil leaves
1 cup (2 sticks) chilled unsalted butter, cut into small pieces
1 recipe Semolina Pasta (recipe follows) or 1 pound commercial pasta

Heat the butter and oil in a medium skillet over medium heat. Add the shallots, garlic, and celery and sauté until tender, about 5 minutes. Add the mussels and wine. Steam, covered, until mussels are open, about 5 minutes. Discard any mussels that do not open. Strain the cooking liquids and reserve ½ cup. Set mussels aside to cool.

Cover the peas with salted water and bring rapidly to a boil. Boil over medium heat until very tender, about 6 to 8 minutes. Drain and puree in a food mill or food processor, then pass through a fine sieve. Set aside.

Combine the shallots and wine in

SEMOLINA PASTA

This calls for an unusually large number of eggs and requires a heavy-duty pasta machine to make because of the semolina.

1 **pound fine semolina flour, plus extra for storing**
5 **whole eggs plus 5 egg yolks**
1 **tablespoon olive oil**
 Pinch of salt

Place semolina in a large bowl, make a well in the middle, and put all other ingredients in well. Mix and then knead dough in a pasta machine. Either use a machine to cut the pasta or cut it by hand.

You can hold this pasta for a few hours by lightly tossing it with extra semolina and placing it in a single layer on a tray. Cover with plastic wrap and refrigerate until ready to use.

Cook the pasta in a large pot of boiling salted water until just tender, several minutes depending on whether you use fresh or dried. To serve, toss hot pasta with a little butter, ladle pea puree into the bottom of warmed individual bowls, and place pasta over each. Arrange 4 to 6 mussels on top of each serving.

Serves 6 to 8

OPPOSITE: **Sally Jordan (left), her daughter Judy, and winery chef John Thomas Caputo.** BELOW: **Formal dinner in the dining room.**

saucepan and whisk in the butter piece by piece over low heat. Keep warm.

Preheat the oven to 450 degrees. Generously coat meat with salt and pepper. Heat a large, heavy ovenproof skillet to very hot over high heat, add butter, and as soon as it has melted and starts to brown slightly, sear the lamb on all sides until nicely browned, about 3 minutes to a side. Leave loins in the skillet and place in the oven and bake for 7 to 10 minutes for medium rare; 12 minutes for medium.

Serve with wine sauce.

Serves 6 to 8

❧

Roasted Lamb Loin with Cabernet Wine Sauce

Lamb prepared in this manner is about as good as it can get.

SAUCE

- 1 bottle Cabernet Sauvignon
- 1 medium onion, finely chopped
- 2 medium garlic cloves, coarsely chopped
- 3 medium shallots, thinly sliced
- 1 to 2 small carrots, thinly sliced
- 3 parsley sprigs
- 1 medium bay leaf
- 2 sprigs fresh thyme, or 1 teaspoon dried
- 3 cups lamb, veal, or chicken stock
- 8 tablespoons (1 stick) chilled unsalted butter, cut into small pieces

MEAT

- 4 lamb loins, about 8 ounces each
  Salt and freshly ground black pepper
- 6 tablespoons (¾ stick) unsalted butter

For the sauce, combine the wine, onion, garlic, shallots, carrots, and herbs in a nonreactive saucepan and bring rapidly to a boil. Boil until reduced to 1½ cups of liquid, about 20 minutes. Add stock and reduce to about 2 cups of liquid, about 30 minutes. Pass through a sieve into a fresh

Roasted Garlic Custard

Here is a dish for garlic lovers. It may be cooked a couple hours in advance, if desired.

- 6 whole eggs plus 3 egg whites
- 2 cups heavy cream
  Salt and white pepper
- 3 to 4 medium garlic heads, roasted (page 65)

Preheat the oven to 250 degrees and put a kettle of water on to boil. Butter ten 3-ounce metal (see Note) molds generously and set aside. Beat the eggs and whites until well mixed, then add the cream. Mix well. Gently squeeze garlic pulp out of heads and into the mixture. Mix, then pass through a fine sieve. Pour into the buttered molds, which should be about three-fourths full. Place molds in a larger pan and add boiling water to come about halfway up the molds. Bake until firm, about 1 hour and 15 minutes. If the blade of a knife is inserted in the center, it should come out clean.

To reheat, place baked custards back into a hot water bath, out of the oven, for 7 to 10 minutes before serving.

Makes 8 to 10

Note: If you use ceramic custard cups, you may have to cook these a little longer.

ABOVE LEFT: **Roasted Lamb Loin with Cabernet Wine Sauce, and Roasted Garlic Custard.** ABOVE RIGHT: **Marinated Goat Cheeses.** RIGHT: **Fresh Figs with Wild Strawberry Sauce.**

Marinated Goat Cheese

As the photograph will attest, these look great while they are marinating. Of course in the picture, we used many more than are called for here. You can, too, because they keep for months. You should use slightly aged (10 to 14 days) cheese. Fresh goat cheese absorbs too much oil.

6 small goat cheeses
2 medium garlic cloves
6 black peppercorns
2 medium dried Japanese or cayenne chiles, coarsely chopped
3 fresh sage leaves, crushed
2 sprigs fresh thyme, or scant 1 teaspoon dried
1 sprig fresh rosemary, or ½ teaspoon dried
1 bay leaf, crushed
Good-quality olive oil
2 red bell peppers, roasted (page 104)

Place goat cheese in a small container with a lid. Sprinkle with the garlic, peppercorns, chiles, and herbs and cover with olive oil. Marinate, covered, in the refrigerator for about 2 weeks before using.

To serve, allow cheese to come to room temperature and place on a triangle of peeled and seeded roasted red bell pepper.

Serves 6

Fresh Figs with Wild Strawberry Sauce

Wild strawberries, or fraise de bois, *have a slightly different texture and taste. Of course, if you don't have wild strawberries, you can substitute the domestic ones. You can also substitute fresh raspberries if they're available.*

1 pint or more fresh strawberries
  Superfine sugar to taste
9 large fresh figs
  Mint or sprigs of strawberry for garnish (optional)

Puree half the strawberries and sweeten to taste with the sugar. If you are using wild strawberries, leave the balance whole; if regular strawberries, slice them thickly.

To serve, cut figs in half lengthwise and arrange 3 halves on individual plates. Heap strawberries in the middle and surround with a few spoonfuls of puree. Garnish with mint or strawberry sprigs if desired.

Serves 6

ABOUT THE WINES

Selection of wines to accompany any meal at the Jordan Winery is a joint affair. So when this meal was first planned, Sally Jordan, hospitality coordinator Jean Reynolds, and resident chef John Caputo went into a huddle and came up with their choices:

"Food and wine pairing is governed by a simple idea: the creation of harmony between the food to be eaten and the wines to be served. Jordan Chardonnay and Cabernet Sauvignon are soft, rich, elegant, and finely balanced wines. They are blended to complement rather than overpower the foods with which they are served.

"The fruitiness and complexity of Jordan's Chardonnay show beautifully when paired with lightly prepared fish and shellfish dishes. In turn, the wine's natural acidity enhances the subtle flavors of the seafood and the fullness of the butter sauce.

"The soft tannins and velvety character of Jordan's Cabernet Sauvignon highlight the richness of the lamb; the wine's lively cassis flavor adds even more enticing nuances to this course. The garlic custard, with its understated cream character, not only complements the lamb but also underscores the smoothness of our Bordeaux-style wine and works in partnership with the wine's lingering, rich finish."

Rollie's Family Favorites

HEITZ WINE CELLARS

THERE IS a little booklet printed for Heitz Wine Cellar that tells about the winery's beginning and describes its wines. Inside, under the name Heitz Cellar, is the line, "A family winery making fine wines in the Napa Valley since 1961." This simple declarative sentence sums up the whole operation about as well as I can imagine any words doing. This is first and foremost a family business; all its members are involved and totally devoted to making the best wine they know how on a scale they are comfortable with.

It all started with Joe and Alice Heitz—but, we'll come back to them in a minute. Of their children there is number one son, David, who is the vice-president and winemaker. He made the 1974 commemorative bottling of Martha's Vineyard Cabernet Sauvignon as his solo effort after he began to work full time at the family winery.

Four years after David began his full-time duties, daughter Kathleen came aboard to involve herself in marketing and general winery operation.

Finally, after the youngest, Rollie, finished at the University of Santa Clara in 1980, he joined the others, having worked in the vineyards and cellar since his grammar school days.

Although they each have titles, you can't help but get the feeling that everybody here does a little of everything—not because they have to necessarily, but because they want to.

Now back to Joe and Alice. Joe, originally from Illinois, got the wine-making bug during World War II, when he was able to moonlight as a cellarman at a San Joaquin Valley winery between shifts as a ground crewman for a fighter squadron. By the time his tour of duty was finished he knew what he wanted to do and prepared himself by going to U.C., Davis. In 1961 he and Alice made a modest start on what had become a dream for them both. It was a very small building on St. Helena Highway, which is now their sales room, with a parcel of land on which to grow their first grapes.

Being determined, and industrious, and knowing what they wanted, Joe and Alice managed by 1964 to acquire the Spring Valley ranch just east of St. Helena. This was the old winery and vineyard established in the 1880s by Anton Rossi. Its original stone winery structure now holds their white wines for fermentation. This was joined in 1972 and 1979 by other buildings for additional fermentation space and bottling facilities, making it possible for the Heitzes to reach their peak goal of 40,000 cases a year.

Along the way the Heitzes bought more acreage, but they also continue to buy grapes from selected local growers, most notable of which are the much-praised Martha's Vineyard near Oakville, from whom they purchase Cabernet Sauvignon grapes, and Bella Oaks Vineyard situated near Rutherford.

Heitz grows most of its own Chardonnay grapes on the famous "Z" property on Zinfandel Lane and on property adjoining the sales room.

Although Alice has created more than her share of memorable meals to be complemented by Heitz wines, Rollie is the man in the family who likes to cook—and what a good cook he is. For this little dinner, with the help of his wife, Sally, and Alice, he prepared food they all like. In these dishes is reflected the Mexican influence that has seeped into local tastes over the years.

Dessert was two kinds of sorbet made from their Grignolino and Grignolino Rosé wines. These were absolutely delicious and are so easy to prepare that you've got to try them.

So this family that likes to make wine together also likes to make merry together. Try their wine and food and you'll see why.

OPPOSITE: **The old stone winery.**
ABOVE: **The whimsical weathervane.**

CHICKEN SALSA PHYLLO
TRIANGLES
PORK TOMATILLO STEW
MUSHROOM RICE
GRIGNOLINO ROSE SORBET

1986 Chardonnay
1984 Cabernet Sauvignon
Grignolino

Chicken Salsa Phyllo Triangles

The family likes these hearty triangles as a first course. They are delicious and would make a good lunch with just the salad and sorbet.

TRIANGLES

2   medium chicken breasts, halved and skinned

4   ounces grated dry Monterey Jack cheese (Parmesan or Romano may be substituted)

1   4-ounce can diced green chiles

½   roasted and peeled red bell pepper, diced (page 104)

1   cup mild or hot commercial salsa

1   package (1 pound) phyllo dough

½ to ¾ pound (2 to 3 sticks) unsalted butter, melted

ACCOMPANIMENTS

Sour cream

Guacamole

Poach the chicken breasts in just enough water to cover until tender, about 20 minutes. Do not overcook. Remove from heat and let cool in the liquid until you can handle them and remove the bones. Shred the meat with a fork and place in a bowl with the cheese, chiles, red pepper, and salsa. Mix well and refrigerate.

Preheat the oven to 350 degrees.

Open the phyllo and immediately cover with wax paper, then a damp towel. It is important not to let the dough dry out. Remove the filling from the refrigerator and place the melted butter in a convenient place so you will be able to brush the sheets of dough with it. Working quickly, place 1 sheet of dough on a flat surface, with the longer edge perpendicular to you, and brush with butter. (You can use a new 2-inch paint brush for this.) Cover with another sheet of phyllo and brush with butter. Repeat with a third sheet, keeping the remaining dough covered while you do this.

With a sharp knife, cut the phyllo sheets lengthwise into 3 equal strips (2 cuts). Place a tablespoon of filling at the bottom end of 1 strip and fold dough over filling to form a triangle, then continue folding triangles (as you would fold a flag) until you reach the top of the strip.

Repeat for another 2 strips. As you finish the triangles, place them on a buttered baking sheet and brush each individually with melted butter. Continue making triangles until all dough and filling are used.

Bake triangles until golden, about 8 minutes. Check once near the end of the cooking time to be sure they are not baking too fast.

These may be made in advance and placed on a lightly greased cookie sheet and frozen on the sheet. When frozen, remove them to a plastic freezer bag. To cook frozen triangles, place them unthawed on a lightly greased cookie sheet and bake until golden, about 10 minutes.

Serve with sour cream and your favorite guacamole.

Makes about 18 triangles

✦

Pork Tomatillo Stew

Rollie tells me this stew can also be made with beef, but he prefers it with pork.

1 ½   pounds fresh tomatillos

2   large tomatoes

3   pounds boned pork loin

3   small jalapeño peppers, stemmed, seeded, and minced

½   teaspoon salt

½   teaspoon pepper

⅓ to ½ cup all-purpose flour

4   tablespoons (½ stick) unsalted butter

⅔   cup beef consommé

½   cup hot salsa

¼   cup water (optional)

1   to 2 tablespoons cornstarch (optional)

Preheat the oven to 300 degrees.

Remove the paperlike husks and drop the tomatillos in a pot of rapidly boiling water. Boil for 5 to 6 minutes. Drain and pull the skins off and stem with a sharp knife. If skins do not come off some of the tomatillos, squeeze them over a bowl and extract as much of the pulp as possible, discarding skins.

Drop tomatoes in boiling water for 20 seconds. Skin and halve, then squeeze out and discard seeds. Dice.

Cut pork into ½-inch thick slices and cut each slice so it is roughly 2 inches square. Place jalapeño peppers, salt, and pepper in a bowl and toss with the pork slices, pressing peppers into the meat. Add the flour and toss again to coat lightly. Melt the butter in a large skillet over medium heat and sauté the pork until golden on both sides. Do not crowd pan.

Transfer browned pork slices to an ovenproof stew pot. Pour out fat and deglaze skillet with the consommé, scraping up browned parts, and pour this over the pork. Add tomatillos and salsa. Cover tightly and bake until pork is tender, about 1½ hours. If stew needs thickening, combine the water with the cornstarch and stir it into the mixture. Cook over medium heat until thickened, stirring. Add tomatoes and heat well. Correct seasoning.

This may be prepared a day in advance without the tomatoes, cooled, and refrigerated. Add tomatoes before reheating.

Serves 6 to 8

Mushroom Rice

There seems to be lots of variety in the rice available hereabouts. This one is called Mixed Grain Rice and is from Lundberg Family Farms (see page 173).

- 4 **tablespoons (½ stick) unsalted butter**
- ¼ **cup olive oil**
- 1 **pound mixed fresh mushrooms (shiitake, oyster, button), finely chopped**
- 1 **large red onion, minced**
- 1 **pound Mixed Grain Rice**
- 2½ **cups double-strength beef stock (or a double amount regular beef stock reduced)**
  Salt and pepper to taste
- 2 **tablespoons minced fresh parsley**

Melt the butter in a deep saucepan and add the olive oil. Add the mushrooms and sauté over medium heat until most of the liquid has evaporated, 10 to 15 minutes. Add the onion and continue to sauté until slightly translucent, about 4 minutes. Add the rice mixture and cook over medium heat, stirring occasionally, for another 5 minutes. Add the broth, cover pan tightly, and simmer over very low heat for 45 minutes to 1 hour, until tender.

Stir in salt and pepper. Toss with parsley and serve.

Serves 6 to 8

Grignolino Rosé Sorbet

Grignolino wine makes a marvelous sorbet. Heitz Cellar produces two kinds, and both are delicious.

- ¾ **cup sugar**
- ¾ **cup water**
- 1 **bottle Grignolino Rosé**

Combine the sugar and water in a small saucepan and place over medium-low heat, stirring occasionally, until sugar melts. Let cool.

Combine this simple syrup with the wine. Pour into a commercial ice cream maker and freeze according to manufacturer's directions.

Makes about 1 quart

About the Wines

Rollie's assessments of their wines' qualities have a refreshing directness. They make it easy to understand his choices:

"The richness of our 1986 Chardonnay comes through nicely with the salsa triangles. It blends well with the crisp phyllo coating and stands up to the more spicy flavors in the chicken and salsa filling. A light and fresh wine—a perfect match here.

"Our 1984 Cabernet Sauvignon is hearty, 100 percent varietal and has three and a half years' of aging in wood. It is an ideal match for, and stands up to the rich flavor of, the pork stew. It goes equally well with other hearty stews, red meats, and game dishes, yet it is still soft and very pleasant to drink."

Of the Grignolino used to make the ices, Rollie says: "It has varietal characteristics; that is, it is extremely fruity. It packs lots of fruit that jumps out at you."

A Special Dinner for Friends

TREFETHEN VINEYARDS

❧

WHILE THE COUNTRY was celebrating and toasting the unveiling of the Statue of Liberty in New York Harbor, a different kind of celebration was going on on the other coast. The Goodman brothers, James and George, were toasting the completion of their new winery building in the Napa Valley. That was in 1886 and they had christened their wine estate "Eschol" after the river where Moses discovered enormous clusters of grapes.

Hopes were running high for the Goodmans because their vineyards had already begun to pro-

duce quality wines; two years later they were winning medals, among them the coveted San Francisco Viticultural Fair Prize for their Eschol Cabernet Sauvignon. Their timing and business acumen seem to have been consistently on the button, but by the turn of the century they had decided to retire. Even in this, their timing seems not to have deserted them. Shortly thereafter that the wine business suffered one setback after another. It started with the decimation of the vines by phylloxera. Prohibition and the Depression almost succeeded in finishing what the vine pest had started.

Gene and Katie Trefethen had been walnut growers but wanted to turn their passion for agriculture to wine making, so they bought the old Eschol Estate in 1968. At this point the valley's wine production had just begun to rise from its nadir of the early sixties, and the town of Napa, two miles away, was still only a small sleepy community.

The task they set for themselves with this purchase was enormous. Aside from the usual uncertainties facing any new venture, the business of simply reclaiming 320 acres of neglected vineyards and orchards would have been understandably daunting for anyone. But their son, John, believed fervently in the estate's wine-making potential and stuck by his beliefs.

It was a long and arduous haul, but by 1973, John and his wife, Janet, managed to produce their first wines: 2,000 cases off what had by then expanded to 600 acres. Today their annual production has increased to more than 75,000 cases and is spiraling upward.

On the land acquired by the Trefethens, the original 1886 wine building, designed for the Goodmans by architect Captain Hamden McIntyre, still stood. Now restored, it has been designated a National Historic Landmark of early Calfornia winery architecture.

With everything else the young Trefethens had to cope with in those early years you'd think they would not have had time for much entertaining. But along the way they have developed a personal style that makes their gatherings distinctive, with cooking for parties a truly family affair; John takes care of the outdoor grilling while Janet is in the kitchen handling the accompaniments.

This meal, in its tasty simplicity, is typical of what you could expect to find on an evening when Janet and John entertain a group of their close friends. Makes you kinda wish you lived nearby so you could wrangle an invitation.

LEFT: **Oyster Tartar with Sparkling Wine Sauce.**
ABOVE: **Shade-dappled winery building.**

Prosciutto with Lemon and Dill

*The lemon and dill turn ordinary pros-
ciutto into a treat. Easy too!*

24 thin slices prosciutto
1 tablespoon minced fresh dill
1 teaspoon minced lemon zest
2 medium limes, cut into thin
   wedges

Roll the prosciutto into a shape of
your choice—trumpet, cylinder, or
flower. Mix the dill and lemon zest
and sprinkle over the proscuitto. Serve
with lime wedges.

Makes 24

❧

Oyster Tartar with Sparkling Wine Sauce

*This may be made in advance and be
ready and waiting in the refrigerator.*

24 oysters, shucked, with shells
   reserved

½ cup champagne vinegar
½ cup sparkling white wine
2 teaspoons minced shallot
1 teaspoon minced fresh
   tarragon
   Freshly ground black pepper
4 hard-boiled eggs, peeled with
   yolks and whites separated
   and finely chopped
   Fresh tarragon sprigs, for
   garnish (optional)

Remove the tough muscles from the
oysters and chop into fine dice. Rinse
and refrigerate empty bottom shells.

Blend the vinegar, wine, shallot,
tarragon, and black pepper. Set aside.

Spoon the oysters back into the
shells, dividing as evenly as possible.
Top each with a teaspoon or more of
the sauce. Chill the oysters well and
then serve in shells over crushed ice.
Garnish each with a bit of egg yolk
and white and a sprig of tarragon.

Makes 24

❧

Red Cherry and Yellow Plum Tomato Soup

Janet Trefethen calls this California Sunset Soup. Look at the picture and you will see why.

- 4 **baskets red cherry tomatoes (about 12 cups)**
- 6 **tablespoons chicken stock**
- 2 **teaspoons white wine vinegar**
- 2 **tablespoons olive oil**
  Sugar
  Salt and pepper to taste
- 4 **baskets yellow plum tomatoes (about 12 cups)**
  Crème fraîche, for garnish (optional)

Cut cherry tomatoes in half and toss with 3 tablespoons of the chicken stock, 1 teaspoon of vinegar, 1 tablespoon of oil, pinch of sugar, and salt and pepper. Process in batches until smooth and strain into a large bowl.

Make another portion of soup using the remaining ingredients and the yellow tomatoes.

To serve, take 2 ladles of the same size. Fill each with one color soup, and pour the soups simultaneously into a bowl. Place crème fraîche in a squeeze bottle and make a design on each serving. (See the photograph.)
Serves 6

OPPOSITE ABOVE: **Red Cherry and Yellow Plum Tomato Soup;**
BELOW: **John Trefethen.**
ABOVE: **Prosciutto with Lemon and Dill.**
RIGHT: **Grilled Herb Squabs, Green Beans, and Brown and Wild Rice.**

Grilled Herb Squabs

Slipping herbs under the skin of the squabs gives them a strong and distinctive flavor. Fresh herbs must be used. Incidentally, if you don't like or can't obtain squabs, substitute game hens.

- 3 **cups fresh oregano**
- 2 **tablespoons fresh thyme**
- 2 **medium garlic heads, roasted (page 65)**
- ½ **cup olive oil**
- 6 **plump squabs**

Prepare grill. Place the oregano, thyme, and garlic pulp in a food processor. Process, adding the oil in a thin stream to form a paste. Slip the mixture under the breast skin of the birds. Thread stuffed birds onto a spit.

Grill for 30 to 40 minutes, to an interior temperature of 160 degrees.
Serves 6

Note: These may also be done in an oven by roasting them at 400 degrees until the desired temperature is reached, about 20 minutes. Turn once during the cooking time.

❧

Brown and Wild Rice

This is referred to as Dad's Rice in the Trefethen household, since Mrs. Trefethen's father farms rice in the Sacramento Valley and uses this method of preparation. It is important to use only short-grain brown rice, which is usually available in health food stores if you don't find it in your local market.

1 cup short-grain brown rice, washed and picked over
½ cup wild rice, washed and picked over
4 cups boiling water
1 teaspoon salt
1 tablespoon oil

Place the rices in a heavy saucepan and pour in boiling water. Stir in salt and oil. Bring quickly to a boil, cover tightly, reduce heat to moderate, and cook until liquid is almost absorbed, about 20 minutes. Turn off heat and let stand for an additional 15 minutes.

This reheats very well.

Serves 6

Green Beans

The trick to this is to cook beans until tender but not mushy.

1 pound young green beans, tipped and stemmed
2 tablespoons minced shallots
1 tablespoon unsalted butter
Salt and pepper to taste

Steam the beans until just tender, 5 minutes or more, depending on the age and size of the beans.

Meanwhile, sauté the shallots in the butter. When the beans are done, refresh under cold water just long enough to stop their cooking. Shake dry and add to shallots. Toss, adding salt and pepper.

Serves 6

The flower gardens.

Green Salad with Red Wine Vinaigrette

Use any combination of fresh, tender garden lettuces you like. Do not over-dress the greens.

- 3 to 4 medium to small heads lettuce, washed, dried, and mixed
- 2 tablespoons red wine
- ¼ cup sherry vinegar
- ⅓ cup olive oil
- 2 tablespoons peanut oil
- 1 teaspoon lemon juice
- Pinch of sugar
- Salt and pepper to taste
- 1 large garlic clove

Place the lettuces in a large bowl and refrigerate until ready to serve. Meanwhile, whisk together the wine, vinegar, oils, lemon juice, sugar, salt, and pepper. Mash the garlic slightly and float on top.

Remove the garlic before using the vinaigrette and toss with the greens. Serve with a wedge of the Savory Cheesecake (recipe follows).

Serves 6

Savory Cheesecake

As with the cheese tart served at Mondavi, this would also make a perfect first course, with or without salad. It's delicious either way.

- ¾ cup toasted bread crumbs
- ¾ cup finely chopped toasted walnuts
- 3 tablespoons unsalted butter, melted
- ¾ pound aged Asiago cheese or aged Tomme, grated
- 1¼ pound cream cheese, at room temperature
- 4 eggs
- 1 medium garlic clove, crushed or minced
- ¼ teaspoon dried tarragon, or 1 tablespoon minced fresh
- Salt and pepper to taste

Preheat the oven to 350 degrees.

Place the bread crumbs, walnuts, and butter in a food processor and process until thoroughly combined. Press into the bottom and slightly up the sides of an 8-inch springform pan. Set aside.

Beat the Asiago and cream cheese with a hand mixer until smooth. Add the eggs, one at the time, beating well after each addition. Add the garlic and tarragon and combine well. Add salt and pepper to taste. Pour into the prepared pan and bake for 45 minutes to 1 hour, checking after 45 minutes. Cake should be golden and puffed, not loose in the center. Remove from oven and let stand for 30 minutes before cutting.

Serves 6 to 8

Note: A variation of this is to use mushroom cheese, if it is available.

Boysenberry Pyramids

This gorgeous dessert is remarkably easy to make and can even be partly made a day before.

MASCARPONE CREAM

- ½ **cup crème fraîche**
- 2 ½ **tablespoons mascarpone cheese**
- 1 **tablespoon sugar**

PYRAMIDS

- 7 **cups large fresh boysen-berries**
- ½ **cup sugar**
- 2 **tablespoons Sauternes**
- 3 **sheets phyllo dough**
- 2 **tablespoons butter, melted**
- 1 **tablespoon ground almonds**
- 1 **tablespoon confectioners' sugar**

Make the cream. Whip the crème fraîche into soft peaks and beat in mascarpone and sugar. Refrigerate until ready to use. This can be done the day before. Stir again before using.

Make the pyramids. Place 3 cups of the berries in a saucepan and sprinkle with the sugar and Sauternes. Mix, stirring lightly over medium heat, until the mixture boils and thickens, about

20 minutes. Be careful not to let this scorch. Cool and refrigerate. This keeps well.

Preheat the oven to 350 degrees.

Brush 1 sheet of phyllo with melted butter. Sprinkle with sugar and ground almonds. Put a second sheet on top, butter it and sprinkle with sugar and almonds. Put on the third sheet and sprinkle with confectioners' sugar.

Cut rounds out of stacked phyllo to fit six 4½-inch pie tins. Lay rounds inside and bake for 5 to 7 minutes or until just golden.

When cool, remove rounds to individual plates and spread with mascarpone cream. Dip remaining berries in the thick boysenberry syrup, individually, and mound on top of the cream to form a pyramid.

Serves 6

※

ABOUT THE WINES

Janet Trefethen, whose recipes for this menu evolved over time, has a lively way of viewing the process of combining wines and food—managing to be informative, light-hearted, and knowledgeable all at once.

"Wine and food are natural combinations. It is relatively easy to put the two together with 'everyday' foods. However, when you are preparing a more elaborate menu for a really special event, you want your wines equal to the occasion.

"It is at these unique meals—when

we take more time in the kitchen and more time lingering at the table with friends—that it is wise and enjoyable to give more thought to wine and food marriages. I have one guideline: The wine should enhance the food, and the food should complement the wine. When you find one of those unique 'made-in-heaven' marriages, the two take each other to ethereal heights that neither could achieve on its own.

"In designing this menu, I knew the wines I wanted to serve and at the same time knew what was fresh in my garden.

"The tomato soup is one of my favorites. It captures the essence of wonderful fresh tomatoes. I use tarragon in it, which is a close friend to the Chardonnay. They like each other. The addition of a little crème fraîche brings everything together in harmony to make a sublime combination.

"Squab, chicken, and game birds are wonderful accompaniments to wine because of their versatility. The sauce or the marinade determines what wine to serve with it. In this case, I wanted to feature Pinot Noir, so I used oregano, thyme, and garlic to marry the bird with the wine. Their flavors bring out the best in each other. The rice has a slightly nutty flavor, which helps to accentuate this quality in the wine.

"The savory cheesecake is a wonderful recipe for any wine buff to have in his or her repertoire. The flavors of the dish marry beautifully with almost any full-bodied red wine, both young and old. The cheese softens any tannins and prepares the palate for the wine. Delicious!"

※

Star Turns

❧

GREAT CLIMATE, abundant produce, fabulous wines, relaxed living, and a growing appreciative audience have all conspired to make the Napa and Sonoma Valley a burgeoning center for food enthusiasts.

First came the wineries, then the constantly expanding group of people anxious to visit them and try their wares. The increasingly sophisticated wine palates created by these visits lead to an increasing demand for good food. A match made in heaven.

Chefs attracted by all these goings on, and the cross-pollination among their growing number, have been responsible for the wonderfully varied cuisine springing up in the area. And as individual as all these professionals are, their interaction creates a connecting thread that is starting to tie together this part of the wine country with its own style.

Here is a sampling of what some of these energetic and dedicated people are doing.

In getting this section together, I specifically asked the chefs to keep in mind the limited time and help the average cook has, so all the recipes that follow would easily be within the capability of us non-professionals who don't have lots of people scurrying around making sauce reductions and creating garnishes.

CASSANDRA MITCHELL

THE DINER
6476 Washington Street
Yountville, California 94599
(707) 944-2626

CASSANDRA Mitchell is that *rara avis,* a native Californian. And she was born on Christmas Day to boot.

Over the years the food at The Diner has evolved, but the place has managed to remain what it was meant to be from the very beginning: "We are a diner, our culture's archetypal local hangout. We do it as well as we can."

Whole Corn Cakes

These tasty cakes may be made as they are here or, if you want to give them a little extra zip, add 2 teaspoons minced or pressed garlic and ¹/₂ cup crumbled feta or Asiago cheese to the batter.

For breakfast serve them with butter, maple syrup, and sausage (and eggs). For a savory lunch or appetizer, serve them with Corn and Avocado Salsa and crème fraîche. For dinner, serve them with Mexican Pork Stew.

1 ¹/₃   **cups yellow or blue cornmeal (medium stone-ground, if possible)**
  ¹/₂   **teaspoon salt**
  ¹/₂   **teaspoon baking soda**
  ¹/₄   **cup all-purpose flour**
  2   **eggs**
  ¹/₃   **cup corn oil**
1 ¹/₂   **cups buttermilk**
1 ¹/₂   **cups grated zucchini or any other summer squash**
  1   **cup corn kernels, drained (fresh, frozen, or canned)**

Sift together the cornmeal, salt, baking soda, and flour. In a separate bowl, mix the eggs, corn oil, and buttermilk until smooth. Add the grated squash and corn, then stir in the sifted ingredients. Blend until smooth.

Cook 3-inch cakes until golden brown on a hot, lightly oiled griddle or heavy skillet.

Serves 4 to 6

Corn and Avocado Salsa

1 medium white onion, cut into ⅛-inch dice
1 tablespoon minced garlic
¼ cup rice vinegar
Juice and grated rind of 1 medium lime
2 tablespoons coarsely chopped cilantro
2 tablespoons finely diced red bell pepper
1 medium jalapeño pepper, stemmed, seeded, and finely minced
1 cup corn kernels
1 medium to large ripe avocado, peeled, pitted, and cut into ½-inch cubes

Place all ingredients except avocado in a glass bowl and toss well. Add avocado and toss, being careful not to mash avocado pieces.

Makes 2 cups plus

Homemade Sausage

This is a basic recipe that makes about 6 patties. If you are going to the trouble of making sausage, consider doubling the recipe at least. Ms. Mitchell tells me the sausage meat freezes well.

1 pound boneles pork shoulder, coarsely ground
1 ¼ teaspoons salt
1 ½ teaspoons rubbed sage
½ teaspoon coarsely ground black pepper
¼ teaspoon ground cloves
¼ teaspoon grated nutmeg
⅛ teaspoon ground allspice
2 teaspoons brown sugar
½ to 1 teaspoon crushed dried red chile (use more or less, depending on how hot you like your sausage)

Place the pork in a ceramic bowl and sprinkle the remaining ingredients over it. Combine well with your hands. Cover tightly and allow to mature in the refrigerator—for several days if possible.

To cook, form sausage meat into 3-inch patties that are ½ inch thick, and fry on a hot, very lightly oiled griddle until they are dark golden brown on both sides, about 2 to 3 minutes per side.

Makes 4 to 6 patties

LEFT: **Whole Corn Cakes, Mexican Pork Stew, and Corn and Avocado Salsa.**
ABOVE: **Whole Corn Cakes, and Homemade Sausage.**

Mexican Pork Stew

Pork stew is good served with brown rice if you don't want to serve it with the corn cakes.

- 1 **pound fresh tomatillos, husked and washed (or 3 cups drained canned tomatillos)**
- ¼ **cup corn oil**
- 1 **large white onion, diced**
- 1 **tablespoon thinly sliced garlic**
- 2 **medium jalapeño peppers, stemmed, seeded, and minced**
- 2 **tablespoons minced cilantro**
- ¾ **cup coarsely chopped and loosely packed romaine**
- 2 **cups chicken stock**
- 3 **pounds boneless pork butt, well trimmed and cut into 1-inch cubes**
- ½ **teaspoon dried oregano**
  Flour for dredging
  Salt to taste

Poach fresh tomatillos in hot water until tender, about 10 minutes. Drain and set aside.

Place 2 tablespoons of the oil in a large heavy saucepan over medium heat and cook the onion, garlic, and jalapeño pepper until limp and golden, about 10 minutes. Add the cilantro, romaine (which adds color but not much flavor), and stock. Heat to a boil, 3 to 5 minutes. Pour into a food processor and puree. Add the tomatillos and process until smooth. Pour out into a bowl and set aside.

Place the pork cubes in a single layer on a sheet and sprinkle with the oregano. Sprinkle with flour and roll cubes around to coat completely.

Place the remaining 2 tablespoons of oil in the same skillet in which you cooked the vegetables and brown the pork cubes in a single layer over high heat. When pork is browned, add tomatillo sauce, scraping the bottom of the pan to incorporate any brown bits. Bring quickly to a boil, then turn back to a simmer. Cook for 45 minutes to 1 hour, until meat is tender. Add more stock if sauce becomes too thick. Stir occasionally. Correct seasoning with salt if necessary.

Serves 8

MARK MALICKI

TRUFFLES RESTAURANT & BAR
234 South Main Street
Sebastopol, California 95472
(707) 823-8448

MARK MALICKI takes yearly trips to Thailand with his wife to study Thai cuisine and consistently has a four-course Thai dinner on the restaurant menu. He's very interested in the local Sonoma County farmers' produce, using exotic mushrooms farmed by partner Bryan Lau, and organic produce whenever possible. He also works in conjunction with the American Heart Association to prepare food for the health conscious.

In addition, Mark created the imaginative dishes for the croquet lunch at Sonoma-Cutrer, pages 69 to 71.

Mushroom, Fennel, and Artichoke Ragout

- 3 **tablespoons olive oil**
- 3 **large shallots, thinly sliced**
- 3 **medium garlic cloves, thinly sliced**
- 1 **medium carrot, scraped and chopped fine**
- 3 **tablespoons unsalted butter**
- ½ **pound fresh porcini mushrooms, cut into 1-inch cubes**
- ½ **pound matsutage mushrooms, thinly sliced**
- ½ **pound chantarelle mushrooms, thickly sliced**

- ½ **pound shiitake mushrooms, thickly sliced**
- 1 **small fennel bulb, trimmed, sliced, and blanched for 5 minutes in salted water**
- 3 **large cooked and trimmed artichoke hearts, cut into quarters**
- ½ **teaspoon fennel seeds, toasted about 30 seconds in a dry skillet over medium heat, shaking all the while**
- ½ **teaspoon minced fresh thyme**
  Salt and pepper to taste

Place oil in a 12-inch skillet and, over low heat, cook shallots, garlic, and carrot until tender but not browned, about 7 minutes. Add the butter and turn heat to high. When butter is melted, add the mushrooms, fennel, and artichokes. Toss and cook until mushrooms give up their liquid and liquid has evaporated and mushrooms are tender. This will take only a few minutes over high heat. Be sure to keep tossing lightly and shaking pan. When almost done, sprinkle fennel seeds and thyme over all, tossing. Correct seasoning.

Serves 6 to 8 as a first course

Happy Pancakes and Prawns with Cucumber Sauce

1 ¾ cups rice flour
2 cups water
Pinch of saffron threads
3 tablespoons minced cilantro
3 tablespoons minced scallions
1 cup finely minced cooked shrimp
3 tablespoons peanut oil plus extra for frying
6 tablespoons minced shallot
6 tablespoons minced garlic
1 cup bean sprouts
½ cup finely diced fresh water chestnuts or jicama
3 large prawns, cut in half lengthwise and grilled, for garnish
Cucumber Sauce (recipe follows)

Whisk together the rice flour, water, and saffron. Mix in the cilantro, scallions, and shrimp thoroughly. Set aside for and hour.

Place 3 tablespoons of peanut oil in a 9-inch non-stick skillet and heat over medium heat. Add 1 tablespoon of the shallots and 1 tablespoon of the garlic, stir and add ½ cup of the reserved batter. Cook until edges begin to curl and crisp, shaking continuously, about 7 or 8 minutes.

Turn out onto a warmed plate and sprinkle 2 generous tablespoons of bean sprouts and 1 generous tablespoon of water chestnuts on half the pancake. Fold over and transfer to a warmed plate.

There should be a bit of oil left in the skillet; if not, add 1 tablespoon and make 5 more pancakes, adding oil when necessary.

Garnish pancakes with half a prawn, and top with Cucumber Sauce.

Serves 6 as a first course

CUCUMBER SAUCE

In the photograph the pancake is topped with a curry sauce, which is simple to make if you have the ingredients handy, but since this is not likely in most kitchens, I asked Mark to give me an alternative; the recipe below can be made in advance.

3 tablespoons white wine vinegar
1 tablespoon sugar
½ cup water
1 medium serrano chile, seeded and very thinly sliced
1 long seedless cucumber, sliced very thin, or 2 regular cucumbers, peeled, seeded, and very thinly sliced

Combine vinegar and sugar in a small saucepan and stir over low heat until sugar dissolves, 1 or 2 minutes. Stir in water, chile, and cucumber off the heat and set aside to cool.

Makes about 1 cup

꒜

HIRO SONE

TERRA
1345 Railroad Avenue
St. Helena, California 94574
(707) 963-8931

IN THE very short time since it opened, Terra has made its mark in an area increasingly known for its concentration of widely acclaimed restaurants. Mr. Sone and his wife, Lissa Doumani, also a chef, are its owners.

Hiro's interest in today's evolving cooking directions has led him to experiment constantly and refine his food, to the delight of his restaurant's ever-increasing sophisticated clientele.

LEFT: **Happy Pancakes and Prawns with Cucumber Sauce.**
OPPOSITE: **Mushroom, Fennel, and Artichoke Ragout.**

Tomato and Bread Salad

I think Hiro's is, hands down, the best version of this Italian classic I know of. Try it. Incidentally, when I make this I make a double batch of the crunchy croutons and freeze them (toasted).

- ½ small baguette (about 12 inches in length)
- 1 large garlic clove, mashed
  Olive oil
- 6 medium to large tomatoes, cut into large chunks
- ½ medium onion, chopped (10 to 12 tablespoons)
- 3 tablespoons coarsely chopped fresh basil
- ¼ cup balsamic vinegar
- ½ cup olive oil

Preheat the oven to 300 degrees.

Split the baguette in half lengthwise. Rub one half very well with the mashed garlic on the cut side. Brush liberally with olive oil. Cut the garlicked half in half again lengthwise and then cut these strips into ¾-inch pieces. Place croutons on a cookie sheet, crust side down. Bake until dark golden, about 30 minutes or more.

If croutons are made in advance, place tomatoes in a large mixing bowl a bit before you intend to mix salad, then drain and discard any juice that may have accumulated in the bottom of the bowl.

To serve, add the croutons, onions, and basil to the tomatoes. Whisk together the vinegar and oil for the vinaigrette. Pour over salad and toss.

Serves 6

Smoked Bacon and Wild Mushrooms in Puff Pastry

Vol au vent is a large flaky pastry shell with a top. You can make them yourself (which I never do) or buy packages of individual ones frozen. (Pepperidge Farm is the brand available most places.)

This is often served as a first course in the restaurant, but it would also make a fine luncheon dish with just a salad and a fruit dessert.

- 6 individual frozen pastry shells
- 1 egg, beaten
- 1 tablespoon unsalted butter
- 5½ ounces smoked bacon strips (about 6 strips), cut into ½-inch pieces
- 12 ounces mixed fresh wild mushrooms (chanterelle, shiitake, oyster, etc.), carefully cleaned and chopped into large pieces
- ½ teaspoon chopped fresh thyme
- ½ teaspoon chopped garlic
  Salt and pepper to taste
- 3 cups heavy cream
- 1 cup chicken or veal stock, reduced to ⅓ cup
  Thyme, for garnish

Preheat the oven to 400 degrees. Place frozen pastries on a baking sheet according to package directions. Mix beaten egg with 1 tablespoon of water and brush on pastries. Bake according to package directions. When golden, remove to a warm spot.

Melt the butter in a large skillet and add the bacon. Sauté over medium to low heat until just transparent, several minutes. Add the mushrooms, thyme, garlic, salt, and pepper. Turn heat up slightly and continue to sauté until mushrooms begin to brown slightly, 3 or more minutes. Add cream and stock. Reduce by half, 10 or more minutes.

Taste and adjust the seasoning if necessary. Cut the tops from the pastry shells and reheat the bottoms in a 400 degree oven for a few minutes. Place

bottoms on individual plates and fill with the mushroom mixture. Return tops to filled shells and garnish each with a sprig of thyme.

Serves 6

❧

OPPOSITE: **Tomato and Bread Salad.** BELOW: **Smoked Bacon and Wild Mushrooms in Puff Pastry.** BELOW RIGHT: **Smoked Salmon and Spinach Risotto.**

DONNA SCALA

RISTORANTE PIATTI
6480 Washington Street
Yountville, California 94599
(707) 944-2070

W HEN Virginia-born Donna Scala moved to Texas as a very young woman, she was intrigued by the local techniques used in grilling, barbecuing, and roasting. As a matter of fact, these methods so interested her that she began to experiment with the first of her many signature dishes based on these techniques.

Then she married Giovanni Scala, and together they joined forces with Ristorante Piatti where she is now the executive chef. Giovanni's Italian influence on her food was a perfect match, and many of the restaurant's most successful dishes are the result of their collaboration.

Smoked Salmon and Spinach Risotto

A mouth-watering blend of ingredients!

- 2 tablespoons unsalted butter
- ¼ medium onion, chopped
- 1 pound Arborio or Carnaroli rice
- 1 cup dry white wine
- 2 ¾ cups chicken stock
- 1 bunch spinach, large stems removed and julienned to ⅛-inch wide
- ¼ cup minced fresh chives
- 6 ounces smoked salmon
- ¾ cup (6 ounces) mascarpone cheese
  Salt and pepper to taste
- 2 ounces tobiko (Japanese flying fish roe) or golden caviar

Heat half the butter over medium heat in a heavy bottomed 6-quart pot. Add the onion and cook until wilted but not brown, about 3 minutes. Add the rice and stir well for 30 seconds. Add the wine and stir. Add 1 cup of the stock, turn up heat, and bring to a boil. Turn heat immediately back to a simmer, stirring with a wooden spoon every minute or so. When rice becomes dry, add another cup of stock. Rice should be covered with a "veil" of stock during cooking. Repeat until all stock is added, about 13 minutes. Add the spinach, half the chives, and the salmon. Mix and cook for another 3 to 4 minutes, stirring constantly so that the rice doesn't stick. Remove from heat and stir in cheese and remaining butter. Season with salt and pepper.

Transfer risotto to individual warmed plates and sprinkle with tobiko or caviar and remaining chives. Serve immediately.

Serves 4 as an entree or 8 as an appetizer

Smoked Salmon and Tobiko Caviar Pizza

Here are the same ingredients, except for the spinach, in another incarnation—and just as mouthwatering.

PIZZA DOUGH

- 1 ¾ cups all-purpose flour
- ⅔ ounce fresh yeast or 1 package dry active yeast
- 1 ½ teaspoons salt
- ⅔ cup warm water (100°F)
- 2 tablespoons olive oil

FILLING

- 1 ½ cups (12 ounces) mascarpone cheese
- ¼ cup chopped fresh chives
- 4 medium shallots, minced
- 2 tablespoons fresh lemon juice
  Salt and pepper to taste

TOPPING

- 6 ounces smoked salmon, cut into ⅛-inch-wide strips
- 2 ounces tobiko or golden caviar

Make the dough. If you are using a mixer, put flour in mixing bowl. Dissolve yeast and salt in the water and let stand for a few minutes. Using a dough hook, combine yeast mixture with the flour at low speed. Add olive oil and continue mixing. When ingredients are well mixed, raise speed to medium and continue mixing for 3 minutes. Switch speed back to slow and finish kneading for another 3 minutes. Turn out onto a floured surface and cover with a damp towel. Let dough rise for 1 hour, then cut into 3 equal pieces. Form into balls with your hands by kneading with a short circular motion. Dough balls should have a smooth and somewhat tense surface. Put dough balls in separate large plastic bags and seal. Refrigerate. For best results, let dough rise the second time in the bags, refrigerated overnight.

If you are mixing the dough by hand, pour the flour out onto a table and form a well in the middle. Add yeast mixture and olive oil. Start pinching the dough together. Knead dough for 6 to 7 minutes, then treat as above.

Make the filling. Mix ingredients together thoroughly, leaving out 1 tablespoon chives for garnish, and set aside at room temperature. Do not overstir or whip the mascarpone or it will break.

Bake the pizzas. Preheat the oven to 500 degrees. If you have a baking stone, the results will be better. Take dough from the refrigerator and let it sit at room temperature for a few minutes. Soften the dough by hand and dip it in flour. Shake off excess. Dust your work surface (which should be smooth; formica will do if you don't have a marble slab) with flour. Roll the dough out with a rolling pin using a light touch, especially as you come to the edge. Start in the middle and roll away from yourself in one motion; do not go back and forth. For each roll, turn dough a quarter turn. Roll the dough out until it is about 7 inches in diameter. Dust the dough and work surface with flour again. Place your hands on top of the dough, side by side with the edges of your hands ½ inch inside the rim. Stretch the dough gently using an outward circular motion, turning the dough about a 1/16th of a turn each time. This will keep your pizza round. Stretch the dough until it is about 10 inches in diameter. The pizza should have a thin middle and the edges should be about 1/8 inch thick.

Place pizza on a pizza paddle or a lightly floured piece of cardboard. If you have cornmeal or semolina flour, sprinkle it on the card so pizza will slide off easier, but plain flour works, too. Spread a thin layer of the filling on the pizzas, leaving about 3/4 inch of rim. Slide pizza onto the baking stone or a heavy baking sheet and bake until dough is golden brown, 8 to 10 minutes. Take pizza out with the pizza paddle or a piece of cardboard and slide it onto a plate.

Add topping. Arrange smoked salmon strips on top of pizzas and sprinkle with caviar and remaining chives. Brush edges with olive oil and cut each pizza into 8 pieces. Serve immediately.

Makes 3 pizzas

❧

CHARLES SAUNDERS

SONOMA MISSION INN & SPA
18140 Sonoma Highway 12
Boyes Hot Springs, California 95416
(707) 938-9000

CHARLES Saunders's current duties give him ample opportunity to stretch his talents in the Inn's two dining facilities: The Grill, which offers both wine country cuisine and the establishment's renowned low-calorie cuisine, and the Big Three Cafe, which specializes in regional Italian cuisine.

Charles also created the luscious menu and recipes for Buena Vista's Balloon Ride Breakfast, pages 49 to 53.

Dungeness Crabcakes with Jalapeño-Lime Mayonnaise

Saunders's own delicious take on the classic crabcakes.

    1/4 cup peanut oil
    1/4 cup (1/2 stick) unsalted
         butter
    1   cup finely diced white onions
    1   cup finely diced celery
    1   pound fresh crabmeat
    1   egg, lightly beaten
  1 1/2 tablespoons Dijon-style
         mustard
    1   tablespoon roughly chopped
         fresh parsley
    1   tablespoon finely chopped
         fresh thyme
         Salt, black pepper, and
         cayenne pepper to taste
    3/4 pound fresh, fine white bread
         crumbs
         Jalapeño-Lime Mayonnaise
         (recipe follows)

Heat half the oil and butter in a small skillet and cook onion and celery over medium heat until tender, about 5 minutes. Place in a food processor and pulse a few times to make mixture finer. Put crabmeat in a mixing bowl and pick over carefully. Scrape in sautéed vegetables. Mix lightly and add egg and mustard. Mix again very lightly and add parlsey, thyme, salt, pepper, cayenne, and half the bread crumbs. Toss but do not overmix. Form into 12 small cakes, handling as little as possible, and roll in the remaining bread crumbs.

Preheat the oven to 350 degrees. Heat a few tablespoons each of butter and oil (more oil than butter) in a large cast-iron skillet over medium heat. Lightly brown crabcakes on each side, 2 to 3 minutes, turning once. Place in the oven for about 3 minutes to finish cooking. Serve with Jalapeño-Lime Mayonnaise.

Serves 12 as an appetizer and 6 as an entrée

JALAPEÑO-LIME MAYONNAISE

    6   saffron threads
    1/2 cup dry white wine
    3   egg yolks
    3   tablespoons fresh lime juice
         (about 1 medium lime)
    1/2 teaspoon Dijon-style
         mustard
    1   teaspoon seeded and minced
         jalapeño pepper
    2   cups peanut oil
         Salt, black pepper, and
         cayenne pepper to taste

Combine the saffron and wine in a very small saucepan and simmer over medium-low heat until reduced to about 1 tablespoon, 8 to 10 minutes. Strain, reserving the wine, and set aside to cool.

Place yolks, lime juice, mustard, and jalapeño pepper in a small bowl and whisk in the oil in a steady stream until mixture makes a thick mayonnaise. You can also do this in a food processor. Adjust seasoning and stir in the reduced wine.

Makes 2 1/2 cups

❧

OPPOSITE: **Smoked Salmon and Tobiko Caviar Pizza.** LEFT: **Dungeness Crabcakes with Jalapeño-Lime Mayonnaise.**

Sautéed Medallions of Antelope with Tomato Wine Sauce and Fresh Gingered Peach Chutney

You should really try antelope; it has a wonderful flavor and is lower in calories than chicken. It can be bought through the Texas Wild Game Cooperative listed on page 173 or you could get your butcher to order it for you.

¼ cup olive oil
  Salt and pepper to taste
12 antelope medallions, 3 ounces each
  Tomato Wine Sauce (recipe follows)
  Fresh Gingered Peach Chutney (recipe follows)

Place olive oil in a large cast-iron skillet or on a cast iron grill. Heat to very hot. Meanwhile, salt and heavily pepper the antelope medallions. When pan is hot, sear meat, for about 1 minute or slightly more per side for medium rare. (For more well done, transfer meat to a preheated 350 degree oven until degree of doneness is reached.)

Serve with Tomato Wine Sauce and Fresh Gingered Peach Chutney.
Serves 6

TOMATO WINE SAUCE

2 tablespoons olive oil
1 pound antelope trimmings
¼ cup coarsely chopped leek
¼ cup coarsely chopped onion
¼ cup coarsely chopped celery
¼ cup coarsely chopped carrot
2 tablespoons minced garlic
1 cup peeled, seeded, and chopped tomato
1 cup dry red wine
1 quart chicken or veal stock
10 fresh sage leaves
½ teaspoon coarsely ground black pepper

Place the olive oil in a deep saucepan and cook antelope over medium heat until lightly browned, about 10 minutes. Add all the vegetables except the tomato and cook until caramelized, 10 to 15 minutes. Add the tomato and deglaze pan with the wine. Add stock and cook over medium to high heat until reduced by half, about 15 minutes.

Add sage and pepper. Simmer for about 1 hour, skimming. Correct seasoning if necessary.
Makes about 3 cups

FRESH GINGERED PEACH CHUTNEY

1 tablespoon roughly chopped fresh ginger
2 ¼ cups unfiltered apple juice
¼ cup apple cider vinegar
¼ teaspoon ground cardamom
¼ cup molasses
6 ounces halved kumquats
10 ounces peaches, peeled, pitted, and thickly sliced
3 ounces medium shallots
1 tablespoon drained green peppercorns
  Salt and pepper to taste
2 tablespoons sliced almonds, toasted (optional)

Combine the ginger, apple juice, vinegar, cardamom, and molasses in a medium saucepan. Bring quickly to a boil and turn back to a simmer. Poach kumquats, peaches, and shallots individually in the syrup about 1 minute. Remove with a slotted spoon. Add the green peppercorns and adjust seasoning if necessary. Reduce liquids over medium heat until it is the consistency of maple syrup, about 10 minutes. Cool. Toss poached ingredients and almonds together and pour syrup over all. Toss again and set aside.

Makes about 3 cups

MICHAEL CHIARELLO

T R A   V I G N E

1050 Charter Oak Avenue
St. Helena, California 94574
(707) 963-4444

Michael Chiarello grew up in a large Italian family whose group activity centered around the growing, cooking, and preserving of good, simple food. He really started his career early—at 14, when he began working in restaurants, but he keeps up with family tradition. In additon to his regular duties, Michael, with his large and seemingly tireless crew, also produces prosciutto, braciola, salami, cured olives, and olive oil.

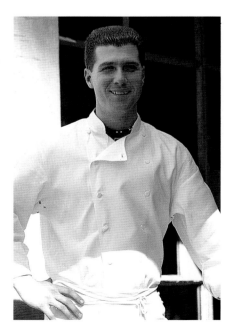

Grilled Radicchio

This delicious first course is a bit time consuming but at least parts of it, such as the sauce reduction and mixing the poaching liquid, can be done ahead of time.

- 2 **cups red Zinfandel wine**
- 6 **medium to large shallots, minced**
- 3 **cups chicken stock**
- 3 **cups veal stock**
- 2 **bay leaves**
- 2 **sprigs fresh thyme**
- 1 **quart water**
- 1 **cup champagne vinegar**
- 1 **cup dry white wine**
- ¼ **cup lemon juice**
- 2 **medium heads radicchio, quartered**
  Olive oil
  Salt and pepper to taste
- 2 **tablespoons black olive paste (see Note)**
- 10 **medium basil leaves**
- 3 **tablespoons chilled unsalted butter, cut into bits**
  Coarsely chopped fresh Italian parsley for garnish

Place red wine and shallots in a large saucepan and reduce over medium high heat to approximately 1⅓ cups, 10 to 15 minutes. Add the stocks, bay leaves, and thyme and reduce to about 3½ cups, 20 minutes or more. Strain and set aside.

Combine the water, vinegar, white wine, and lemon juice and bring to a boil. Turn back to a simmer and drop radicchio quarters in to poach for 1 minute, being sure they are submerged all the while. Carefully remove radicchio and place in a bowl of ice water to stop cooking. Drain. Brush radicchio lightly with olive oil, sprinkle with salt and pepper, and grill (or broil) lightly until hot and marked by the grill. Set aside covered lightly.

Bring sauce to a boil and add olive paste and basil. When slightly viscous, about 5 minutes, stir in butter.

Serve radicchio on top of a pool of sauce and sprinkled with parsley.

Serves 8

Note: Olive paste is available a specialty food stores or Italian markets.

OPPOSITE: **Sautéed Medallions of Antelope with Tomato Wine Sauce and Fresh Gingered Peach Chutney.**
TOP: **Grilled Radicchio.**

Pizzettas with Herb-Roasted Garlic

This is for all the garlic lovers. If garlic is not for you, then this pizza isn't, either. Incidentally, you can compare this pizza dough recipe with the one that Donna Scala of Ristorante Piatti uses and make the one you are most comfortable with.

1 tablespoon olive oil
2 teaspoons salt
1 egg
1 cup warm water
(110° to 115°F)
3 ½ cups bread flour
Olive oil
Fresh rosemary leaves
Grated Parmesan cheese
3 garlic cloves, minced
3 Herb-Roasted Garlic bulbs
(recipe follows)

Combine the oil, salt, egg, and warm water in a warm mixing bowl. Crumble in yeast and stir to dissolve or mix with dough hook for 30 seconds. Add flour and mix until dough comes away from the bottom of the bowl. Dough should be slightly moist. Turn out onto a lightly floured surface. Knead 1 minute. Let rise until doubled in bulk, about 45 to 60 minutes. Punch down and cut into 3 equal pieces. Roll each dough into a ball. Brush lightly with olive oil and let rise until doubled in size, another 45 to 60 minutes.

When ready to bake, preheat the oven to 500 degrees. Knead the dough from the center outward, pressing with thumb and forefinger and rotating the dough in your hand to make a 6-inch flat, uniformly thick circle. Brush dough with olive oil and sprinkle with rosemary leaves and Parmesan cheese, using about 1 tablespoon of rosemary leaves, 1 clove garlic, and 1 tablespoon grated cheese for each pizzetta. Bake 5 minutes, then place a roasted garlic bulb in the center of each pizzetta. Continue to bake until golden brown, about 5 minutes more. When cool enough to handle, pick up garlic bulbs and squeeze pulp and juice out onto the pizzettas. Serve at once.

Makes 3 pizzettas

HERB-ROASTED GARLIC

3 bulbs (heads) red garlic
1 cup olive oil
1 ½ teaspoons minced fresh thyme
1 tablespoon minced fresh rosemary
Salt and white pepper

Preheat the oven to 350 degrees.

Cut tops off garlic bulbs to expose cloves. Brush generously with olive oil and place in a small-lipped pan with remaining olive oil. Sprinkle with the thyme, rosemary, salt, and pepper. Roast for 1 hour, covered, until garlic within cloves is tender and spreadable.

⟋

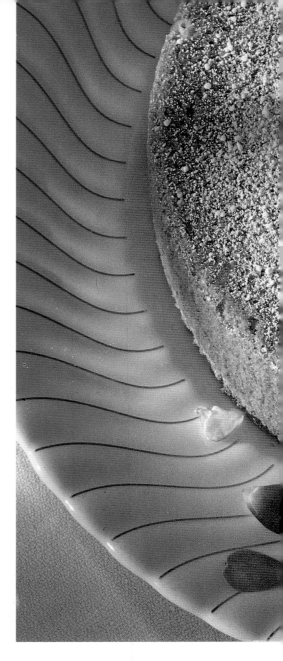

ABOVE: **California Nut Torte.**
BELOW: **Pizzettas with Herb-Roasted Garlic.**

JOHN ASH

JOHN ASH & CO
4330 Barnes Road
Santa Rosa, California 95403
(707) 527-7687

EARLY YEARS spent with his grandparents on a California ranch gave John Ash a keen awareness of nature's beauty—and of good food, which he carried with him through a series of jobs and finally to John Ash & Co. located in Santa Rosa, which he opened in 1987. All you have do is look at the pictures of how his food is presented to know he started out to be an artist—which, of course, he still is.

California Nut Torte

I've got to say this about one of the best nut cakes I've ever had, and I'm a nut cake nut.

CRUST

½ cup medium-ground hazel nuts

½ cup medium-ground toasted almonds

3 ½ tablespoons pastry flour

2 ½ tablespoons granulated sugar

⅓ cup unsalted butter, cut into bits

FILLING

1 cup plus 2 ½ tablespoons light brown sugar, packed

2 whole eggs plus 1 egg yolk

½ teaspoon baking powder

1 ¾ cups coarsely chopped walnuts

1 cup shredded, sweetened coconut

½ cup all-purpose flour

Confectioners' sugar, for dusting (optional)

Crème Anglaise (page 17) or whipped cream

Preheat the oven to 350 degrees.

Make the crust. Mix the hazelnuts, almonds, flour, sugar, and butter with a paddle in a mixer until just combined but slightly crumbly. Press into a 2-inch-deep 8-inch-round cake pan, going about one-third up the side of the pan.

Make the filling. Place the brown sugar, egg and egg yolk, and baking powder in a mixer with a paddle and blend. Mix in remaining ingredients and pour into prepared crust. Bake 50 minutes, until golden but soft and caramelly in the middle. Allow to cool and set in the pan for about 15 minutes before inverting onto the serving plate.

Dust with confectioners' sugar if desired and serve with Crème Anglaise or whipped cream.

Serves 8 to 10

Pork Loin Marinated to Taste like Wild Boar and Roasted with a Mustard Coating

Ash tells me this is especially good served at room temperature or cold as part of a picnic.

ROAST AND MARINADE

- 2 tablespoons olive oil
- 3 medium carrots, roughly chopped
- 1 large onion, roughly chopped
- 2 large shallots, chopped
- 3 medium garlic cloves, minced
- 5 cups hearty red wine
- ½ cup good red vinegar
- 4 medium bay leaves
- 6 parsley stalks, roughly chopped
- 16 juniper berries
- 2 teaspoons salt
- 12 black peppercorns
- 5- to 6-pound boneless, center-cut loin of pork with fat removed to ¼ inch of the meat

MUSTARD COATING

- 3 large garlic cloves, roughly chopped
- ⅓ cup coarsely chopped scallions
- ¼ cup dry white wine
- ½ teaspoon dried sage
- ½ teaspoon dried thyme
- 1 cup Dijon-style mustard
- ¼ cup olive or light salad oil
- 1 teaspoon salt
- ½ teaspoon freshly ground black pepper
- 2 tablespoons olive oil

Make the marinade. Heat the oil over medium heat and cook vegetables until lightly browned, 3 to 4 minutes. Add the wine, vinegar, and seasonings, then bring to a boil. Simmer for 10 minutes and allow to cool. Place meat in a ceramic bowl and cover with the marinade. Refrigerate for 2 to 3 days, turning once or twice.

Make the coating. In a food processor, quickly process the garlic, scallions, wine, and herbs until smooth. Add remaining ingredients and process just until combined. Mixture should be very thick.

To roast, preheat the oven to 400 degrees. Remove the meat from the marinade. Pat dry. Heat olive oil in a large skillet over medium to high heat and lightly brown pork on all sides, about 5 minutes or more. If you don't have a skillet large enough to do this, cut meat into 2 equal pieces. Place roast on a rack in a baking pan and coat well with mustard mixture. Bake until just done, about 30 minutes, until juicy and slightly pink, with an internal temperature of 160 degrees. Allow to rest 5 minutes before serving.

Serves 12 or more

AARON BOWMAN

LA PLACITA RESTAURANT
1304 Main Street
St. Helena, California 94574
(707) 963-8082

I SUPPOSE on the face of it, there would seem to be a long stretch from an Amish family background to a stylish California-Mexican restaurant, but chef Aaron Bowman, who traveled extensively in Europe, the Middle East, and Asia as a young adult, has managed to marry his family's food traditions based on abundance, freshness, and generosity to the culinary experience he gleaned during his travels—in the process creating a distinctive cuisine that apparently can be comfortable with many ethnic foundations.

RIGHT: **Pork Loin Marinated to Taste like Wild Boar and Roasted with a Mustard Coating.** OPPOSITE LEFT: **Caramel-Coated Tortillas;** RIGHT: **Cheese and Herb-Stuffed Pasilla Chiles,** garnished with avocado and purple basil.

Caramel-Coated Tortillas

A surprising, crunchy treat. Aaron gives a recipe for flour tortillas, but I suspect most of you would use the store-bought kind for this—as I do.

FLOUR TORTILLAS

- 3 tomatillo husks (optional)
- 1¼ cups water
- 1½ cups all-purpose flour
- ½ teaspoon baking powder (optional)
- 2 tablespoons corn oil

ASSEMBLY

- 1 cup plus 6 tablespoons corn oil
- 1 pound *pilonsillo* (see Note) or light brown sugar
- ½ cup water
- Ground cinnamon to taste

Make the tortillas. There are two ways to do this. First is to cover the husks with 1¼ cups of the water and bring to a boil. Simmer for about 5 minutes until you have only ¾ cup water. Allow to cool and discard husks. Use this water with the flour and eliminate the baking powder since the husks take its place, and follow the balance of the recipe. If you use baking powder, simply place flour and baking powder in a bowl and mix.

Stir ¾ cup water and the oil into the flour. Mix rapidly to make a soft elastic dough. Do not overmix.

Break off walnut-size pieces of dough and roll them out into approximately 10-inch circles. Stack tortillas with wax paper in between.

Assemble. Heat oil in a large skillet and fry tortillas—homemade or store-bought—over medium-high heat until golden on each side, about 30 seconds. Drain on paper towels.

Combine *pilonsillo* or brown sugar with the water. Simmer a few minutes at low heat, then dip each tortilla in the mixture to coat. Sprinkle with cinnamon to taste, then cool on wax paper. These will crisp as they cool.

Makes several dozen

Note: *Pilonsillo* is a type of raw brown sugar found in Latin markets.

❧

Cheese and Herb-Stuffed Pasilla Chiles

The basic work on these may be done in advance so I think they would make a terrific lunch dish—all you need is sliced avocados and salsa.

CHILES

- 6 to 8 large pasilla chiles (see Note)
- 4 medium garlic cloves, minced
- 3 tablespoons minced scallions or shallots
- 3 medium pieces oil-packed sun-dried tomatoes, minced
- ½ cup loosely packed cilantro, finely chopped
- ¼ cup tightly packed fresh basil, minced
- ½ cup mild dry goat cheese, crumbled
- 1 cup grated soft Monterey Jack cheese
- ½ teaspoon dried thyme
- ½ teaspoon dried dill
- Salt and pepper to taste

ASSEMBLY

- 1 egg
- 2 to 3 tablespoons heavy cream
- 1 cup blue cornmeal (yellow can be substituted)
- 2 or 3 tablespoons peanut oil

Roast and peel chiles as you would bell peppers (page 104). Leave stem on and after they are peeled, carefully slit the chiles starting at the stem to about halfway down their length. Lift out seeds and discard. Set aside.

Combine all the other ingredients, mixing well. Gently place enough cheese mixture into each chile to fill the cavity without overstuffing. Close by overlapping the seams. Put stuffed chiles on a tray and refrigerate, covered, until needed.

Remove chiles from refrigerator at least 30 minutes before continuing with the recipe.

Assemble. Lightly beat together the egg and cream. Spread the cornmeal on a sheet of wax paper. Dip each chile in the cream mixture, letting excess run off; dredge in cornmeal, lightly shaking off excess. Place coated chiles on a plate or a sheet of wax paper next to the stove as you finish them.

Heat the peanut oil in a large skillet and gently sauté chiles until golden brown on all sides and cheese mixture has softened and warmed. This will take several minutes, depending on how hot the heat is. Don't cook these too fast or they will burn before the stuffing is heated through. Serve at once.

Serves 6 to 8

Note: Pasilla chiles can be found in specialty markets or Latin markets.

DIANE PARISEAU

T R I L O G Y
1234 Main Street
St. Helena, California 94574
(707) 963-5507

JUST around the corner from Hiro Sone's Terra is another comparative newcomer to the local restaurant scene in Napa. Owned and operated by the husband and wife team of Diane and Don Pariseau with partner Tim Masher, it has quickly established itself as a trend and pacesetter.

Diane is the chef and culinary inspiration for the very elegant dishes that have made Trilogy one of the several must-visit places to dine when touring the wine country.

Scallop Seviche

Quick and simple and delicious.

1 ½ pounds sea scallops (3 to 4 ounces per serving)
Juice of 4 limes
¼ cup finely diced red onion
4 medium tomatoes, peeled, seeded, and diced small
2 tablespoons finely chopped cilantro
6 tablespoons olive oil
Freshly ground black pepper to taste
6 sprigs cilantro, for garnish

Remove the small muscle from the side of each scallop and discard. Marinate the scallops in the lime juice for 3 hours, refrigerated.

Drain and thinly slice the scallops. Arrange in a circle, slices overlapping on individual plates. Heap some diced onion in the center of each circle and arrange tomato pieces around scallops. Sprinkle with cilantro. Drizzle a tablespoon of olive oil over each serving and top with a grinding of black pepper. Garnish with a sprig of cilantro.

Serves 6

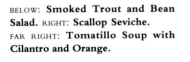

BELOW: **Smoked Trout and Bean Salad.** RIGHT: **Scallop Seviche.** FAR RIGHT: **Tomatillo Soup with Cilantro and Orange.**

Smoked Trout and Bean Salad

This delightful salad makes a perfect first course, but could easily be expanded to be the centerpiece of a light lunch.

3 medium smoked trout, deboned
1 ½ pounds very thin string beans (haricots vert)
Salt
½ cup hazelnut oil
¼ cup whole-grain mustard
1 tablespoon champagne vinegar
1 tablespoon minced fresh tarragon
3 tablespoons finely diced red onion
12 toasted and peeled hazelnuts
Chive blossoms, for garnish

Make sure the trout have no bones by running your finger along the fish to check. Remove with a tweezers.

Blanch the beans in salted water for about a minute and refresh with ice water, drain, and set aside.

1½ quarts rich chicken stock
   Salt and freshly ground black pepper to taste
1 tablespoon olive oil
1 small onion, chopped
1 medium garlic clove, sliced
½ medium jalapeño pepper, thinly sliced (optional)
½ pound tomatillos, husked and coarsely chopped (page 107)
1 teaspoon orange zest, loosely chopped
⅓ cup fresh orange juice
3 corn tortillas
1 cup coarsely grated soft Monterey Jack cheese
   Cilantro sprigs, for garnish

In a large pot, bring stock to a boil over medium heat. Add salt and pepper to taste.

Meanwhile, heat the olive oil in a large skillet over medium heat and gently sauté the onion, garlic, and jalapeño pepper until wilted, about 5 minutes. Add the tomatillos, then season with salt and pepper. Cover and let cook slowly for 5 minutes. Add the boiling stock, then the orange zest and juice. Taste for seasoning.

Simmer very gently, uncovered, over lowest heat for 15 minutes. At this point, you can turn the heat off, cover, and let soup sit until serving time, up to about 2 hours.

To serve, bring back to a simmer. In the meantime, heat the tortillas over an open flame, turning often until they begin to form bubbles and show brown flecks. (A griddle or heavy skillet will work if you have an electric stove.) Cut tortillas into thin strips.

Heat the soup bowls and divide tortilla strips among them. Ladle the soup in and sprinkle grated cheese over each. Garnish with cilantro.

Serves 6

Whisk together the oil, mustard, vinegar, and tarragon. If this separates before serving, stir again.

Divide the beans among 6 plates, then arrange trout in 1-inch pieces around beans. Dress beans with 1 tablespoon each or more of the vinaigrette. Sprinkle with diced onion and hazelnuts. Garnish with chive flowers, if desired.

Serves 6

Tomatillo Soup with Cilantro and Orange

Here are some of Sally's hints. Use more jalapeño (than I call for) if desired. A gentle heat is best.

The richer the stock, the richer the soup. Use whatever your conscience and your refrigerator may dictate. I use a little pork or duck stock combined with the chicken stock if I have it on hand.

SALLY SCHMITT

FRENCH LAUNDRY
6640 Washington Street
Yountville, California 94599
(707) 944-2380

THE French Laundry restaurant is the brainchild of Sally Schmitt and her husband, Don. Housed in a marvelous old stone building that is listed on the register of historic places, it was actually a laundry in one of its earlier incarnations. Although strongly influenced by French cuisine, Sally long ago took her own personal direction.

Peach and Berry Shortcake with Warm Cream Sauce

This really is as good as it looks.

SHORTCAKE

- 1 cup all-purpose flour
- 1 ½ teaspoons baking powder
- ¼ teaspoon salt
- ¼ cup sugar
- ⅛ teaspoon grated nutmeg
- 4 tablespoons (½ stick) unsalted butter, softened
- ¼ cup milk
- 1 small egg

CREAM SAUCE

- 4 tablespoons (½ stick) unsalted butter
- ¼ cup sugar
- 2 cups heavy cream

ASSEMBLY

- 3 large peaches, peeled, pitted, and sliced
- 2 baskets mixed berries

Preheat the oven to 400 degrees.

Make the shortcakes. Measure the dry ingredients into a mixing bowl. Cut in the butter with a pastry blender until very fine, like cornmeal. In a large measuring cup, measure the milk, then drop in the egg and mix with a fork. Make a well in the dry ingredients and pour in milk-egg mixture all at once. Mix with a fork just long enough for all ingredients to gather together. Drop in 6 portions by large forkfuls onto a greased cookie sheet.

Bake for 15 minutes or until nicely browned.

Make the cream sauce. Combine ingredients in a heavy bottomed saucepan large enough to have room for the cream to boil up. Simmer over low heat until cream boils. Whisk down and let boil up at least once more, then let simmer very gently for a few minutes. This can be done several hours ahead. It takes about 15 to 20 minutes to cook. For thicker cream, simmer it longer. Should it get too thick, thin out with a little extra cream.

Assemble. Reheat the shortcakes, uncovered, until warm and crisp on top. Split the biscuits and place bottoms on individual serving plates. Top with sliced peaches. Replace tops, then spoon berries over each and spoon warm cream sauce over all.

Makes 6

GARY DANKO

THE RESTAURANT AT
CHATEAU SOUVERAIN
400 Souverain Road
Geyserville, California 95441
(707) 433-3141

ARVEY Steiman, respected columnist for the *Wine Spectator*, neatly summed up Gary Danko's current direction at the Chateau Souverian restaurant in a recent article about him: "The kitchen under the direction of Gary Danko turns out some of the most artfully conceived, creative, and soul-satisfying food anywhere. Here is sophistication without an ounce of pretense. Danko's food leans toward powerful flavors, but the style is reined in and remarkably refined." Amen.

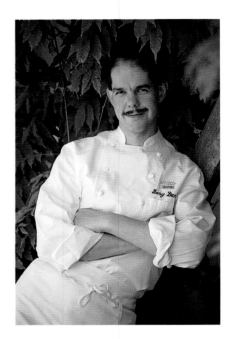

Oven Polenta, Tomato Fondue, and Sonoma Jack Cheese

Golden Pheasant, the kind of prepared polenta grain used here, is very easy to use and may be purchased from the company listed on page 173.

OVEN POLENTA

- 4 tablespoons (½ stick) unsalted butter
- ½ medium onion, minced fine
- 1 cup large cracked polenta (Golden Pheasant, if available)
- 1 tablespoon coarse salt
- 1 teaspoon cracked black peppercorns
- 4 cups boiling water

TOMATO FONDUE

- 1 **tablespoon unsalted butter**
- ¼ **cup extra-virgin olive oil**
- 1 **medium garlic clove, minced**
- 2 **medium shallots, minced**
- 1½ **pounds tomato concasse (peeled, seeded, and finely chopped tomatoes); this will require 3 to 4 medium tomatoes**
- 1 **tablespoon tomato paste**
- ¼ **bay leaf**
- 1 **tablespoon sugar**
  Salt and pepper to taste

ASSEMBLY

- 6 **ounces dry Sonoma Jack cheese, shaved**
- 1½ **cups heavy cream**

Preheat the oven to 350 degrees.

Make the polenta. In an ovenproof pan, melt the butter. Sauté the onion over low heat until translucent, about 5 minutes, then remove from heat and add the polenta, stirring. Add salt and pepper to boiling water and pour over polenta. Mix lightly. Bake for about 30 minutes. Polenta should be firm, but still liquid enough to spread with a spatula. Spread polenta on an oiled 10 by 15-inch jelly roll pan; smooth the top. This will give you a layer approximately ½ inch thick. Cool and refrig-erate, covered, until ready to assemble. This may be done 2 days in advance.

Make the tomato fondue. Place the butter and olive oil in a medium skillet over medium heat. Sauté shallots until translucent, about 5 minutes. Add remaining ingredients and simmer 20 minutes. Salt and pepper to taste. Remove bay leaf.

Assemble. Preheat the oven to 350 degrees. Butter an 8-inch-square gratin dish and smear the bottom with some of the tomato fondue. Cut the cold polenta into 8 strips (see Note) ap-proximately 7½ by 2½ inches. Place the first strip up against one side of the dish. Spoon tomato fondue along the length of the strip leaving about ½ inch uncovered (by the fondue) along the side that touches the edge of the dish. Sprinkle cheese on top of the line of fondue you have just put on the strip of polenta. Overlap the next polenta strip to cover just the line of fondue and cheese. Proceed as with the first strip, overlapping as you go, until you use all the strips. You may have to push the strips more tightly together to make them all fit. Drizzle the cream over all and bake until the top is golden and bubbly, about 35 to 40 minutes.

If you have any cheese left over after assembling the dish, sprinkle it over the top before baking. Any extra leftover fondue may be passed when the dish is served.

Serves 6

Note: Obviously you may cut the cold polenta into any shape you choose as long as the shape is one that will overlap the piece underneath easily when the dish is assembled. Danko sometime does this with triangles of polenta, which looks very nice.

OPPOSITE TOP: **Peach and Berry Shortcake with Warm Cream Sauce.** BELOW: **Oven Polenta, Tomato Fondue, and Sonoma Jack Cheese.**

Chocolate Mousse Cake

Now this is sinfully delicious. All you chocolate lovers rejoice!

- ¾ cup sugar
- ¾ cup water
- 1 ½-inch-thick chocolate cake layer or the same of chocolate sponge cake
- 1 pound semi- or bittersweet chocolate (preferably Callebaut), chopped fine
- 10 eggs, separated
- ¼ cup liqueur of choice (such as Chartreuse or Grand Marnier)

Make a simple syrup by combining the sugar and water, bringing to a boil, and boiling slowly for 5 minutes. (This makes more than needed.)

Line the bottom of a 9-inch springform pan with the chocolate cake. You can patch this. Set aside.

In a double boiler, combine the chocolate and 1 cup of the simple syrup. Melt over boiling water. Pour into a mixing bowl and add egg yolks, one at the time, mixing until just blended after each. Mix in the liqueur with the last egg yolk. Beat egg whites to soft peaks and lightly fold in until just incorporated. Gently pour into pan. Refrigerate overnight. (This cake freezes well.)

To serve, unmold by running a warm knife around the edge of the pan to loosen before unsnapping side. Place on a serving platter and decorate with unsweetened whipped cream and fresh fruit if desired.

Slice with a warm knife.

Serves 12

FATHER STEPHEN STEINECK BROTHER ALLAN RICHARDSON SISTER GERALDINE FOSTER

Brother Juniper's Bakery

6544 Front Street

Box 1106

Forestville, California 95436

(707) 887-7908

YEARS AGO there was a Brother Juniper who started the bakery; now the faithful carry on their work through it. And this work contributes to the perpetuation of a truly worthy enterprise; for almost all the proceeds from the order's food-related projects go toward maintaining Raphael House on San Francisco's Sutter Street. This establishment is the area's only 24-hour shelter for homeless families, which also reaches out to aid and bring companionship to the elderly in the neighborhood.

Raphael House has been ministering to the community's needs for almost two decades, and with the assistance of Brother Juniper's dedicated band, should continue to as long as its services fulfill the community's needs.

So if bread—the bread of life—is the symbol of both life and charity, this group has managed to turn this symbol into a way not only of giving nourishment but of bringing comfort as well.

Country Buttermilk Whole Wheat Bread

Hearty and dense, this bread is a classic.

- Approximately 2 cups lukewarm water
- 3 tablespoons honey
- 1 tablespoon rapid-rise yeast
- 4 cups unbleached all-purpose flour or high-gluten bread flour
- 2 cups coarse-ground whole wheat flour
- 1 tablespoon salt
- 1 cup buttermilk, at room temperature
- 1 egg
- 1 cup water
- Poppy seeds (optional)

Combine the water, honey, and yeast in a bowl and set aside in a warm, draft-free spot for about 5 minutes. In a large bowl mix flours and salt together. Combine buttermilk with the yeast mixture. Pour into dry ingredients, mixing. When combined, knead for appoximately 10 minutes on a floured surface (or in a mixer with a dough hook) until soft and elastic, but not sticky. Turn into a greased clean bowl and allow to rise in a warm draft-free place, covered with a dish towel or plastic wrap, until double in bulk, about 1½ hours. Punch down and allow to rise for another hour.

Form dough into 2 balls and then

into loaves. Place in greased loaf pans and allow to rise until dough crests just above the pan or is double in size.

Preheat the oven to 350 degrees.

Whisk the egg with the water, then brush tops of loaves. You may sprinkle them with poppy seeds if you like. Bake for approximately 45 minutes, or until golden and hollow sounding when thumped on the bottom.

Allow to cool at least 45 minutes before slicing.

Makes 2 loaves

Cajun Three-Pepper Bread

This spicy bread is wonderful when buttered and served with soup.

- 8 cups unbleached all-purpose flour or high-gluten bread flour
- ³⁄₄ cup polenta or coarse cornmeal
- 1 cup finely chopped roasted sweet red bell pepper (page 104)
- ¹⁄₄ cup Tabasco or Louisiana Hot Sauce
- 2 tablespoons dried parsley flakes
- 2 tablespoons granulated garlic
- 2 tablespoons active dry yeast (rapid-rise, if possible)
- 1 ³⁄₄ tablespoons salt

- 1 teaspoon black pepper
  Approximately 3 cups water

Mix all the dry ingredients, then add 2¹⁄₂ cups water. Mix well. Knead for about 8 minutes, or until a soft tacky dough is formed, using the remaining ¹⁄₂ cup water if needed. Dough should be tacky by not sticky.

Place dough in a clean greased bowl, cover, and allow to rise approximately 1¹⁄₂ hours in a warm, draft-free spot. Punch down and allow to rise again for another hour.

Divide the dough into 4 balls and roll out into rectangles. Fold each into thirds, pinching seams closed and turn over, seam side down. Roll out again and fold again. The rectangles should be getting longer. Repeat one more time and pinch off seam carefully. You should have 4 baguette shapes. Sprinkle polenta or cornmeal on 2 baking sheets and put 2 loaves on each, at least 2 inches apart. Allow to rise 1 hour, lightly covered with a tea towel.

Preheat the oven to 425 degrees.

Makes 3 diagonal slashes across the top of each loaf with a serrated knife. Spray tops with cold water from a flower mister. Place loaves in the oven and spray 3 more times, every 2 minutes. Bake, checking in about 10 minutes after the last spraying. Bread should turn deep golden; when it does, turn heat off and allow to cool for 10

OPPOSITE BOTTOM: **Chocolate Mousse Cake.**
ABOVE FROM LEFT: **Country Buttermilk Whole Wheat Bread, Cajun Three-Pepper Bread, and Oreganato Bread.**

minutes more in the oven. Remove from oven and let rest at least 15 minutes before cutting.

Makes 4 loaves

Oreganato Bread

Another spicy treat, also good with soup and for sandwiches.

- 8 cups unbleached all-purpose flour or high-gluten bread flour
- ³⁄₄ cup polenta or coarse cornmeal
- 3 tablespoons dried oregano
- 1 ¹⁄₂ tablespoons dried parsley flakes
- 2 tablespoons granulated garlic
- 1 tablespoon ground black pepper
- 2 tablespoons active dry yeast (rapid-rise, if possible)
- 2 tablespoons salt
  Approximately 3¹⁄₂ cups water

Follow the directions for Cajun Three-Pepper Bread.

Makes 4 loaves

Wine Do's and Don'ts

Tasting Wine with Food

Jamie Morningstar of Inglenook was kind enough to share her personal general guide to pairing wine with food. Always remember, though, that there is room for your own taste and preferences when deciding what wines to serve with your food.

WHEN TASTING wine with food, always begin by tasting the wine first to become familiar with its flavor and texture characteristics. Then taste the food. Return to taste the wine again to see how the wine's various components (acid, tannin, sugar, fruit, and tuexture) are changing because of the flavor of the food.

Does the wine become more sweet or tart? Does the wine feel more full in your mouth or thinner? These are the changes that occur owing to various food flavor combinations. Some will improve the wine's flavor and make you want to keep returning to this pairing, whereas some will detract from a wine and make it less pleasant.

When tasting the food with the wine, consider the method of preparation involved in making the dish. Is the food smoked, roasted, or grilled? What are the herbs used? The main ingredient of the dish serves as the medium for transmitting the other flavors, and it is these flavors that you need to concentrate on when selecting a wine that will best complement your meal.

Also keep in mind the weight of the wine versus the richness of the food involved. A rich, buttery Chardonnay works better with foods that are equally rich. A crisp, herbaceous Sauvignon Blanc requires something much lighter and more refreshing.

The main thing to remember is that everyone tastes food differently; there are no right or wrong answers. Food and wine are the background for good friends and great occasions. We are trying to show some simple guidelines to make these occasions easier for you to enjoy.

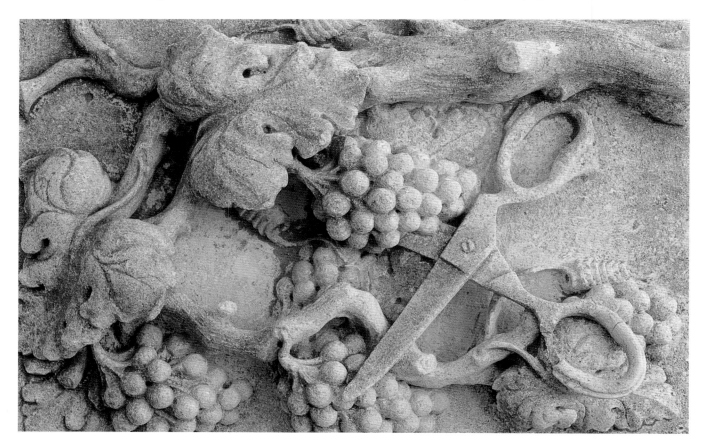

CABERNET SAUVIGNON

DO

1. Cabernets in which the tannins are tamed and smooth need foods that are simple yet elegantly prepared:

   • Full-flavored meats with simple wine reduction sauces: lamb, marbled beef, duck, or squab.
   • Rich earthy flavors: olives, roasted garlic, walnuts, mustard, and mushrooms.
   • Pungent herbs and spices: rosemary, thyme, garlic, mint, peppercorns, and parsley.
   • Cheeses: cheddars when the intensity of the wine is matched to the sharpness of the cheese; soft ripening cheeses like Brie and Camembert, hard grating cheeses like dry Monterey Jack, Parmesan, and Romano.

2. Cabernets bold in tannins need foods that are generously seasoned and rich to help ease that tannic bite:

   • Foods that have bolder emphasis on their seasonings; go heavier on the pungent herbs in preparations.
   • Spices and berry flavors combined in rich brown sauces: cherry, blackberry, and cassis with allspice, nutmeg, mace, and juniper.

DON'T

1. Seafood, vinegar, and salty foods.
2. Delicate flavored meats and poultry: pork, veal, chicken, and turkey.
3. Pungent cheeses: Gorgonzola, Gruyére, and young goat cheese.
4. Flowery herbs: dill, cilantro, and ginger.

CHARDONNAY

DO

1. Rich, full-flavored foods that are subtle in taste: toasted pine nuts, pistachios, mushrooms, and saffron.
2. Rich, full-flavored meats and poultry: veal, pork loin, quail, duck, and pheasant.
3. Rich, full-flavored seafood: lobster, prawns, salmon, scallops, swordfish, crab, and trout.
4. Orange, lemon, and apple with some rich ingredient to balance the acid.
5. Aromatic herbs: tarragon, sage, rosemary, roasted garlic, dill, and basil.

6. Mustard, melon, peach, apricot, and small amounts of ginger also work.

DON'T

1. Acidic ingredients without some rich base such as cream, butter, or mayonnaise.
2. Vinegar, tomatoes, and peppers.
3. Cilantro, oregano, raw garlic, and heavy spices.
4. Heavily smoked and salty foods.
5. Cheese by itself without an ingredient with zing to cut through the butterfat; apple or mustard would do.
6. Pungently flavored dishes.

GRAVION

DO

1. Acidic foods: tomatoes, lemon, lime, grapefruit, orange, goat and feta cheeses.
2. Pungent herbs: cilantro, thyme, oregano, garlic, and mint.
3. Seafood that is not high in fat: mussels, clams, oysters, snapper, sole, bass, and squid.
4. Chicken or pork, especially grilled cuts.
5. Olives, roasted peppers, mild curries, melon, and black pepper.
6. Mexican or Cajun dishes that use tomatoes and not-too-hot seasonings.

DON'T

1. Cream or other rich ingredients unless there's an equal amount of acidic ingredient to balance.
2. Heavily smoked or salted foods.
3. Dishes that are sweet in flavor.
4. High butterfat cheeses.
5. Dill, ginger, cinnamon, or other flowery flavors.
6. Dishes that are heavy with vinegar.

LATE HARVEST GEWÜRZTRAMINER

DO

1. Always keep the dessert less sweet than the wine. The dessert should have a good balance of tartness and sweetness. Watch the amount of sugar used in the dessert.
2. Fruit-based desserts work best: fruit tarts, fresh berries, apricots, pears,
3. or apples poached in the wine. Spices work well in flavoring poach-

ing liquids or whipped cream for garnishes: cinnamon, nutmeg, clove, allspice, vanilla, ginger, bay, and cardamom.
4. Crème caramel or crème brûlée with the addition of citrus work well.
5. Cheeses that have some saltiness or smokiness to them, like mild blue cheeses, blue Bries, smoked cheddars, or Goudas. The addition of fruit to these cheese courses works nicely where it doesn't with most other wines.

DON'T

1. Rich buttercream desserts.
2. Chocolate in any form.
3. Vinegar, pungent herbs, dishes high in acid.

MERLOT

DO

1. Full-flavored meats and poultry with simple wine reductions sauces: lamb, marbled beef, squab, duck, quail, and rabbit.
2. Berry flavors—blackberry, raspberry, black cherry—that are balanced by rich ingredients like butter, cream, or stocks.
3. Rich, earthy flavors: mushrooms, caramelized onions, roasted garlic, mustard, walnuts, and olives.
4. Pungent herbs: bay leaf, thyme, summer savory, mint, parsley, peppercorns, and raw garlic.
5. Spices like allspice, nutmeg, and mace.
6. Cheeses: cheddars when the intensity of the wine is matched by the sharpness of the cheddar, soft ripening cheeses like Brie and Camembert, hard grating cheeses like dry Monterey Jack, Parmesan, and Romano.

DON'T

1. Acidic ingredients without some rich ingredient like cream, butter, or a stock for balance.
2. Flowery herbs: dill, cilantro, basil, and ginger.
3. Heavily salted foods or seafoods.
4. Vinegar.
5. Pungently flavored cheeses: blue, Swiss, feta, and so on.

MUSCAT BLANC

DO

1. Always keep the dessert less sweet than the wine. The dessert should have a good balance of tartness and sweetness. Watch the amount of sugar used in the dessert.
2. Fruit based desserts work best: fruit tarts, fresh berries, apricots, pears, or apples poached in the wine, and the like.
3. Spices work well in flavoring poaching liquids or whipped cream for garnishes: cinnamon, nutmeg, clove, allspice, vanilla, mint, bay, and cardamom.
4. Crème caramel or crème brûlée with the additon of citrus work well.
5. Cheeses that have some saltiness or smokiness to them like mild blue cheeses, blue bries, smoked cheddars, or goudas. The addition of fruit to these cheese courses works nicely where it doesn't with most other wines.

DON'T

1. Rich buttercream desserts.
2. Chocolate in any form.
3. Vinegar, pungent herbs, dishes high in acid.

PINOT NOIR

DO

1. Smoked meats and poultry: ham, veal, beef, duck, chicken, quail, and turkey.
2. Berry flavors—blackberry, raspberry, black cherry, and strawberry—that are balanced by a rich ingredient like butter, cream, or stocks.
3. Earthy, rich flavors: mushrooms, caramelized onions, tomatoes, bell peppers, mustard, and walnuts.
4. Pungent herbs and spices: rosemary, thyme, summer savory, tarragon, peppermint, spearmint, and peppercorns.
5. Spices like allspice, nutmeg, clove, and cinnamon.
6. Trout or salmon smoked over herbs and hickory or poached in pinot with a slice of lemon.
7. Game: lamb, rabbit, quail, duck, and squab.
8. Cheeses that are mild and butter; havarti, Monterey Jack, Gouda, aged cheddar, Brie, and Camembert.

DON'T

1. Acidic ingredients without some rich ingredient like cream, butter; or stocks.
2. Flower herbs: dill, cilantro, basil, and ginger.
3. Heavily salted foods or salty seafoods: mackerel, anchovies, and the like.
4. Vinegar.
5. Pungently flavored cheeses: blue, Swiss, feta.

SAUVIGNON BLANC

DO

1. Acidic foods make the best complements: tomato, lemon, lime, grapefruit, goat and feta cheeses.
2. Pungent herbs: rosemary, thyme, oregano, and garlic.
3. Seafood that is not high in fat: mussels, clams, oysters, snapper, sole, bass, and squid.
4. Chicken or pork, especially grilled cuts.
5. Olives, roasted peppers, mild curries, and black pepper.
6. Mexican or Cajun dishes that use tomatoes and hot seasonings.

DON'T

1. Cream or other rich ingredients, unless there's an equal amount of an acidic ingredient for balance.
2. Heavily smoked or salted foods.
3. Dishes that are sweet in flavor.
4. High butterfat cheese.
5. Dill, ginger, cinnamon, or other flowery flavors.
6. Dishes that are heavy with vinegar.

ZINFANDEL

DO

1. Pungent herbs and spices: rosemary, garlic, thyme, oregano, fennel, sage, and peppercorns.
2. Full-flavored meats and poultry: venison, beef, wild boar, lamb, rabbit, duck, squab, and quail.
3. Rich, earthy flavors: roasted peppers, roasted garlic, mushrooms, tomatoes, olives, and eggplant.
4. Italian dishes: lasagna, eggplant parmigiano, polenta, Italian sausage, and pizza.
5. Cajun dishes like gumbo and jambalaya.
6. Aged hard cheeses: Parmesan, dry Monterey Jack, aged cheddar, or aged Gouda.

DON'T

1. Delicate flavored meats and poultry—pork, veal, chicken, and turkey—without some flavorful herbs or spices from list above.
2. Flowery herbs and spices: dill, cilantro, cinnamon, allspice, and nutmeg.
3. Seafood and vinegar.
4. Heavily salted food.
5. Pungently flavored cheeses: blue, Swiss, and feta.

The Pantry

WINE COUNTRY

AIDELLS SAUSAGE CO.
Sausages of all kinds
1575 Minnesota Street
San Francisco, CA 94107
(415) 285-6660

EXOTICA NURSERY
Rare and unusual fruit trees
2508B East Vista Way
P. O. Box 160
Vista, CA 92083
(619) 724-9093

FRANKS' FRESH FOODS, INC.
Smoked fowl, meat, fish, and seafood
461 Crystal Springs Road
St. Helena, CA 94574
(707) 963-8354

G. B. RATTO & COMPANY
International grocers
821 Washington Street
Oakland, CA 94607
(800) 325-3483;
in California, (800) 228-3515

GOLDEN PHEASANT POLENTA
Packaged dry polenta
139 Mitchell Avenue
South San Francisco, CA 94080
(415) 589-2280

GOURMET MUSHROOMS, INC.
Dried and fresh mushrooms of all kinds
P. O. Box 391
Sebastopol CA 95473
(707) 823-1743

LAURA CHENELS'S CHEVRE
Goat cheeses
1550 Ridley Avenue
Santa Rosa, CA 95401
(707) 575-8888

LUNDBERG FAMILY FARMS
Packaged brown rice and blends of rice types
P. O. Box 369
Richvale, CA 95974
(916) 882-4551

NAPA VALLEY MUSTARD CO.
Mustards and country ketchup
P.O. Box 125
Oakville, CA 94562
(800) 288-1089

SMITH & HAWKEN
*Garden supplies and tools, vegetable
and flower seeds*
25 Corte Madera Avenue
Mill Valley, CA 94941
(800) 777-4556

SONOMA FOIE GRAS
Duck foie gras; deboned, smoked duck breasts
P. O. Box 2007
Sonoma, CA 95476
(707) 938-1229

THANKSGIVING COFFEE CO.
Coffees
Box 1918
Fort Bragg, CA 95437
(800) 648-6491

TIMBER CREST FARMS
Dried tomatoes and fruits, nuts
4791 Dry Creek Road
Healdsburg, CA 95448
(707) 433-8251

WILLIAMS-SONOMA
Cookware, utensils, and food items
P. O. Box 7456
San Francisco, CA 94120
(415) 421-4242

NATIONWIDE

AMERICAN SPOON FOODS
*Dried fruits, and cherries, jams,
preserves, and honeys*
P. O. Box 566
Petoskey, MI 49770
(800) 222-5886

TEXAS WILD GAME COOPERATIVE
*Fresh venison, antelope, and wild boar;
smoked wild game*
P. O. Box 530
Ingram, TX 78025
(800) 962-4263

THE COOK'S GARDEN
Vegetable, herb, and edible flower seeds
P. O. Box 535
Londonderry, VT 05148
(802) 824-3400

WAGNER & SON
Black walnut extract
900 Jacksonville Road, Box C5013
Ivyland, PA 18974-0576
(215) 674-5000

*For information on California wineries,
write or call:*
THE WINE INSTITUTE
425 Market Street; Suite 1000
San Francisco, CA 94108
(415) 512-0151

Index